EXTREME GARDENING

How To Grow Organic
In The Hostile Deserts

David Owens

Printed in the United States of America with soy based ink on recycled paper.

FIRST EDITION

Cover and book design by Corey Lewis

Edited by Paul Howey
Research assistance by Selby Saubolle
Illustrations and diagrams by Jeremy La Mesa

Library of Congress Cataloging-in-Publication Data

The Garden Guy® is the registered trademark of David Owens and the property of Poco Verde Landscape, Inc.

ISBN 0-9705016-0-9

Published and distributed by Poco Verde Landscape.

EXTREME THANK-YOUS

My loving children deserve special thanks for their encouragement and for their understanding during the countless hours I've spent working on this book and on my "Garden Guy" segments for television and radio.

I want to thank my mother and father, Bill and Judy Owens, for spending so many hours gardening with me as a child, teaching me to love the soil and plants.

My loving grandmother, Jane Overstreet, taught me to appreciate the birds and other wildlife that inhabit our lives. John B. Overstreet was the man who so many years ago encouraged me to follow my dream when no one else believed in me. Thanks, Granddaddy.

Arnie and Helen File, I want to thank you for your immense generosity. My family and I will never forget the support you gave, while asking for nothing in return. For their inspiration to me, I thank A. Wayne Smith, Samantha Mohr, and Sensi Shojiro Koyama. For their trust and friendship, I thank Pam Bates, and Narciso Valenzuela. And for her example of perseverance in hard times, I thank my aunt Joan Jaynes.

My brothers Bob Owens and Bill Owens are icons in my life and business and the three of us blend like the roots of trees, bushes, and grasses intermingle, each energizing and protecting the others.

CONTENTS

Section I-Concepts
  Introduction 7
  Garden Design Principles 10
    Design 11
    Watering 13
    Tools 16
  Southwest Desert Soils 18
    Fertilizer 20
    Compost 23
    Companion Plants 27
    Alternative Gardens 41
Section II-Garden Goodies
  Vegetables 47
    Artichokes 49
    Beans 52
    Beets 54
    Black-Eyed Peas 56
    Bok Choy 57
    Broccoli 59
    Brussels Sprouts 61
    Carrots 62
    Cauliflower 64
    Corn 66
    Cucumbers 69
    Eggplant 71
    Garlic 73
    Kale 75

Leeks 76
Lettuce..78
Melons 80
Okra...83
Onions..84
Peas..87
Peppers...89
Potatoes..91
Pumpkins 93
Radishes..96
Spinach..98
Squash...100
Swiss Chard 103
Tomatoes 105
Turnips 109
Fruit and Nuts 111
Almonds 113
Apples..115
Apricots...117
Blackberries.......................................120
Figs..122
Peaches 124
Pears 127
Pecans...129
Pineapple Guavas..............................132
Plums...134
Pomegranates....................................135
Strawberries 137
Subtropical Fruit................................140

Citrus 149

Flowers 158

Roses 171

Sunflowers 183

Herbs 185

Grass and Lawn 199

Section III-Controlling Extreme Pests

Organic Controls..203

Organic Pest Control.............................204

Part One-Insect Identification...............205

Part Two-Damage Assessment.................229

Part Three-Helpful Plants 231

Organic Animal Control 235

Section IV-Looking Ahead

Afterword...242

INTRODUCTION

EVER since I was a kid, I've loved the soil and the plants that spring from it. My earliest childhood memory is being in a garden in Hawaii with my father. I was five years old at the time, and the youngest in what you might call a dynasty of gardeners.

I have spent a lifetime studying, working, and traveling, and have learned to admire how nature — when left on its own — works at near perfection. The Earth consists of symbiotic relationships that make it possible for us and all other living things to coexist. Why am I telling you about this grand scheme of things? Because what I've seen in far-off lands can also exist in your own backyard!

No, you won't be able to plant a tree from the rain forest and attract a toucan. But you can grow ruellia and expect a Hummingbird to show up and start eating insects for you. You can build a simple water garden that will draw Butterflies and dragonflies. You can create plant cultures that sustain themselves, and you. The amazing thing about all of this — it's easy! You don't need decades of gardening experience or a degree in horticulture.

I landscape and garden thousands of homes every year. If there's one thing I've learned, it's that you don't need to pay a guy like me to get a bountiful garden. You just need to set aside a space, put in a few trees, a few herbs, a few vegetables and flowers and . . . BAM! You've got a new environment. You can do it. It's easy. I'll show you how.

I find in gardening a connection to the Earth that cannot be found in any other endeavor. By working the soil and caring for the plants and trees, you'll learn as I have that gardening not only affects the very environment in which you live, but it generates an immense personal satisfaction at the same time. It is one of the most therapeutic things you can do for yourself, and it's an adventure that safeguards our future.

The only thing you need is a desire to feel better. The bonus is that you'll be helping everyone else in the process! Here's a short list of the benefits of gardening: exercise, grow your own food, create beauty, and combat pollution. Not bad, eh? While you're watering your Snap Beans and picking your Carrots, you're relaxing. Gardening relieves stress more efficiently than almost any other activity. It's a scientific fact!

Your yard will be the place for you to grow food and create a beautiful and relaxing environment. I know it's hard to believe, but home gardening and proper landscaping will literally change your environment. Not *can* change, but *will* change.

As gardeners, we can gently guide nature, but we cannot force her without paying a price. Today's standard farming and landscaping practices are outdated, and in some cases harmful to our environment. After many years of spraying insecticides and herbicides, many insects and diseases have become resistant to them. It's important that we design our homes, businesses, and landscapes using natural elements for a safer, more productive solution. By creating mini-ecosystems, landscaping can come to reflect our naturally beautiful and safe environment.

I remember when I was 24 years old and in New Mexico working with an old man who had a garden at his small rural home. He taught me that the soil, the plants, the insects, and the wildlife each have something to contribute to the others. And he had found a way to become an integral part of it. By tending his beautiful place, he provided a sanctuary for himself, his family, and for nature.

Since then, I've had the good fortune to study in the Bahamas, Hawaii, Mexico, and South America with some of America's foremost horticulturists, and for the last quarter-century, I have gardened the unique Arizona soil. Above it all, it's that old man's example that sticks with me.

What he was doing back then would eventually get a name: Organic Gardening. His soil-building fertilizers came from natural materials. He controlled pests by achieving a balance of predators, prey, and plants. Each of the elements of his garden was in harmony with the others — no synthetic chemicals, no extermination, no waste. As is the case with most important things in life, it was simple. From him, I learned that a successful garden requires sharing, give-and-take, and balance.

From the comfort our own homes, we can create balanced microcosms that reflect the natural world. We can get Birds, insects, Lizards, Toads, and Snakes to work on our behalf. We can nurture plant life and promote beauty and sustenance in our own living spaces. A vibrant garden is an interactive, diverse environment, not an unhealthy mishmash of synthetic fertilizers, pesticides, and herbicides.

I'm going to ask that you use this book in your garden for just a few weeks. In addition to your regular routine of cutting the grass, pick one of my example gardens and plant it. Give yourself two hours a week (that's about 15 minutes a day, with a little extra on Saturday) to introduce a whole new world to your home. Soon, you'll be taking vacations in your own backyard to get away from it all!

For the last several years, I've been on TV and radio talking about how, with just a little effort, you can create a productive and beautiful environment. This book brings together all of the gardening concepts I believe in. They boil down to this: design to your needs, forego chemicals for natural techniques, water deeply and infrequently, practice companion planting, and finally, enjoy yourself!

Gardening is an art, not a science and I consider myself blessed to be working as an artist in the field I love. If this book helps you to share in that blessing and find the artist in yourself, then I'll know it was all worth it.

Get relaxed, get healthy, and get in the garden.

This is not a coffee table book. It's meant to be used, so I've tried to make things as user-friendly as possible. For one thing, I've capitalized certain words. When you see one of these, you'll know that it's described in detail elsewhere in the book. Check the index for page numbers.

Also, the binding is designed for easy access and use. Open it up and lay it flat and go to work. Take it into the garden for easy reference. Or take it with you to the nursery or garden store. I want the information to be right where you need it! The paper is a sturdy stock and can take a little rough-housing, just don't drop it in the pool.

GARDEN DESIGN PRINCIPLES

HAVE you ever been driving down the road and noticed row after row of crops flashing from a field next to you? You've just witnessed Monoculture. That means only one plant (or one dominant type of plant) is being grown year after year in the same place. Monoculture drains the soil of nutrients, and most farms — whether they grow Corn, Lettuce, or cotton — are Monocultures. They often depend on massive amounts of insecticides, herbicides, and chemical fertilizers which fosters unhealthy soil. Eventually, Monocultures produce food with fewer nutrients and more chemical content. They create a measurable negative impact on our environment. We don't like Monocultures.

Environments that encourage plants, insects, and animals to strengthen one another and their soil are called Polycultures. It's the way to go for home gardens and lawns. A Polyculture in your landscape and garden will provide organic-style vegetables, fruits, flowers, nuts, and herbs. They will be more nutritious, taste better, and will contribute to a healthier environment. Plus, organic gardening is cheaper.

The way I'd like you to look at it is this: *when you feed the soil, the soil will feed the plant.* In the pages ahead, you'll find all you need to know to design strong organic gardens.

Nature can do it herself, but you need a plan. If you start planting things without a preconceived notion of how they're all going to fit in with the rest of the yard, you're likely to end up changing it again when the next project rolls around. In the wild, Nature has a long time span to produce her Polycultures. Don't worry that you don't have centuries to work things out. It's just a matter of choosing what you want. I'll help you create a master plan and work at completing it a little bit at a time.

DESIGN

Creating a landscape or garden design means combining various elements into a productive microcosm. In a good outdoor home environment, these elements work together in symbiotic relationships, complementing one another and contributing to the overall health and beauty of the space.

Begin with healthy soil. If you're just starting a garden, build up the soil with plants like Beans and Peas (I'll show you how). Then begin creating the aboveground environment you want. A canopy of trees on the west side of the garden comes first (preferably in the Legume family), then pathways, raised gardens, and sheet mulching to create a wonderful Polyculture made up of a variety of flora and fauna.

Everything that goes into your design must add to the integrity of the plan. There's almost nothing that you can't put to use. Plants, flowers, trees, lights, and lawn furniture are a few of the things you have to work with. Nature can create mini-ecosystems, working from designs we don't fully understand. When we look at the outcome of that design, however, we're able to copy nature's work and modify it to fit our own needs.

The challenge is to know *where* and *how* to use them. You can plant flowers that draw pollinators, strengthen crops, and feed the soil to produce vegetables that end up on your table. Flowering vines attract predator insects and Birds that gobble up pest populations. The cycle starts and restarts every hour of every day.

You don't have to begin and finish your entire design all at one time. Gardening can and should be a part of the rest of your life. Figure a way to balance the beauty of possibility with the constraints of need and time. Work on one section at a time, always with the big picture in mind. What's "the big picture"? Simply put, it means your home and garden is a self-sustaining mini-ecosystem.

Natural mulches and organic fertilizers will make plants, trees, and grass strong enough to resist diseases, so you won't have to spend time diagnosing and fighting them with chemicals. Companion plants will help the soil to grow nutritious, tasty vegetables and fruits. There are plants that can even make your home more secure! Cacti and agaves make good burglar barriers.

Along with produce, beautiful scents, and glorious views, a well-designed yard and garden has another benefit — namely, your family's health. With a balanced haven for plant life and beneficial wildlife, you can stop using deadly chemicals around the house. Besides the bugs, who breathes and absorbs those harmful substances? Every living creature, including your kids and pets, that's who.

We still don't know all of the long-term consequences of chemical use. Substituting natural techniques for synthetic ones will help you and everyone else in the long run. It's your landscape and garden design that's going to help you get there.

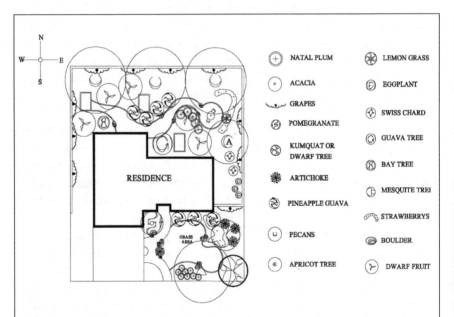

Edible Landscape. Here's just one idea for a home yard and garden design that gives you fruit, nuts and vegetables year-round. It provides micro-environments all around the home.

WATERING

More than anything else we do to our plants, how we water them determines how healthy they'll be. For decades, we've been told to conserve water in our arid climate. That's because water is a scarce, precious resource that deserves careful distribution. So when it comes to irrigating plants, the best way to conserve might surprise you.

Water deeply and infrequently. By giving grass, plants, and trees long, wet drinks, you don't have to do it as often. Watering deeply and infrequently will actually use far less water over time. Reducing the number of times you irrigate also means cheaper water bills. You're saving water *and* money.

It also means healthier plants. The soil in the low desert has a high pH and also tends to hold a lot of salts. The best way to combat this is to turn the hose, or drip system on low and let it run for a good long while. If irrigation is on so high that water is pooling on top of the soil, turn it down. You want it soaking in.

When water goes into the soil it percolates down, pushing away dangerous salts. But then as the water dries and evaporates, it moves back *up* again through the soil to moisten roots. If you've got moisture down deep, evaporation takes longer and you get more bang for your buck.

Did you know that plants "sweat"? It's called "evapotranspiration" and just like us, plants use it to keep themselves cool. The direct sun can force a plant to speed up that process, using more water. Wind will also make fast work of plant moisture. It's known as "desiccation."

Imagine getting out of a pool and standing in the sun on a windy day. You dry off real fast. But if you're in the shade and away from the breeze, you stay wet longer. The same rule applies to plants. If they hold moisture longer, they use it more efficiently.

There are more ways to reduce water use. Keep a deep layer (six to eight inches) of mulch around all plants. Mulch can be rock, or it can be organic things such as shredded bark or compost. It acts as insulation, cooling the soil and reducing evaporation. There are some rules to applying mulch — read more about it in the "Southwest Desert Soils" chapter. Later in the book, I'll tell you when and how to shade plants to protect them from dehydration.

I have included an irrigation schedule below with approximate amounts of water. Always check your plant and soil to confirm that the schedule works for your needs. And if not, modify.

To check the soil, get yourself a Soil Probe (see "TOOLS" chapter). Wet soil will let you push the probe into the ground. If the soil's dry, though, the probe will stop dead. Measure the probe to see how deep the water has gone. Different plants (trees, flowers, grass) require different depths of water penetration. I list those depths below, and in other places throughout the book.

WATERING SCHEDULE GUIDELINES

Plant Type		Spring (Mar. - May)	Summer (May - Oct.)	Fall (Oct. - Dec.)	Winter (Dec. - Mar.)	Watering Depth
Trees	Desert-adapted	14-30 days	7-21 days	14-30 days	30-60 days	3-4 ft.
	High-water-use	7-12 days	7-14 days	7-12 days	14-30 days	3-4 ft.
Shrubs	Desert-adapted	14-30 days	7-21 days	14-30 days	30-45 days	2-3 ft.
	High-water-use	7-10 days	5-7 days	7-10 days	10-14 days	2-3 ft.
Groundcovers and Vines	Desert-adapted	14-30 days	7-21 days	14-30 days	21-45 days	1 ft.
	High-water-use	7-10 days	2-5 days	7-10 days	10-14 days	1 ft.
Cacti and Succulents		21-45 days	14-30 days	21-45 days	if needed	1 ft.
Annuals		3-7 days	2-5 days	3-7 days	5-10 days	1 ft.
Warm Season Grass		7-10 days	3-5 days	7-10 days	30 days	6-8 in.
Cool Season Grass		3-5 days	none	3-5 days	5-10 days	8-10 in.

Guidelines for established plants (2 yrs. for shrubs, 5 yrs. for trees). Additional water is needed for new plantings, sandy soils, and extremely hot, dry weather. Water to the depth indicated and 1.5 times the plant canopy width.

Chart provided by Arizona Municipal Water Users Association.

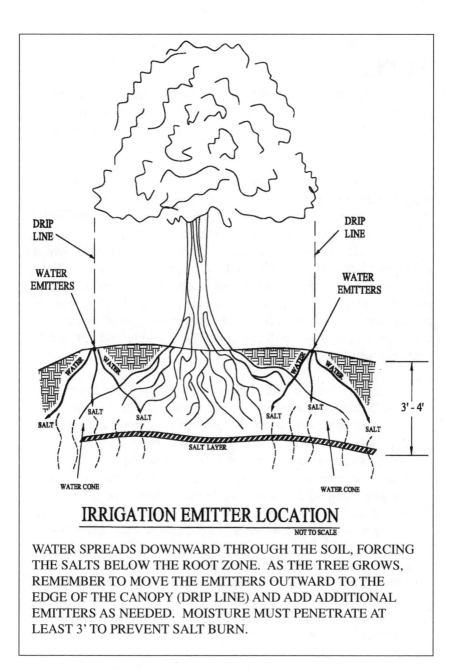

IRRIGATION EMITTER LOCATION

NOT TO SCALE

WATER SPREADS DOWNWARD THROUGH THE SOIL, FORCING
THE SALTS BELOW THE ROOT ZONE. AS THE TREE GROWS,
REMEMBER TO MOVE THE EMITTERS OUTWARD TO THE
EDGE OF THE CANOPY (DRIP LINE) AND ADD ADDITIONAL
EMITTERS AS NEEDED. MOISTURE MUST PENETRATE AT
LEAST 3' TO PREVENT SALT BURN.

TOOLS

There are a few tools that every gardener should have in the shed. Some of the items on the list might seem obvious, but I have to include everything to make the list complete, so please bear with me.

For working outside on your lawn and garden, you'll need two shovels (a round-head and a flat nose), two rakes (a leaf rake and a hard rake), a pick, a hula hoe (it has a stirrup-like attachment that makes it easier to work our hard desert soils), hand pruners, clippers for shrubs, and lopping shears.

In addition to the list above, there are a few other things you should have. These tools will be a huge help, trust me. The good thing is that they're not going to cost a lot of money. Get yourself a soaker hose, at least one spray bottle for "recipes," a soil temperature gauge, a Soil Probe, a turkey baster, and a magnifying glass. I know that sounds like a pretty odd list, but I'll explain everything.

- The soaker hose is good for irrigating deeply and directing water where you want it. You can water the yard or an individual plant with a soaker hose. It's the best way to go
- You'll use your spray bottle (or bottles) for my organic "recipes" for insect control and for fertilizing
- A soil temperature gauge can be more helpful than you can imagine. Planting dates are really based on soil temperatures. So instead of relying on a wide range of planting dates, a soil temperature gauge can tell you precisely when it's the best time to plant
- Get a turkey baster that you will use *exclusively* to spread some of my "recipes" for insect control. Never, ever use the same turkey baster on food
- The magnifying glass is helpful when you are inspecting for pests or damage

- A Soil Probe will help you decide when things need water. You need a thin piece of metal that you can push into the soil to check for moisture. How far you can push the rod into the soil determines if the plant needs water. To make your own, buy a four-foot piece of rebar for a couple bucks. Bend one end at a 90-degree angle to use as a handle. Use tape or white paint to mark one-foot increments down the rest of the rebar. For smaller plants, you can use a screwdriver (if the "blade" is at least ten inches long). This is the best way to keep from over-watering or under-watering. All of the "WATER IT" headings in this book give you a depth for a Soil Probe.

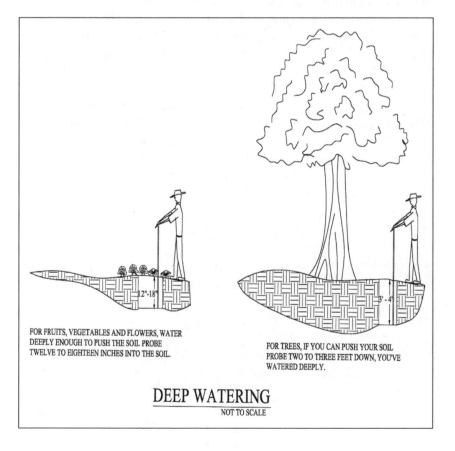

FOR FRUITS, VEGETABLES AND FLOWERS, WATER DEEPLY ENOUGH TO PUSH THE SOIL PROBE TWELVE TO EIGHTEEN INCHES INTO THE SOIL.

FOR TREES, IF YOU CAN PUSH YOUR SOIL PROBE TWO TO THREE FEET DOWN, YOU'VE WATERED DEEPLY.

DEEP WATERING
NOT TO SCALE

SOUTHWEST DESERT SOILS

THERE is some variance to the composition of soils in the low desert Southwest; but overall, the soils' contents are about the same. Regardless of where you are, the soil is high in pH (meaning the soil is alkaline rather than acidic), it's packed with caliche and clay, and contains a lot of salts.

A very dense layer of clay sits just two to three feet beneath the topsoil, blocking good drainage. The clay layer must be broken up before you can plant anything with deep roots. Wherever you plant, dig through that layer with a pick or other tool to remove the clay (see diagram).

Good drainage is imperative to a healthy environment. Whether you're planting Citrus to grow for another decade or a flower that will last four months, the water must drain away. Otherwise, soggy soil invites disease and rot. If you have soil that doesn't drain well, consider a raised garden (see the "ALTERNATIVE GARDENS" chapter later in this section).

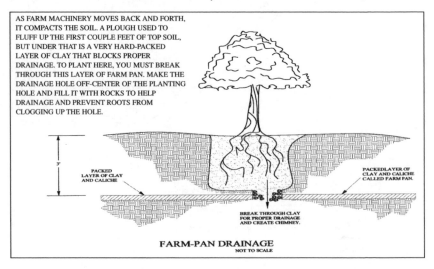

AS FARM MACHINERY MOVES BACK AND FORTH, IT COMPACTS THE SOIL. A PLOUGH USED TO FLUFF UP THE FIRST COUPLE FEET OF TOP SOIL, BUT UNDER THAT IS A VERY HARD-PACKED LAYER OF CLAY THAT BLOCKS PROPER DRAINAGE. TO PLANT HERE, YOU MUST BREAK THROUGH THIS LAYER OF FARM PAN. MAKE THE DRAINAGE HOLE OFF-CENTER OF THE PLANTING HOLE AND FILL IT WITH ROCKS TO HELP DRAINAGE AND PREVENT ROOTS FROM CLOGGING UP THE HOLE.

3'

PACKED LAYER OF CLAY AND CALICHE

PACKED LAYER OF CLAY AND CALICHE CALLED FARM PAN.

BREAK THROUGH CLAY FOR PROPER DRAINAGE AND CREATE CHIMNEY.

FARM-PAN DRAINAGE
NOT TO SCALE

Don't get the idea that our soil is bad for growing. This area has some of the best soil in the country, but it's so dry that most plants don't get the benefit of it. The single most limiting factor is water. When plants are young and establishing themselves here they need ample irrigation — but that water must be able to drain away. Young plants also require a lower pH, so utilize compost, gypsum, or soil sulfur.

If you're putting native plants in the ground, you don't need to add anything to the soil. For non-native plants popular opinion pushes the idea that you need a lot of rich soil additives. Not true. For the long-term health and growth of the plant in the low desert, it's actually better to *not* apply anything to the soil. Keeping the indigenous soil next to the roots helps the plant develop a strong root system.

No matter what you plant though, you'll want to add a ground cover or mulch to the surrounding area. Ground covers can include granite, compost, shredded bark, or even large river rock (see next diagram). A thick layer of ground cover or mulch (four to eight inches deep) will help protect the soil in a number of ways: it keeps it cool in the summer and warm in the winter, it retains and evenly distributes moisture and holds it longer in the soil, and organic mulches such as compost act as slow-release fertilizers and help with disease control. However, keep mulch away from the stems of the plants, or it can cause stem-rot problems.

Shredded bark works great in play areas for kids or in Dog pens. A lot of people believe this attracts insects, but if you get Citrus or Eucalyptus bark, the scent wards off a lot of the bugs in your soil. It's fairly soft, so it won't hurt the kids if they fall in it.

If you choose granite, I recommend you do *not* put plastic down. Over time, sheets of plastic suffocate and kill soil. To prevent weeds under the granite, use organic methods like corn gluten. This keeps the soil alive and breathing, without providing weeds with a place to grow.

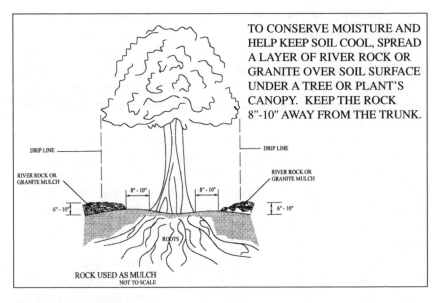

TO CONSERVE MOISTURE AND HELP KEEP SOIL COOL, SPREAD A LAYER OF RIVER ROCK OR GRANITE OVER SOIL SURFACE UNDER A TREE OR PLANT'S CANOPY. KEEP THE ROCK 8"-10" AWAY FROM THE TRUNK.

DRIP LINE   DRIP LINE

RIVER ROCK OR GRANITE MULCH   RIVER ROCK OR GRANITE MULCH

8" - 10"   8" - 10"

6" - 10"   6" - 10"

ROOTS

ROCK USED AS MULCH
NOT TO SCALE

FERTILIZER

Once you've spent the time planting and caring for your plants and grass, you'll want to make sure they're growing strong and healthy. Maybe you're thinking fertilizer. Well, one of the most common mistakes in home gardening is to *overfertilize*.

How you fertilize your yard and plants directly affects the health and vitality of everything (including insects, pets, children and adults) in your yard and home environment. You must be careful about what you spread around your lawn and plants! Some common chemical fertilizers use "filler" materials that are potentially carcinogenic. It's difficult to tell what those "filler" materials are, because there is no law that requires manufacturers to give a detailed list of ingredients.

I'm very leery of chemical fertilizers because so much of what goes in those big bags has the potential to make people and plants sick. The materials in the fertilizer are "systemic," meaning they are absorbed right through the leaf structure of the plants. But it also means that your skin absorbs the same stuff. If you touch it, it goes directly into your body. There are all kinds of studies that show the materials in many fertilizers lead to cancer. Of course, there are also many studies from chemical companies that show no direct relationship between fertilizers and cancer. In my opinion, it's far better to be safe than sorry.

To minimize any potential for health risk, go organic. I often hear about problems with fertilizers "burning" and actually killing surrounding grass and other vegetation and trees. That can come from several things, including the high salt content of most artificial fertilizers.

There's much less chance of "burning" things with organic or natural fertilizers, because ingredients work more slowly on the soil. And that's really the trick: micronutrients working to stimulate soil activity. It makes plants healthy in the long run. Repeat the mantra after me: *Feed the soil, not the plant.*

Many chemical fertilizers on the market have active ingredients (such as nitrogen, phosphorus, and potassium) which head straight for the roots to stimulate plant growth. Once the plant absorbs the material, there's nothing left. You have to fertilize again to give it more food. Then fertilize again. And again. It's like a drug — once the plant gets some, it can't stop using. Once the plant gets its meal, there's nothing left in the soil to maintain microbiotic activity. You end up with plants that have thick, rich growth that is prone to insect infestation and disease. Most synthetic materials not only prevent healthy soil, they can actually kill the beneficial microorganisms in the soil that make plants stronger.

When you think about how to help a plant grow, think natural. Compost, manures, cottonseed meal, bonemeal, fish emulsion, Milorganite, liquid seaweed, or even some of my homemade fertilizer recipes are safe bets. But more than that, natural fertilizers feed the soil, which in turn feeds and strengthens the plant.

For plants native to the area, you don't even want to feed the soil. For things like cacti and mesquite, fertilizer can actually harm them. The natural soil has enough to sustain indigenous plants. For those plants that do need the extra food, check the FERTILIZE IT information listed with each item in Section II — Garden Goodies.

Fertilizers around your home

Alfalfa

- Grind (in a blender) and spread 20 pounds of Alfalfa meal per 1,000 square feet
- Kills soil-borne diseases
- Alfalfa meal is great for Roses
- Contains nitrogen fixing bacteria in the roots

Coffee grounds:

- High in nitrogen, they lower pH and attract earthworms
- Spread in soil or compost

Epsom salts

- Essentially magnesium sulfate. Drench the soil around plants and flowers with a solution of one tablespoon of Epsom salts per gallon of water
- Great for Roses: two tablespoons per bush (just before blooming)
- Great for Queen Palms: five to ten tablespoons per palm
- Sprinkle over root zone and water in

Garlic

- Adds trace elements to soil. Blend cloves of Garlic with water, spread around garden
- Also repels insects, fungus (see "Organic Controls").

Hydrogen peroxide

- Oxygen helps increase microbial activity on leaves. Spray plants with one tablespoon of hydrogen peroxide per gallon water

Rabbit pellets (rabbit food)

- Helps all plants. Two to four cups per plant, then water in
- Or spread 10 to 25 pounds per 100 square feet on grass (about one dollar per pound)

Vinegar

- Lowers pH, and is great source of trace elements
- Add a tablespoon to water to make cut flowers last longer

Great organic fertilizers
- Manure: chicken or steer
- Compost
- Earthworm castings
    - Apply 20 pounds per 1,000 square feet
- Fish emulsion. Spray foliage and the ground. (One of my favorite recipes:
    - ¼ cup fish emulsion
    - ¼ cup liquid seaweed
    - 1-gallon water
    - splash of vinegar
    - (1 tablespoon of molasses will reduce smell)
- Gypsum counteracts salt buildup, lowers pH (for soil use only)
- Liquid seaweed. Spray foliage and ground. See recipe above
- Mauget is a great fertilizing system for trees — environmentally friendly, low water use, pinpoint accurate. Works directly into the bark layer
- Natural apple cider vinegar. Spray foliage and the ground
    - 1 tablespoon per gallon water (for extra kick add 3 aspirin and a ¼ cup of hydrogen peroxide)
- Soil sulfur counteracts salt buildup, lowers pH

COMPOST

If there were only one thing I could use in the garden, it would be compost. There's just about nothing better for your yard and garden. Straight compost takes care of all your fertilizing needs for anything and everything! Flowers, vegetables, shrubs, and lawns all love it. Weeds, disease, and pests hate it. Anything with friends and enemies like that is good in my book. Heck, I like it so much I'll sometimes sprinkle it on my ice cream.

Compost is what you get when organic material breaks down and decomposes in an enclosed space. Within that space, moisture is held in to help the process. In a composting bin, the chemical reactions of decomposition create the heat that essentially cooks the organic material into a big, dark brown hill of rich compost.

It's nature's way of recycling. In the wild, things decompose over time and turn themselves into compost. Look under layers of pine needles in a forest and you'll find some. In the desert, look under the leaf pile at the base of a bush and there's some compost. Before industrial-style farming started in the Midwest, everything was all a big pile of compost. It's everywhere!

And it's all good stuff. Nitrogen and more than a dozen essential elements pack it full of nutrients and micronutrients. It provides soil with a kick in the pants to get microbiotic activity going. That in turn makes the soil more hospitable to plants, helping it to provide roots with more food, like iron. This is one of the great benefits of organic additives.

These days, chemical fertilizers and additives are formulated with pure versions of things like nitrogen, phosphorus, and potassium. Most of these synthetic materials don't contain micronutrients. In fact, they can actually kill the beneficial microorganisms that make plants stronger! As far as I'm concerned, all of these big words mean I don't put synthetic chemicals anywhere near my garden or lawn.

As much as I like using compost as mulch on top of the soil, what I really love to do is garden in pure compost. It makes the best growing environment and virtually guarantees success for the plant. My all-time favorite gardening method is to make a raised garden (see "ALTERNATIVE GARDENS" chapter) and fill it with 12 to 18 inches of compost. There ya go. Your plants are set for life. Well, almost.

Whether compost is only topdressing or it's the lone soil source, you need to replenish it every so often. Upcoming chapters suggest you put a thick layer (four to eight inches) of compost around your plants. About every six months (ideally in spring and fall) topdress with additional compost. If you put four inches down, almost half of it will be gone six months later. Replace it.

And in those container gardens, add enough to maintain a level of 12 to 18 inches.

If you want to make your own compost, good for you. Start now and you'll have a batch of well-composted material in about six months. I say "well-composted," because you don't want to use it too early. When it's fluffy to the touch, smells like fresh Apples, and is so dark brown it's almost black, then it's ready to use. Otherwise, put it back in the bin.

How To Make Compost Work

Ingredients: Chicken or Steer Manure: 20%

Browns: 40%   Greens: 40%

Dry Leaves	Grass Clippings
Sawdust	Fruit Peels
Straw	Vegetables
Twigs	Landscape Trimmings

Shredded Newspaper or Junk Mail

- Blend manure into the green material and brown material.
- Layer greens and browns in a composting bin in the yard. Do not let the pile get too dry — add water to keep it as moist as a wrung out sponge.
- Turn the pile weekly. Remember to always layer so browns cover greens.

There are essentially two ways to compost: with earthworms or without. Earthworms speed up the process and they add castings (earthworm castings are little bits of magical soil) to the end product. You can let the earthworms migrate through the bottom of the compost during cooler months to help speed up the process. Red Wiggler earthworms work great. Get them from a bait and tackle shop or order them from my website. Without earthworms, you'll still get compost, it just won't happen as fast.

If you don't have the space or the time to make your own, you can buy compost. It's available at most nurseries and gardening centers.

WORM COMPOST BIN

- To start, take an old wine case and drill one-inch holes to provide circulation. Line with fiberglass screen (fiberglass won't rust) and use a lid so worms don't escape.
- Order up to 1,000 Red Wigglers. Drop them and their packing soil in with shredded newspaper and vegetable scraps.
- They consume about ½ their body weight per day.
- Keep the worms at 60-90° (F) — (your kitchen is a perfect place).
- You can add the worms to your large compost heap, so long as you maintain temperatures.
- Worm castings fertilize and ward off disease in garden plants, potted plants, and new seedlings.

No matter where compost comes from, you should have it in your garden and on your lawn. It helps activate and strengthen the soil. It holds and evenly distributes moisture. It cools the soil. It prevents weeds, keeps diseases from spreading, and it's the best fertilizer you can buy. It's the perfect investment. No risk and high yields. It's like a dream come true.

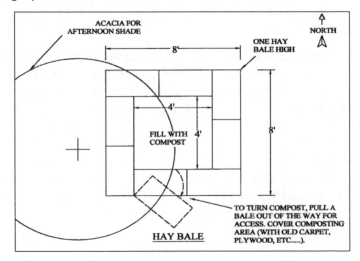

ACACIA FOR
AFTERNOON SHADE

ONE HAY
BALE HIGH

NORTH

8'

4'

FILL WITH 4'
COMPOST

8'

TO TURN COMPOST, PULL A
BALE OUT OF THE WAY FOR
ACCESS. COVER COMPOSTING
AREA (WITH OLD CARPET,
PLYWOOD, ETC.....).

HAY BALE

COMPANION PLANTING

Ever had a roommate you didn't like? How about moving in with that messy co-worker? Doesn't sound too good. But what if Bob Vila moved in and started remodeling your house for free? Would you mind if Michael Jordan used your extra bedroom and gave you basketball lessons? Not so bad, eh?

Well, Sunflowers are the Michael Jordans of a Melon patch. And Peas are the Bob Vilas of a Cornfield. Putting plants together that help one another to grow and thrive is called Companion Planting.

In nature, plants grow together as a community. Distinctive to any climatic region or elevation are the canopy plants, the mid-range plants, the ground covering plants, and the accent plants. These plants exist in a symbiotic relationship, all doing their part to support their mini-ecosystems. We want to mimic those systems. Growing a wide diversity of plants helps ward off pests and diseases, heightens crop flavor, and increases yields. In making these synergistic combinations, you are creating polycultures (a favorite word of mine). And that's a very good thing.

There are a few types of plants that protect their neighbors from insect pests. Some emit a scent that pests try to avoid. Such plants include the beautiful smelling Lavender, Rosemary, and Sage. Another type of pest control plant acts as a "trap crop." Consider trap crops your sacrificial frontline of defense in the fight against garden pests. It's similar to giving the kids paper plates while the adults use the fine china. If the paper plate gets dropped, who cares? Same thing with trap crops — they get eaten to protect the finer plants. Plant Lantana or Nasturtiums as an Aphid trap crop, protecting Roses and other plants.

Pest control plants can work in the opposite direction, too. Instead of dealing directly with a pest, these plants call for help. With flowers or scents, they attract bugs that are known as beneficial insects. They can be predators of other insect pests or they can be pollinators. Many herbs and other flowering plants attract beneficial insects.

Companion plantings also include plants that directly influence and enhance the growth of nearby plants. Most Legumes, (plants in the Pea family) are able to "fix" — or hold — nitrogen in the soil. They store the nitrogen in their roots. That's why I leave the roots buried and just cut off the tops when I'm done growing them. The soil can then utilize nitrogen from the withering roots. Nearby plants can then use this nitrogen.

Another helpful pairing involves plants with opposite root systems. The larger roots of a big plant can loosen the soil for smaller plants. Or plants with deep taproots, such as dandelions and alfalfa, bring minerals up to the surface where shallowly rooted plants can get at them.

Some plants provide physical benefits to plants grown nearby. Tall plants do triple duty by creating shade for smaller plants, supplying wind protection, and contributing humidity from evapotranspiration (plant sweat).

Then there are the plants that enjoy the same growing conditions and are good companions because one grows faster than the other, preventing their roots from competing for food and water. Carrots and Lettuce enjoy this type of companionship.

Additionally, when you're ready to remove a plant, think about what should replace it. As vegetable crops grow and produce, they extract nutrients from the soil. But some use more than others. As a rule of thumb, "light feeders" like Beets, Carrots, and Garlic should follow "heavy feeders" such as the cabbage family, Corn, and Tomatoes. When you rotate the next time, use things like Beans and Peas that will help build the soil back up, instead of depleting it.

Conversely, some plants should neither be planted together nor follow one another, because they are susceptible to the same diseases. Here in the desert, don't plant a member of the Solanaceae family (Tomatoes, Eggplants, and Peppers) in the same place you just had another Solanaceae. Keep family members clear of the area for at least three years. Petunias and Vincas also share diseases. These two flowers are often in the same beds, Petunias in the winter and Vincas in the summer. It's okay to do that for one year. Then something else needs to rotate in, to minimize a buildup of soil diseases.

As companions go, some of the combinations I sug[
will be a benefit to one plant over the other. Onions and Ga[   ]
great companions to Roses and keep Aphids away. No Rose should
be without its good buddy Garlic nearby! Roses, however, flourish in
moist soil, while Onions and Garlic need dry soil to cure (develop an
edible bulb). If you want edible Garlic and Onions, you'll need an
additional place to plant them. My list puts it all together.

Companion plants

Alyssum
- Attracts Butterflies, Ladybugs (also known as Ladybird Beetles) and beneficial insects that pollinate Squash and Tomato crops
- Attracts predaceous insects that eat Mealybugs, Scale insects, Spider Mites, Thrips
- Plant with Okra, Plum trees, Roses

Artemisia
- General insect repellent. Plant by doorways, throughout the garden
- Repels Ants, Aphids, Fleas, Mosquitoes, Moths, Ticks
- Dogs will avoid it
- Plant with Carrots, Eggplant, Roses. Do not plant with Fennel
- Repellent recipe: Steep $1^1/_2$ cups of Artemisia leaves in one gallon of water, strain and spray on plants

Bachelor's Button
- Attracts beneficial pollinators for Corn, Melons, Squash
- Attracts predaceous insects that eat Mosquito larvae, Scales, Thrips
- Plant with flowers, Pear trees

Basil (including Opal Basil)
- Attracts beneficial pollinators
- Plant throughout garden to repel Aphids, flies, Mosquitoes, Moths, Spider Mites, Tomato Hornworms
- Plant with Cauliflower, Tomatoes, Apricot, Peach trees
- Do not plant with Rue

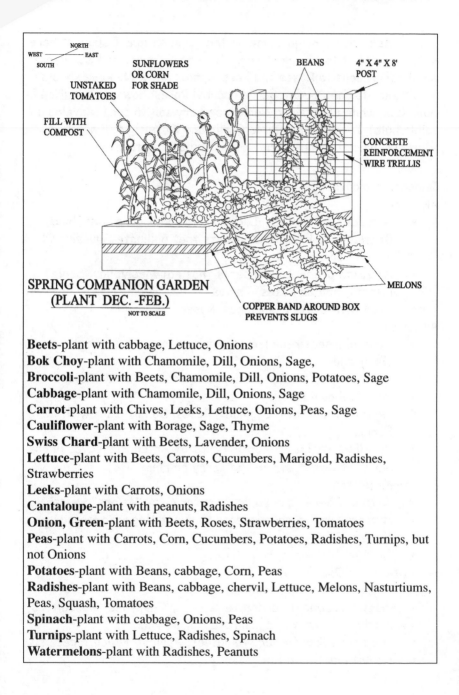

SPRING COMPANION GARDEN (PLANT DEC. -FEB.)
NOT TO SCALE

Beets-plant with cabbage, Lettuce, Onions
Bok Choy-plant with Chamomile, Dill, Onions, Sage,
Broccoli-plant with Beets, Chamomile, Dill, Onions, Potatoes, Sage
Cabbage-plant with Chamomile, Dill, Onions, Sage
Carrot-plant with Chives, Leeks, Lettuce, Onions, Peas, Sage
Cauliflower-plant with Borage, Sage, Thyme
Swiss Chard-plant with Beets, Lavender, Onions
Lettuce-plant with Beets, Carrots, Cucumbers, Marigold, Radishes, Strawberries
Leeks-plant with Carrots, Onions
Cantaloupe-plant with peanuts, Radishes
Onion, Green-plant with Beets, Roses, Strawberries, Tomatoes
Peas-plant with Carrots, Corn, Cucumbers, Potatoes, Radishes, Turnips, but not Onions
Potatoes-plant with Beans, cabbage, Corn, Peas
Radishes-plant with Beans, cabbage, chervil, Lettuce, Melons, Nasturtiums, Peas, Squash, Tomatoes
Spinach-plant with cabbage, Onions, Peas
Turnips-plant with Lettuce, Radishes, Spinach
Watermelons-plant with Radishes, Peanuts

Bay
- Leaves repel Ants, Caterpillars, grubs, Moths

Beans
- Attract nitrogen to surrounding soil
- Plant with Corn, Eggplants, Petunias, Strawberries
- Plant with Sunflowers for shade
- Repel Moths
- Do not plant with Fennel, gladiolus

Borage
- Plant with Strawberries, Tomatoes
- Repels Moths, Tomato Hornworms

Calendula
- Interplant with Lettuce, Peas, Tomatoes
- Good with Alyssum, Marigolds, Pansies, Vincas
- Deters Beetles, Caterpillars, Moths

Catmint
- Repels Beetles including flea Beetles

Catnip
- Plant near pet runs to deter Ants, Beetles, Fleas
- Plant with crops to keep mice, insects away

Chamomile
- Improves flavor of Onions, cabbage family
- Once known as the Doctor Plant because it improves health of nearby plants
- Attracts beneficial pollinators, predaceous insects

Chives (also Onion chives and Garlic Chives)
- Plant with Carrots, Parsley
- Plant with Roses to protect from Black spot, Mildew
- Plant thickly around trunks of stone fruit trees to deter fruit tree Borers
- Deter Aphids, Crickets, Grasshoppers

Chrysanthemum paludosum
- Works great with Lettuce, Roses, and all other plants
- Repels most insects
- Reseeds easily

Citrus
- Bark chips repel Fleas, Ticks
- Juice (especially Lemon juice) kills Ants

Coreopsis
- General insect deterrent
- Attracts many pollinators, predaceous insects including those that eat Mealybugs, Scale insects, Spider Mites, Whiteflies

Coriander (cilantro)
- General insect deterrent
- Attracts beneficial pollinators, predaceous insects, including Trichogramma wasps and others that eat Mealybugs, Scale insects, Spider Mites, Thrips, Whiteflies

Corn
- Plant with Dill, Nasturtiums
- To fight Earworm Caterpillars, attract Birds by planting Sunflowers
- Provides shade for Bush Beans, Bok Choy, Cucumbers, Melons, Potatoes, Pumpkins, Squash
- Do not plant Artichokes after Corn or vice versa

Cosmos
- General insect deterrent
- Attracts Ladybugs, Green Lacewings, many other beneficial insects that feed on Mealybugs

Cucumbers
- For sweeter Cucumbers, plant with Sunflowers

Dandelion
- Good with grasses. Extremely long roots bring minerals up to the surface
- Encourages vigorous growth in other flowers, triggers fruit to ripen faster
- Full of all kinds of vitamins
- I love Dandelion salads

Dill
- Attracts beneficial pollinators, predaceous insects including Trichogramma wasps and others that eat Mealybugs, Scale insects, Spider Mites, Whiteflies
- Helps Corn produce bigger ears

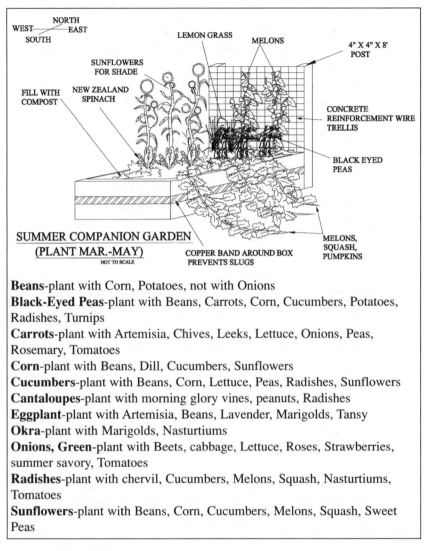

WEST — NORTH — EAST
SOUTH

LEMON GRASS

MELONS

SUNFLOWERS
FOR SHADE

4" X 4" X 8'
POST

FILL WITH
COMPOST

NEW ZEALAND
SPINACH

CONCRETE
REINFORCEMENT WIRE
TRELLIS

BLACK EYED
PEAS

SUMMER COMPANION GARDEN
(PLANT MAR.-MAY)
NOT TO SCALE

COPPER BAND AROUND BOX
PREVENTS SLUGS

MELONS,
SQUASH,
PUMPKINS

Beans-plant with Corn, Potatoes, not with Onions

Black-Eyed Peas-plant with Beans, Carrots, Corn, Cucumbers, Potatoes, Radishes, Turnips

Carrots-plant with Artemisia, Chives, Leeks, Lettuce, Onions, Peas, Rosemary, Tomatoes

Corn-plant with Beans, Dill, Cucumbers, Sunflowers

Cucumbers-plant with Beans, Corn, Lettuce, Peas, Radishes, Sunflowers

Cantaloupes-plant with morning glory vines, peanuts, Radishes

Eggplant-plant with Artemisia, Beans, Lavender, Marigolds, Tansy

Okra-plant with Marigolds, Nasturtiums

Onions, Green-plant with Beets, cabbage, Lettuce, Roses, Strawberries, summer savory, Tomatoes

Radishes-plant with chervil, Cucumbers, Melons, Squash, Nasturtiums, Tomatoes

Sunflowers-plant with Beans, Corn, Cucumbers, Melons, Squash, Sweet Peas

Dutch White Clover
- Great cover crop. It helps the soil rest and rejuvenate. Plant in pockets of bare soil or where you're waiting to plant something. When it's about one inch high, till it into the soil for a quick nitrogen fix

Eggplant
- Plant with Tarragon, Thyme to improve flavor, yield
- Plant Artemisia, Lavender, Marigolds, Tansy, Thyme to repel Aphids
- Plant with Beans
- Do not plant with Onions, Garlic, Potatoes

Eucalyptus
- Use bark and dried leaves to deter Fleas, Ticks

Fennel
- Attracts beneficial pollinators, predaceous insects
- To repel Fleas, rub juice of crushed leaves on pet's fur, place dried leaves and seeds in pet's bedding
- Do not plant with Artemisia, Bush Beans, Coriander, Tomatoes

Feverfew
- General insect repellent
- Attracts beneficial pollinators and predaceous insects, including ones that eat Scale insects, Whiteflies

Fleabane
- Attracts beneficial insects that eat Scale insects
- Easy to grow. Great looking flower is good throughout garden
- Old wive's tale: Fleabane repels Fleas. Miners planted Fleabane around their shacks to deter Fleas

Flowering Onion
- Protect Roses from Aphids, Black spot, Mildew

Garlic
- Protects Roses from Aphids, Black spot, Mildew
- Protects stone fruit trees from fruit tree Borers
- Deters Crickets, Grasshoppers

Geranium (Pelargonium)
- General insect repellant
- Scented Geraniums deter Ants, Moths

Lantana
- Use this trap crop in a sunny corner as a leafy banquet for many insect pests including Whiteflies

Lavender
- Plant with Eggplant, Swiss Chard
- General insect repellant. Plant throughout garden
- Repels Ants, Aphids, Fleas, Ticks, Mosquitoes, silverfish
- Discourages Crickets, Grasshoppers, mice, Moths, Rabbits
- Bees and Butterflies love Lavender

Leeks
- Plant Leeks with Onions, Carrots
- Since Leeks are slow growing, interplant with cabbage family, Lettuce, herbs to use space productively
- Protect Roses from Aphids, Black spot, Mildew

Lemon Balm (Melissa officinalis)
- Attracts bees to pollinate Melons, Cucumbers
- Attracts beneficial pollinators and predaceous insects including ones that eat Scales, Whiteflies

Lettuce
- Plant with Beets, cabbage family, Carrots, Cucumbers, Marigolds, Strawberries
- Plant Radishes to deter Aphids

Marigold (Tagetes)
- Helps Tomatoes produce better yields
- Interplant with bulbs, Potatoes, Roses, Strawberries to fight disease, increase plant vigor
  - Must do this for at least two years
- Strong fragrance deters many pests, including Aphids, Crickets, Grasshoppers, Whiteflies
- Attracts Hoverflies, Butterflies, other beneficial insects

Mexican Primrose
- The pink flowers of this trap crop protect Roses from Aphids and Flea Beetles

Mints (including Pennyroyal and Spearmint)
- General insect repellant
- Repel Ants, Aphids, Moths, Whiteflies
- Flowers attract predaceous insects
- Sink bottomless pots of mint near cabbage to deter Moths

Nasturtium
- Repels Aphids for Broccoli
- Repels squash bugs. (Because Squash grows fast, plant Nasturtiums several weeks earlier than Squash)
- Repels Beetles, striped pumpkin Beetles, Cucumber pests, Moths, Whiteflies
- Plant around stone fruit trees to confuse insects' sense of smell
- Attract beneficial insects that eat Scale

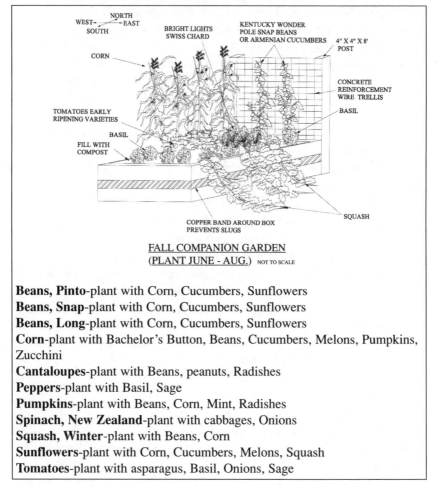

FALL COMPANION GARDEN
(PLANT JUNE - AUG.) NOT TO SCALE

Beans, Pinto-plant with Corn, Cucumbers, Sunflowers
Beans, Snap-plant with Corn, Cucumbers, Sunflowers
Beans, Long-plant with Corn, Cucumbers, Sunflowers
Corn-plant with Bachelor's Button, Beans, Cucumbers, Melons, Pumpkins, Zucchini
Cantaloupes-plant with Beans, peanuts, Radishes
Peppers-plant with Basil, Sage
Pumpkins-plant with Beans, Corn, Mint, Radishes
Spinach, New Zealand-plant with cabbages, Onions
Squash, Winter-plant with Beans, Corn
Sunflowers-plant with Corn, Cucumbers, Melons, Squash
Tomatoes-plant with asparagus, Basil, Onions, Sage

Onions
- Gardener's best friend
- Great with Beets, Lettuce, Roses, Strawberries, Tomatoes
- Plant thickly to protect fruit trees from Borers
- Deter Ants, Aphids, Crickets, Grasshoppers, Moths, Slugs
- Plant Chamomile to give Onions more vigor
- Do not plant Onions with Beans, Peas, Peppers

Parsley
- Plant with asparagus, Carrots, Chives, Tomatoes
- Protects Roses from Rose Beetles
- Let some plants flower to attract pollinators and predaceous insects that will eat Mealybugs, Scale, Whiteflies

Pennyroyal
- General insect deterrent
- Deters Ants, Crickets, flies, Grasshoppers, Mosquitoes
- Plant in pots or in ground around patio areas in part shade
- After testing for skin sensitivity, rub leaves over your skin as insect repellent

Peppers
- Interplant among flowers to deter insects
- Don't plant with Onions

Petunia
- Plant with Broccoli, Lettuce, Tomatoes
- Plant with Beans and Potatoes to repel Beetles
- Repels Aphids

Radishes
- Protect Cucumber, Lettuce, Nasturtium, Peas, Squash from Aphids
- Repel Carrot flies, cucumber Beetles, Spider Mites
- Lettuce on either side helps Radish grow strong

Rose
- Plant with Artemisia, Catnip, Coriander, Fennel, Geraniums, Mints, Rosemary, Tansy, Thyme
- Plant Garlic, Nasturtiums, Onions, Parsley, Petunias to repel Aphids
- Onions and Garlic help prevent Black spot, Mildew
- Plant with Marigolds to help deter non-beneficial nematodes

Rosemary
- Plant throughout garden with Brussels Sprouts, Melons, Squash, and other fruits or vegetables that need pollinating
- Wonderful at attracting bees and other pollinators
- Good at disrupting the sensory mechanisms of most insects, including Beetles, Crickets, Fleas, Grasshoppers, Moths
- Put sprigs with woolens to deter Moths

Rue
- Plant Rue with Roses
- Deters Fleas, flies. Put in pet areas, especially near food and water dishes
- Rub on furniture to keep Cats from clawing
- Do not combine with Basil in the garden

Sage
- Plant with cabbage family, Carrots, Rosemary, and Tomatoes
- Don't plant near Cucumbers. It makes cukes taste bitter
- Strong fragrance repels many pests including Crickets, Grasshoppers, Mice, Moths
- Put dried leaves in with woolens to repel wool Moths
- Botanical name Salvia means "to save" (Roman)
- Used for centuries to promote health and healing

Santolina
- General pest deterrent. Repels Crickets, Fleas, Grasshoppers, Rabbits
- Plant with Roses

Society Garlic
- Protects Roses from Aphids, Black spot, Mildew

Squash
- Plant with Corn, Nasturtium, peanuts

Sunflowers
- Easy to grow. Great addition to almost any garden
- Good companions to Corn, Cucumber
- Plant on west side of garden to provide afternoon shade for sun-sensitive plants, such as Tomatoes
- Attract bees and Birds to garden. Birds then stick around to feast on insects
- Do not plant with pole Beans, Potatoes

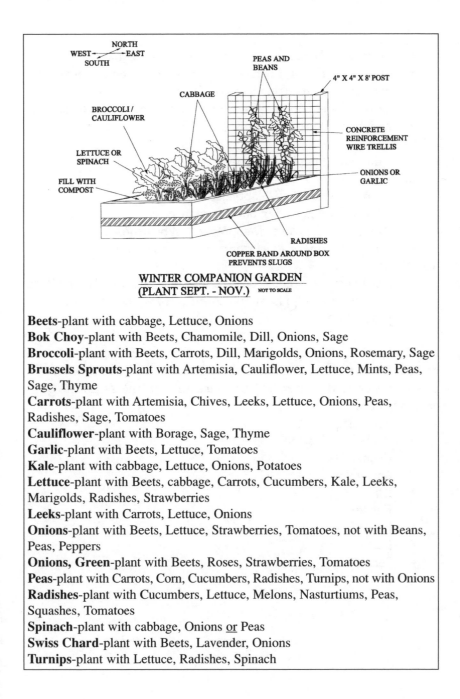

WINTER COMPANION GARDEN (PLANT SEPT. - NOV.) NOT TO SCALE

Beets-plant with cabbage, Lettuce, Onions
Bok Choy-plant with Beets, Chamomile, Dill, Onions, Sage
Broccoli-plant with Beets, Carrots, Dill, Marigolds, Onions, Rosemary, Sage
Brussels Sprouts-plant with Artemisia, Cauliflower, Lettuce, Mints, Peas, Sage, Thyme
Carrots-plant with Artemisia, Chives, Leeks, Lettuce, Onions, Peas, Radishes, Sage, Tomatoes
Cauliflower-plant with Borage, Sage, Thyme
Garlic-plant with Beets, Lettuce, Tomatoes
Kale-plant with cabbage, Lettuce, Onions, Potatoes
Lettuce-plant with Beets, cabbage, Carrots, Cucumbers, Kale, Leeks, Marigolds, Radishes, Strawberries
Leeks-plant with Carrots, Lettuce, Onions
Onions-plant with Beets, Lettuce, Strawberries, Tomatoes, not with Beans, Peas, Peppers
Onions, Green-plant with Beets, Roses, Strawberries, Tomatoes
Peas-plant with Carrots, Corn, Cucumbers, Radishes, Turnips, not with Onions
Radishes-plant with Cucumbers, Lettuce, Melons, Nasturtiums, Peas, Squashes, Tomatoes
Spinach-plant with cabbage, Onions or Peas
Swiss Chard-plant with Beets, Lavender, Onions
Turnips-plant with Lettuce, Radishes, Spinach

Tansy
- Plant with Roses, deciduous fruit trees, veggies
- Plant near doors. Spread a layer of Tansy leaves on the ground or on a patio to ward off insects
- Deters Ants, Aphids, Beetles, Fleas, Moths, squash bugs
- Ladybugs flock to it

Tarragon
- Plant with Eggplant, Peppers

Thyme
- Plant with Eggplant, cabbages
- Attracts bees, other beneficial insects
- Deters Caterpillars, flies, Moths, Whiteflies
- Sprigs of Thyme in winter woolens repel Moths

Tomatoes
- Plant with asparagus, Basil, Chamomile, Marigolds, and Peas
- Plant with Basil, Nasturtiums, Sage for general insect protection

Here is a list of flowers and herbs that are great at attracting beneficial insects to the garden. Whether you want pollinators or pest hunters, plant these early in the season to get an upper hand.
- Alyssum
- Bachelor's Button
- Chamomile
- Coriander
- Dill
- Fennel
- Feverfew
- Lemon Balm
- Parsley

ALTERNATIVE GARDENS

Getting the soil to work *for* you can require a lot of work *from* you. The consistency of clay and high pH content of our soils here in the low desert of Arizona require you to till soil, which can be hard work. Planting things in hard-packed dirt demands more care and effort.

Things aren't so hard though, when you garden above the soil line. In bypassing the native soil, different rules apply and you take complete control over all aspects of the process. You dictate 100% of soil content, irrigation, drainage, etc. These aboveground gardens work best when filled entirely with compost. Flowers, vegetables, herbs, and most other plants love to root in the rich organic material.

Alternatives include:
* No-till gardens
* Tire gardens
* Raised gardens

They raise plant life up and into a soil that has lots of nutrients and room to root. They also drain very well. My preferred method of growing things is in a raised garden. There's no tilling and it saves your back some strain because you don't bend down as far to tend the garden.

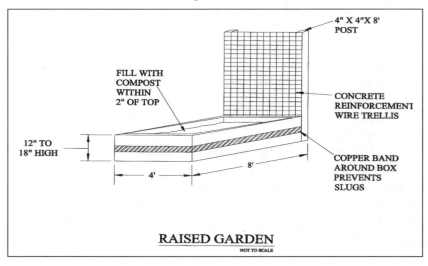

FILL WITH COMPOST WITHIN 2" OF TOP

4" X 4" X 8' POST

CONCRETE REINFORCEMENT WIRE TRELLIS

COPPER BAND AROUND BOX PREVENTS SLUGS

12" TO 18" HIGH

4'

8'

RAISED GARDEN
NOT TO SCALE

There is also no need to aerate the soil, because the simple act of pouring compost in will provide plenty of fresh air and oxygen. Gardening in the compost of raised beds allows you to eliminate chemical fertilizers, insecticides and herbicides, because the compost provides enough nutrients to the soil and plants that they don't require chemical help. This natural, organic way of gardening provides so many benefits there is really no argument against using them.

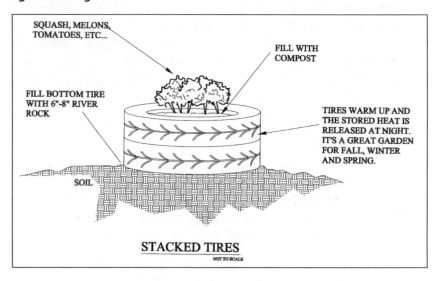

I've included a few diagrams here to show you what they can look like. The size and shape are up to you, but I've found that they should be no wider than four feet at any point, or else it's difficult to get at plants in the middle. The ideal height is about 18 inches, but you can go higher. Don't go any lower than 12 inches off the ground.

And speaking of the ground, give yourself enough space. You'll want room to build the garden and then when it's done, have at least three feet around each side. You need room to move and work. Make sure that the soil underneath your alternative garden drains fairly well. Use a hard rake or pick to break through it if you have to.

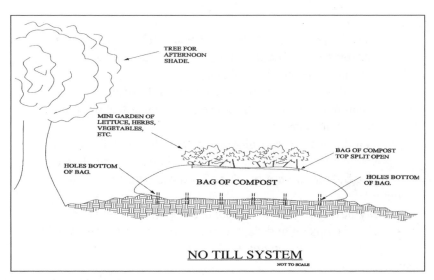

TREE FOR
AFTERNOON
SHADE.

MINI GARDEN OF
LETTUCE, HERBS,
VEGETABLES,
ETC.

BAG OF COMPOST
TOP SPLIT OPEN

HOLES BOTTOM
OF BAG.

BAG OF COMPOST

HOLES BOTTOM
OF BAG.

NO TILL SYSTEM

NOT TO SCALE

Container Gardens

No land? No space? Wrong sun exposure? Even without a plot of land, you can grow a beautiful and productive garden entirely in containers. You've got the potential for an explosion of vibrant colors or veggies, and you can put them anywhere you want them. It's simple, easy, and inexpensive.

Containers can dry out quickly in the heat of summer. So be prepared to water often (daily, if necessary).

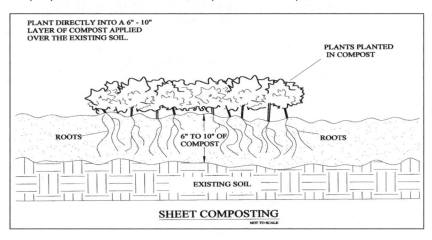

PLANT DIRECTLY INTO A 6" - 10"
LAYER OF COMPOST APPLIED
OVER THE EXISTING SOIL.

PLANTS PLANTED
IN COMPOST

ROOTS

6" TO 10" OF
COMPOST

ROOTS

EXISTING SOIL

SHEET COMPOSTING

NOT TO SCALE

The Container
- The bigger, the better. Anything smaller than a five gallon container lets the soil heat up so much that water can "steam" the roots in summer
- Soil stays cooler in light colored containers
- Foam pots and wooden barrels are insulated better than plastic or terra-cotta
- For decorative containers without drainage holes, put a smaller pot inside and plant in it. Raise the smaller pot off the bottom with a brick or inverted saucer

Placement
- My pots get eastern exposure for afternoon shade
- For dimension and depth, group together three to five pots of varying sizes

Drainage
- Drill two ¾-inch holes per square foot of container bottom
- Add one to two inches of pea gravel or Styrofoam beads, then cover with a piece of hardware fabric or mesh
- Lift the pots off the ground with bricks, pot feet (specially made to raise pots), or moveable dollies. Do this BEFORE pots are filled with soil and plants

Soil
- Use commercial soil-less potting mix, or make your own inexpensive, fast-draining, nutrient-holding mix
- Recipe for homemade potting mix:
  - 1 part vermiculite (absorbs then releases nutrients)
  - 1 part peat moss (lowers pH, adds organic material)
  - 1 part perlite (keeps mix fluffy, holds oxygen in mix)
  - 1 to 2 handfuls compost (activates soil microbes for healthy, vigorous plant growth)
  - A little "Soil Moist" (see package for amounts)
- Fill the container partially with the soil mix and tamp down.

The Plant
- Don't mix plants that have conflicting needs. In each pot, use plants with similar sun and water requirements
- Leave two inches of clearance from top of root ball to top of pot to allow for layer of mulch and for watering
- For color, plant densely
  - Put tallest plant in the center. Mature height shouldn't be more than 1½ times the height of pot
  - Fill in around the central plant, adding those that trail or drape over edges of container
  - A touch of white in any grouping emphasizes colors of other plants
- For vegetables, choose bush or dwarf types. Look for the early ripening varieties that will produce quicker
  - The following vegetables need six hours of sunlight daily (morning sun is preferred)
  - The climbing or vining type veggies may be grown up a trellis placed in the pot when the soil is added
  - Warm weather crops (plant in warm weather)
    - Beans
    - Corn (get large containers and group pots together for pollination)
    - Cucumbers
    - Eggplants
    - Melons
    - Patio or cherry Tomatoes
    - Peppers
    - Swiss Chard
  - Cool weather crops (plant in cool weather)
    - Beets
    - Broccoli, cabbage, Cauliflower
    - Carrots
    - Lettuce
    - Peas
    - Spinach

- Herbs
  - Many herbs lend themselves to pot culture
  - Tuck them in with flowers and veggies (they attract beneficial insects and help repel pests)
    - Basil
    - Chives
    - Marigold
    - Marjoram
    - Mint
    - Nasturtium
    - Parsley
    - Rosemary
    - Sage
    - Savory
    - Thyme

Watering
- Irrigate daily when temperatures exceed 90° (F)
- Two to three times a week in fall, spring
- One to two times a week in winter

Fertilizing
- With frequent watering, use organic fertilizer (fish emulsion, liquid seaweed, etc.) every two weeks (or use a more diluted solution every time you water)
- Liquid seaweed improves plants' heat/cold resistance and has the amazing ability to help plants ward off disease

Pest control
- Check plants often for insect damage (don't forget to look on the undersides of the leaves)
- For infestations, mix a homemade solution of 1 to 2 tablespoons of blue dishwashing liquid to 1 gallon of water
- Potted plants often attract fungus gnats (They're irritating, but harmless. To repel, drench soil with mixture of 1 capful of yellow Listerine to 1 gallon of water)
- NOTE: weakened, stressed plants attract pests (the stronger the plant, the fewer pest problems)

VEGETABLES

WHEN dinnertime rolls around and you want to avoid an expensive restaurant or a long trip to the grocery store, where do you go? If you've owned this book for long, you just take a few paces out the back door for fresh organic produce! Pick and choose from your vegetable garden to enjoy the things that you've cultivated.

Whether you use vegetables in small salads or as full entrees, it's satisfying to know that gardening is one of the healthiest things you can do for your family and for the environment. And I promise you that the food you grow will be tastier than anything you can buy at the store.

There is a vast array of veggies that thrive in the low deserts of the Southwest. Our abundant sunlight and moderate temperatures make anything possible! In the pages ahead, I've got all the information you need to get healthy veggies from Artichokes to Zucchinis and everything in between.

For each item, I'll explain: how to CHOOSE IT, the best way to PLANT IT, how to WATER IT, how to CARE FOR IT, the right stuff to use to FERTILIZE IT, how to know when it's ripe enough to ENJOY IT, and what to do to PROTECT IT.

I'll also give you a list of Companion Plants that work best together, and what tools and ingredients you'll need for each item. In short, this section will teach you how to get a vibrant and healthy plant while avoiding the pitfalls.

One of the best things you can do for *any* garden is to put it above ground. A raised garden eliminates the need to till — a difficult, and sometimes ineffective, technique of working the native soil. By using organic material, maintaining a balance of beneficial insects and animals, and abolishing synthetic chemicals, you'll go a long way to creating a fantastic and healthy garden.

Before you get going, I want to define a few words and phrases to make things easier as you plan your garden.

- Direct Seed

   Plant the seed directly into the garden. Generally, the quickest Germination occurs when the soil temperatures are above 55°.

- Germination

   This is the point when the seed has sprouted, emerged through the surface of the soil, and grown a few leaves.

- Seedling Transplant

   This is when seed is started away from the garden (maybe in a greenhouse) so that it can grow to a transplantable size. When the seedling is a couple of inches tall, it's ready to go into the garden.

- Nursery Stock

   Vegetable, flower and herb varieties are often available in a size range from 6-packs to 5-gallon containers. Plant them as soon as they are available from nurseries.

- Heirloom

   Simply put, Heirlooms are tried-and-true varieties that are open-pollinated. What does that mean to you? With Heirloom varieties, the seed you gather from the plant will produce another plant just like the original. With hybrid varieties (which are very common), you don't know what the second-generation seed will produce.

Now get your cookbook ready for the tasty vegetables to come.

ARTICHOKES

THERE are two main varieties of Artichoke: Globe and Jerusalem. The Globe is a relative of the thistle family and grows very fast. The mature flower resembles a very large dark blue/purple thistle. The Jerusalem grows quite differently. It's actually a member of the Sunflower family, but grows as a tuber, like a Potato. To grow Globes from seed, try the Imperial Star Artichoke.

Globes

If you're able to find one in the fall, transplant it then. Otherwise, plan to plant mid-January through mid-March as edible vegetables or as landscape plants. The large, silvery-gray foliage is great as an accent in the back of the garden bed. In the low desert, Globe Artichokes usually produce for several seasons, with heavier production starting the second year.

CHOOSE IT: When buying a transplant, make sure the leaves are an even color (without spots or discoloration) and that there aren't any Aphids or other insects lurking on the undersides of the leaves or on the stems. If you plant from a one-gallon container in January, Artichokes produce a light crop by June.

> Artichokes are good accent plants for landscaping. I let mine go dormant in summer, then bring them back in fall.

> Artichokes need a nutrient-rich soil, so don't plant them in the same place you had Corn, Tomatoes, or cabbages. Those crops are heavy feeders that deplete the soil of nitrogen. Put Artichokes somewhere else.

PLANT IT: Put Globes in an eastern exposure to give them some afternoon shade. Plant in compost rich soil when soil temperatures are 60-85° (F). Space them about three to four feet apart. Artichokes planted in fall have a heavy crop the first spring.

WATER IT: Artichokes need a lot of water. Maintain moisture two to three feet down. Irrigate when the top inch of the soil is dry.

CARE FOR IT: Harvest often because if the buds open and flower, the plant will quit producing Artichokes. As the weather gets warmer, flowers start opening sooner and sooner. That's when Artichokes get tough and inedible. When this happens, leave the buds on the stalk and let the tops grow. The plant will start to die back in June. At that point, I like to chop off 90% of the plant, leaving just a stub sticking out of the ground. Drop the leaves around the plant to act as mulch. During this summer dormancy, reduce watering. In August, resume watering and apply fish emulsion or manure to encourage good fall growth.

> Artichokes do not have specific companion plants, but you can grow them with various flowers and herbs.

FERTILIZE IT: Once they're planted, apply a thick layer (four to six inches) of mulch around the Artichoke, but don't let the mulch touch the plant stem.

ENJOY IT: Harvest Artichokes when they reach softball-size, and the leaves are still tightly closed.

PROTECT IT: Protect Artichokes from hard frosts. Aphids are the most common pests. See "Organic Pest Control" for solutions. Diseases don't generally bother Globes.

Jerusalems

The Jerusalem Artichokes are also known as Sunchokes and can be found in most grocery stores sold in little mesh bags like Onions. Two pounds gives 32 tubers (cut into pieces one and one-half inches long), so you might not need to plant them all.

What You Need To Start
Tuber with eye
Trowel or shovel
Compost or manure
Mulch

CHOOSE IT: Jerusalems need a long growing season of up to 120 days from Germination. From seed, Mammoth French White and French White Improved varieties do very well here.

PLANT IT: Between mid-January and mid-May, when soil temperatures are 50-85° (F), plant this perennial tuber about four inches deep and 18 inches apart. Cover with four to six inches of mulch. Be careful where these veggies are located, though. They can spread aggressively and quickly. Keep them in a separate area.

WATER IT: When the top one-inch of the soil is dry, water until it's moist to two feet deep. Jerusalem Artichokes cannot tolerate drought.

CARE FOR IT: Think "shallow" when it comes to the Jerusalem. Tubers grow close to the soil level, so be careful not to damage them when you're weeding. On the flip side, they get six to seven feet tall.

FERTILIZE IT: There is a steady supply of nutrients from the decomposition of the compost or manure you used as organic mulch. But it's important to supplement every couple of weeks with a solution of fish emulsion or liquid seaweed. Follow these fertilizations with a deep irrigation.

ENJOY IT: These tubers are great for salads, relishes and pickles, and the yellow flowers are real nice. When you see flowers starting to wane (usually toward the end of September), harvest all Sunchoke tubers at once. This prevents regrowth in the fall.

PROTECT IT: Be careful not to damage by weeding too deeply. Don't let the soil dry out. Diseases and pests leave the Sunchoke alone.

BEANS

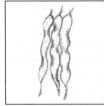

THIS vegetable grows fast as a bush or vine, and is full of vitamins A and C, calcium, and iron. It takes up a lot of space and is very prolific. Usually the bush varieties produce more quickly than the pole varieties. I suggest also trying the Asparagus or Chinese yard-long Bean. Once Beans are ready to harvest, be prepared to pick them often!

Companion Plants
Calendula
Carrots
Corn
Cucumbers
Fennel
Petunias
Potatoes
Radishes
Rosemary
Sunflowers

CHOOSE IT: There are two classes of Snap Beans: bush types or pole types. Each class has many varieties. Generally here in the low desert, you'll plant bush Beans in the spring, because it's a short season. Pole Beans get planted in the summer to produce during the longer fall season. Bush varieties include: Rolande (56 days from Germination), which has superb quality and taste and grows to about six inches long, and Tri-Color Mix (55 days). The gold, royal purple, and dark green of Tri-Color makes it a great garden accent as well as a tender, juicy veggie. Baby Bush varieties include: Mini Bean Yellow (52 days) and Mon Petite Cheri (58 days).

Several dependable pole varieties include Kentucky Blue (58 days from Germination), Blue Lake (60 days) and Trueblue (54 days). They thrive in warm weather and will actually rot in soils too cold or wet. Choose varieties that are resistant to bacterial diseases and wilts. Selecting these resistant types make growing Beans much easier.

PLANT IT: From mid-March through April when soil temperatures are 60-85° (F), and again from mid-July to mid-September when soil

Factoid
Bean roots add nitrogen to the soil. When the Bean season is over, cut the Beans down leaving the roots in place.

temps start to fall from the 100° (F) range, plant the seeds about one inch deep and two to three inches apart. Plant successive crops of bush types every two weeks to prolong the harvest. In the summer, plant pole Beans anytime. Unlike Peas, you should NOT presoak Beans prior to planting because they might rot.

WATER IT: Instead of overhead sprinkling, water at the soil level. Wet leaves lead to disease. Deep water to 18 inches when the top one-half inch is dry.

CARE FOR IT: Beans need good air circulation so don't crowd them. As plants grow, they should not touch. Thin them until they're six inches apart. Avoid handling plants if they are wet, because it's easy to spread disease. Beans take between 45 to 70 days to fruit. Radishes are an especially great companion crop, as they help repel bean Beetles and are very easy to grow. Sow them along with the Beans.

Pole Beans need to grow up on trellises or something. I like to make a teepee out of four bamboo poles and let the vine wind its way upward. Cornstalks are also useful — let the Corn grow to one foot tall, then plant the Beans. Corn and Pole Beans make good companions. But don't put Sunflowers with Pole Beans.

Factoid
You can store Bean seeds up to three years, so save some for a later crop.

FERTILIZE IT: Although Beans are not heavy soil feeders, they do like a shot of fish emulsion or liquid seaweed every two weeks. Also, keep a thick layer of alfalfa hay over the bed to discourage soil-borne diseases from splashing up during irrigation. The hay also evens out moisture in the soil and encourages microbial activity.

ENJOY IT: Pick the pods when they're small and tender. Cut or pinch, but don't tear them off the vine. If you don't harvest frequently (daily or every other day), the plant will quit producing. Pick them before seeds are visible through the pod. Wash and eat!

PROTECT IT: Mold, fungus, and powdery Mildew are very common and can be avoided by watering at the soil level and keeping the plant dry. Remove and dispose of any infected Bean plants. Do not compost diseased Beans, as this can spread disease. Also, plant varieties that are resistant to these diseases.

BEETS

MAYBE your mom made you eat your Beets when you were a kid and you swore you would never do that to your own children. Think again. When you serve one picked fresh from your garden, the tasty, succulent roots and tender delicate leaves will have your kids asking for seconds! I've found Beets easy to grow in first-year gardens.

CHOOSE IT: There are many varieties of Beets, from baby to golden and white types. I recommend you plant early ripening varieties in late winter/early spring.

PLANT IT: Sow seed directly into the garden from mid-September to mid-March, when soil temperatures are 50° to 85° (F). Beets are a compound seed within an outer shell; more than one seed may sprout. Plant short rows every two weeks for a continuous supply of Beets and greens. Transplants don't usually work, because it's so easy to damage the roots when planting. Beets grow great under a layer of four to six inches of compost or mulch on top of the soil.

What You Need To Get Started
Seeds
Shovel
Composted manure or compost

WATER IT: When the top one-half inch is dry, irrigate 12 inches down into the soil. Keep the soil evenly moist for the most tender and flavorful Beets.

CARE FOR IT: Thin frequently so there's room to develop their familiar round shape. Snip off the plants at the soil level instead of pulling them out because you don't want to disturb adjacent Beets.

FERTILIZE IT: If the Beets were planted in compost-rich soil, they won't need fertilizer. Otherwise, fertilize with fish emulsion or compost tea every two to three weeks.

Remember to save some seed to plant again in mid-September

ENJOY IT: They're ready to harvest when the Beet itself is about $1\frac{1}{2}$ inches in diameter, or marble size. Remove the leaves, keeping about two inches of the stem. Wash off the soil and steam them quickly. When tender, eat the entire Beet and stem, or slice off the stems and gently "pop" it out of its skin by squeezing the root end. Add the Beet thinnings (tops and roots) to fresh spring salads or steam them quickly, and serve with butter. If you let Beets get too big (three inches in diameter), they get a woody taste.

PROTECT IT: Beets don't need sun protection, if you plant short season varieties in the late winter/early spring. Caterpillars occasionally chew leaves (handpick and drop them into a bucket of soapy water). Use Bacillus thuringiensis occasionally.

Companion Plants
cabbage
Lettuce
Onions

BLACK-EYED PEAS

THEY go by the names of cowpea and field pea, too. But it's a little misleading, because the Black-eyed Pea is actually a Bean. Whatever the name, though, consider them the workhorses of the garden. They provide nutritious food, gather nitrogen to help other plants grow, and the roots aerate the soil and break up salts that accumulate from irrigation. When used as a "cover crop" for empty garden spaces, they enrich the soil. Almost anything grows with Black-eyed Peas!

CHOOSE IT: Several varieties are available as seed: Banquet (52 days from Germination), California Black Eye, Mississippi Silver, and the Calhoun Purple Hull take about 65 days. The California Black Eye will keep producing until frost or cold weather hits.

PLANT IT: When soil temperatures are 75-95° (F) in April through mid-August, plant seeds about 1½ inches deep, spaced 12 inches apart. Set rows about three to four feet apart. Pods will mature in three to four months.

> Black-eyed Peas are especially nutritious. During the lean days of the depression, my granddad planted "cowpeas" on his Kentucky fields and let neighbors harvest them for food.

WATER IT: Keep soil moist 12 to 18 inches deep. You'll probably have to water two to three times per week. A layer of compost or mulch four to six inches thick will keep soil evenly moist. Don't let the mulch touch the stem.

CARE FOR IT: Besides deep irrigation and a thick layer of mulch, Black-eyed Peas don't require any special care. Most varieties carry their pods above the foliage, so don't worry about staking or trellising. The plant itself will shade the ground and keep it cool.

FERTILIZE IT: They do not need fertilizer.

ENJOY IT: To eat as fresh Snap Beans, harvest the pods when they are thin and straight. For shelled Beans, harvest when the pods have swelled with the Bean seed. Shell them like Peas from the pod and use fresh. For dried Beans, harvest the pods when they have dried or begin to break open. Separate the seeds from the pods, and then dry and store for later cooking.

PROTECT IT: Black-eyed Peas will rot if they are planted in wet, cold soils. Otherwise, no special protection is necessary. These plants revel in the heat and will produce until frost.

My Dad's Black-eyed Pea Recipe

Ingredients
1 cup Black-eyes, dried
1 piece of salt pork, 1"x 1"
¹/₂ of a small Onion
¹/₄ teaspoon dried mustard
³/₄ teaspoon sugar
salt and pepper to taste

Soak Peas overnight. Dice salt pork and Onions and cook in a pot until soft (about seven minutes). Add Peas and water until water level is three inches over the Peas. Boil on medium heat until Peas are soft-not mushy (about an hour and fifteen minutes). Enjoy!

BOK CHOY

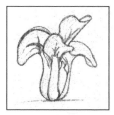

BOK Choy, Pak Choi, however you spell it, these non-heading Chinese cabbages taste wonderful! Add them to stir-fry dishes, salads, or simply serve them braised in some butter until crunchy tender. Another bonus is that this cabbage family member is easy to grow, maturing in about six weeks from Germination. They grow like weeds (but they taste much better!).

CHOOSE IT: If this great veggie isn't in the regular seed category, look for it with the Oriental vegetables. Try Pak Choi Joe Choi Hybrid (45 days from Germination) or Mei Quing Choi Pak Choi (45 days). You might find it just labeled as Bok Choy.

PLANT IT: Sow seed one-quarter inch deep from mid-August to the end of February when soil temperatures are 45-95° (F). Plant in compost or manure-rich soil, spacing seeds about three inches apart. Make continuous plantings every two weeks to provide a long harvest.

What You Need To Start
Seeds
Shovel
Compost/manure
Mulch

WATER IT: Keep the seedbed moist at all times. Water to 12 inches deep when the top one-half inch of the soil is dry. Apply a layer of four to six inches of mulch between rows of Bok Choy to conserve moisture and keep roots cool.

CARE FOR IT: Keep these tasty veggies growing vigorously. Late summer plantings should be made in light shade and protected from the afternoon sun with 50% or less shade cloth. Rows of Sunflowers or Corn can also provide shade. Cabbage family crops benefit from extensive companion plantings. Lots of flowering herbs will encourage beneficial insects into the garden as well as insect-gobbling Birds. Some crops that can be planted along with Bok Choy include Beets and Green Onions. If you plan to harvest the leaves from the Bok Choy, thin to about four to six inches apart. If you prefer to harvest the entire head, thin to about eight to 12 inches apart.

Companion Plants
Beets
Chamomile
Dill
Onions
Peppermint
Rosemary
Sage

FERTILIZE IT: Apply solutions of fish emulsion every two weeks to keep the Bok Choy growing vigorously. And keep the bed mulched!

Factoid
No need to cook these babies, just chop into salads or eat the stalks like celery.

ENJOY IT: One great thing about this veggie is that you can harvest it within 20 days. Carefully cut off the outer leaves when they are still tiny for use in many dishes and salads. Baby Bok Choy is delicious and will grow new leaves to replace the ones you have cut.

PROTECT IT: These tasty members of the cabbage family have their share of bugs determined to get to them before you do. Night-feeding cutworms eat newly sprouted seedlings. To deter, put a collar made of milk carton sections over each plant and push firmly into the soil. Watch for Caterpillars and handpick to dispose of them. Trap Slugs and Snails with the method described in "Organic Pest Control."

BROCCOLI

WITH its cancer-preventive properties and rich flavor, Broccoli is even more delicious when it's homegrown. I eat the florets right off the plant. Yum!

CHOOSE IT: Select varieties that are quick ripening so the harvest will be complete before the onset of hot summer weather. Try Green Comet, an All-America winner that matures in 55 days from Seedling Transplant. Another choice is Super Blend, which combines early, mid-season, and late varieties together so that you may harvest Broccoli for a long period of time.

What You Need To Start
Seeds or transplants
Shovel
Compost or
Mulch

PLANT IT: For transplants, set them out when they first become available in the fall, as early as the middle of September, if you can find them. Plant in compost-enriched soil that has not been previously planted (within the last three years) with other members of the cabbage family (Brassica is its scientific family name). To enhance Broccoli's flavor, plant with flowering herbs such as Chamomile, Dill, Rosemary, and Sage. Broccoli needs sun for good production, so interplant with Carrots because they won't create shade. Seedling Transplants and Nursery Stock

Let some flowers open to attract beneficial insects

can go in when soil temperatures are 45-85° (F) (usually mid-September through January). Direct seed from late August to mid-January when soil temperatures are 45-90° (F).

WATER IT: Broccoli needs to be kept well watered to a depth of 12-18 inches. Do not let more than the top inch dry out between irrigations. A layer of mulch four to six inches deep will help keep the soil evenly moist.

Companion Plants	
Beets	Brussels Sprouts
Carrot	Cauliflower
Chamomile	Dill
Marigolds	Nasturtiums
Onions	Rosemary
Petunias	Sage

CARE FOR IT: Keep soil well mulched and moist. A soil high in organic matter will prevent nematodes from becoming a pest.

FERTILIZE IT: Since Broccoli is a heavy feeder, fertilize every two weeks with fish emulsion or compost tea. A thick layer of compost conserves moisture in the soil while providing constant nutrition as it slowly decomposes.

ENJOY IT: Harvest when the florets are still small, tightly packed, and deep green. Harvest the center florets first, then the side-branching florets as they mature.

PROTECT IT: Nematodes can become a pest, infecting the soil and possibly preventing future plantings of the Brassica family. Discourage nematodes by thickly interplanting with Marigolds and Nasturtiums. Additionally, planting in compost-rich soil prevents nematodes from getting a foothold in the vegetable

Cabbages are another great vegetable for the desert. Choose quick ripening varieties. Plant them under Sunflowers for shade, and enjoy them right through the summer. Follow my directions for Broccoli and Cauliflower (they're all in the same family).

garden. Aphids are the other pests of Broccoli. Control them by planting a variety of flowering shrubs and herbs to encourage beneficial insects such as Ladybug larvae and Green Lacewing larvae.

BRUSSELS SPROUTS

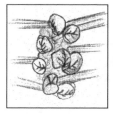

THIS unusual looking vegetable should be planted in the garden more often. Not only do the homegrown varieties taste far superior to the over-strong flavor of those found in the grocery store, it is another cancer-fighting member of the cabbage family.

CHOOSE IT: Generally, Sprouts require a long growing season, 100 to 150 days. So plant early and choose quick ripening varieties such as Jade Cross (85 days from Seedling Transplant), Prince Marvel (90 days), or Valiant (110 days). Brussels Sprouts can also be started by seed – just add 25 days to the "days to harvest."

PLANT IT: These long-growing veggies can be started by seed when soil temperatures are 45-95° (F) from mid-August until the end of October. Use Seedling Transplants from the first of September until the first of December (same soil temperature as seed). Planting every two or three weeks will ensure a continuous harvest. Plant in compost-rich soil, allowing enough space for future growth and development, about one to two feet per plant. Apply a four to six inch layer of mulch.

What You Need To Start
Seeds or transplants
Shovel
Compost or Mulch

Companion Plants
Artemisia
Cauliflower
Pennyroyal
Potatoes
Rosemary
Sage
Thyme

WATER IT: When the top one-half inch of the soil is dry, irrigate until water penetrates 12 to 18 inches down.

CARE FOR IT: As the sprouts begin to develop, break off the bottom leaves to encourage heavier production. Alternate with Peas and Lettuce. Plant with Artemisia and Peppermint (planted in bottomless pots for control), Southernwood, or other aromatic herbs that will encourage beneficial insects to visit your garden.

FERTILIZE IT: Brussels Sprouts are heavy feeders and require additional nitrogen. Apply a thick layer of mulch over the bed so there will be a continuous supply of nutrients as the mulch decomposes. Also, apply an organic fertilizer such as fish emulsion every two weeks or cottonseed meal every month.

ENJOY IT: Begin harvesting the sprouts when they are the size of marbles and still tightly closed. Either twist or cut the sprouts off the stalk, beginning with the lowest ones.

Factoid
Brussels Sprouts are even tastier if they are nipped by cold weather or a frost before harvesting.

PROTECT IT: Watch out for Aphids, Caterpillars, Slugs, and Snails. Hose off Aphids with a stream of water. Check leaves for Caterpillar damage, handpick and dispose of any you find. Collect Slugs and Snails by trapping them under a board or old piece of carpet. Dispose of them in a bucket of soapy water.

CARROTS

WHAT'S up, Doc? Eyesight, crunch, color, and variety. What more could you ask for from a vegetable? Carrots are rich in calcium and phosphorus and make a satisfying snack anytime.

CHOOSE IT: Babette (85 days from seed) is a French baby Carrot that works well here. Another good baby is Minicor (50 days). Nantes (60 to 70 days) are also delicious, nearly coreless, and very tender. For areas with heavy clay soils, try the Chantenay varieties (75 days). For the most part, keep away from large Carrots and plant the smaller, quick-maturing varieties instead.

PLANT IT: Prepare the soil deeply (eight to 12 inches) with organic material such as compost because the root develops into the Carrot. This veggie does not transplant well, so Direct Seed from August through April when soil temperatures are 45-85° (F). Since Carrots need light to germinate, cover seeds lightly with no more than one-quarter inch of soil. Another approach is to mix the seed with sand and then sow. The sand promotes good drainage and indicates where you have sown the seed. You may also mix 30% Radish seed with the Carrot seed. The Radishes encourage Germination and also reduces thinning. DO NOT use fresh manure as it causes Carrots to develop hairy roots.

Factoid
Carrots do best in raised beds with pure compost. Fertilize with fish emulsion every two weeks.

WATER IT: It's important to keep soil moist. Because the seed is practically on the soil surface, water through a layer of cheesecloth, burlap or other thin fabric (remove as soon as seeds germinate). As they grow, provide even moisture to 12 to 18 inches deep and do not let the bed dry out.

CARE FOR IT: Thin often to keep two inches of space between them. Thinning allows for proper growth. For very early thinning, snip off the Carrots so adjacent ones are not damaged. As they mature, you can use thinnings in salads or steam them and serve with butter and snipped Dill.

FERTILIZE IT: If they're planted in a compost-rich soil, don't add extra fertilizer. Keeping a mulch of compost or alfalfa hay will supply a steady stream of nutrients. If the soil doesn't have a lot of organic material or is very sandy, fertilize every two weeks with fish emulsion.

Companion Plants	
Artemisia	Chives
Leeks	Lettuce
Onions	Parsley
Peas	Radishes
Rosemary	Sage
Tomatoes	

ENJOY IT: If you're growing the baby variety, harvest when they are a rich orange color and are about finger length, three to four inches. For regular-sized Carrots, wait until they are about six to eight inches long with a deep color and sweet taste. Always pull the largest Carrots first, so the smaller ones have room to develop.

PROTECT IT: Carrots are virtually pest-free, making them a fun and easy veggie to grow. When you plan your garden, don't put Carrots near Dill, Fennel, or Potatoes.

CAULIFLOWER

CREAMY white, tender, and tasty, homegrown Cauliflower is definitely superior to the grocery store product. And they are very easy to grow. The plants are unusual looking and add great diversity to a garden. Cauliflower is often thought of as the white Broccoli but it's got its own distinct character and flavor. Steamed or eaten raw, Cauliflower is a garden delight.

CHOOSE IT: I suggest using Seedling Transplants or Nursery Stock. By using quick ripening varieties, you can harvest Cauliflower for several months. Try Milkyway Hybrid (45 days from Seedling Transplant), Montano (57 days), Snow Crown (53 days), and White Corona Hybrid (30 days) whose heads are only three to four inches across. Planting by seed will add three to five weeks additional time to harvest dates. Get self-blanching varieties, which protect themselves against the sun.

PLANT IT: From mid-August to the end of January when soil temperatures are 45-85° (F), set transplants 15 to 18 inches apart or plant seeds one-half inch deep in compost-rich soil.

Vigorous growth is necessary for the best heads. For extended harvest, plant early-ripening varieties every two weeks. Apply thick layer of mulch (four to six inches) over the soil.

Companion Plants
Basil
Borage
Sage
Thyme

WATER IT: Consistent moisture is key to developing the sweet, nutty heads. Water deeply (to 8 inches) when the top one-half inch of soil is dry.

Strong-smelling herbs confuse the sense organs of many pests causing them to leave and look for an easier food source.

CARE FOR IT: The cabbage Butterfly larva is a pest to watch for. Inspect plants for Caterpillars, if you notice leaves being chewed. Also watch for Aphids on the tender young shoots and hose them off before they can do much damage.

FERTILIZE IT: Cauliflower is a heavy feeder that needs additional nitrogen. Fertilize by putting down a thick layer of mulch over the soil and feeding monthly with cottonseed meal. Or apply a 50-50 mixture of fish emulsion and liquid seaweed every two weeks.

What You Need To Start
Seeds or transplants
Shovel
Compost
Mulch

ENJOY IT: Harvest when the heads are creamy white and compact. Don't let the Cauliflower get yellowish, or the flavor won't be nearly as tasty.

PROTECT IT: Don't grow Tomatoes or Strawberries near Cauliflower. Plant a diversity of flowering shrubs and herbs to encourage beneficial insects as protection for your veggies.

CORN

HAVING Corn in your garden has lots of advantages. You know it makes a tasty and healthy addition to your dinner table, and I can't think of a better way to shade plants and vegetables. When planted on the western side of the garden plot, the tall stalks provide afternoon shade for other, smaller vegetables. To keep Corn healthy, watch out for two common pests that can cause a lot of damage. There are quick and simple solutions (be sure to read "PROTECT IT").

CHOOSE IT: It's not just "Corn" anymore. Although the choices can seem endless, here's a simple rundown on them. There is Sweet Corn, Sugar-Enhanced hybrids, and Super Sweet hybrids. Once you choose from among these, then pick either white or yellow Corn. In all cases, you should get the early maturing varieties for spring planted Corn. The Casino is a sweet early Corn that I've had great success with. Other varieties to consider: Honey and Cream, a bicolor variety (73 days from Direct Seeding), Early and Often (65 days), and Early Sunglow (63 days).

Companion Plants
cabbage family
Cucumbers
Melons
Nasturtiums
Peas and Beans
Potatoes
Pumpkins
Zucchini Squash
Bachelor's Button or Dill strengthen Corn
Sunflowers attract Caterpillar-eating birds

PLANT IT: Sow Corn seed directly into very rich, well-drained soil. It's a heavy feeder, so prepare the soil with lots of compost, bonemeal, ground rock phosphorus, and composted manure. Plant the seed between mid-February and the first of April when soil temperatures are 60° to 95° (F). Plant a second crop between mid-July and the first of September. Put the seeds one to two inches deep, and about two inches apart. Plan to thin the stalks.

Unless Corn is pollinated, the stalk won't produce ears. For effective pollination, plant in a square block ten feet by ten feet. But if you want Corn to just assist other veggies in the garden, like Pumpkins and Squash, plant Corn on the west side. In this symbiotic relationship, the tall Corn will shade the Pumpkin and Squash fruit, while the large leaves of the Pumpkin and Squash help the soil stay cool and moist.

In order to keep certain varieties from crossbreeding, they need to be isolated from each other by distance or time. If you want to sow two different varieties of Corn and you don't have room to keep them 100 feet apart, plant an early maturing variety first. Then a week later, you can plant a late maturing variety.

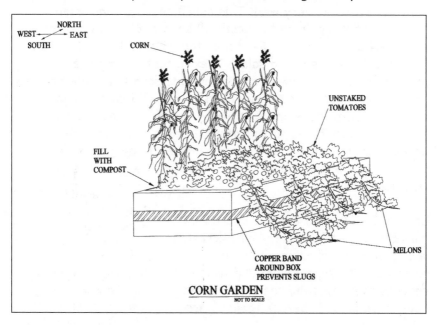

CORN GARDEN

NOT TO SCALE

WATER IT: Corn needs lots of water. Always water at ground level, as overhead irrigation washes pollen off the tassels and ruins the yield. When the top one-half inch of the soil is dry, irrigate to at least 18 inches deep.

FERTILIZE IT: Corn likes a drink of fish emulsion every couple of weeks. When the plants are about six inches tall, side dress with a three to four inches of compost about six inches from both sides of the stalks (you don't want it to touch the stalks). Then place a thick layer of alfalfa hay over everything to act as mulch.

CARE FOR IT: Place four to six inches of mulch over the soil. Alfalfa hay works very well. This mulch and the companion plantings of Pumpkin and Squash will keep the soil shaded and moist. When the Corn is six inches tall, thin to ten inches apart. Toss the thinnings into a salad. They're tasty! Complete pollination of the Corn is very important. Each little silk of the tassel is connected to an individual kernel, and each kernel must be pollinated to develop. This is why "block" planting rather than "row" planting is so important. Because Corn is such a heavy feeder, follow it with Peas or Beans to help restore nitrogen to the soil. Do not follow Corn with Artichokes or vice-versa.

ENJOY IT: Harvest when silks are very dark brown, but NOT dried out. Kernels should be milky when popped with a fingernail. The super sweet and sugar-enhanced varieties will keep from seven days after harvest before their sugars turn to starch.

> **Factoid**
> Early American settlers learned from Native Americans how to get Corn to thrive, after watching them put a dead fish under the Corn seed they planted. The fish is full of natural nitrogen, which fertilizes the soil.

PROTECT IT: Two pests that always seem to find Cornstalks are the Corn Borer and Earworms (see "Organic Pest Control" for information about getting rid of them). They can destroy a crop quickly, and all of your hard work with it. Diseases are usually not a problem with Corn in the low desert. Choose varieties that are resistant to bacterial wilt. Occasionally, a fungus called corn smut occurs. It appears as a grayish mass on the ear of Corn itself. Remove and destroy any stalks that have the disease. Interestingly, Europeans relish corn smut and will prepare and enjoy it just like they do mushrooms!

CUCUMBERS

 CUKES are wonderful in salads and relish trays, and really beautify the garden. They love the warm days of spring, and will rot if planted in soil that's too cold. Use your soil thermometer to make sure ground temperature is above 65° (F).

CHOOSE IT: If space is tight, try the bush varieties, or grow the vining varieties up a trellis to save space and produce straight fruit. The Mediterranean and Garden Oasis produce fruit that is eight inches long with very tender skin, juicy flesh, and good resistance to Powdery Mildew and mosaic virus. The Long and Armenian varieties should be planted in June.

Companion Plants
Beans
Corn
Lemon Balm
Peas
Lettuce
Radishes
Sunflowers

PLANT IT: When soil temperatures hit 65° to 95° (F), from mid-February up until May, plant in soil enriched with manure or compost, and with an eastern exposure. Or set out Seedling Transplants or Nursery Stock when they first become available, usually March through mid-May. Early plantings might require cold weather protection. Grow the plant up a trellis or provide thick mulch for it to sprawl over. Try using Tomato Set for a higher yield. Cukes are sweeter when you plant

Sunflowers with them. Avoid planting them with Sage. To help keep the soil evenly moist, apply a thick layer of four to six inches of mulch or compost.

WATER IT: Water to a depth of 12 to 18 inches when the top one-half inch of the soil is dry. Keep soil evenly moist. Cucumbers have shallow roots and need to be watered frequently. Don't let soil moisture fluctuate between wet and dry. That can cause a bitter taste.

> **Factoid**
> Cucumbers soothe sunburn. They also release a root substance that inhibits weed growth. Cucumber skins ward off Cockroaches.

CARE FOR IT: Place a thick layer of alfalfa hay around the plant to keep the soil moist and cool, and keep the growing fruit off the ground. Cucumbers stop producing fruit halfway through the summer, but the plant will grow all summer long. When the weather cools in the late summer/early fall, production will pick up again. To enhance pollination, plant lots of flowers and herbs to attract beneficial pollinators.

FERTILIZE IT: When planted in compost-rich soil and mulched with a thick layer of alfalfa hay or compost, you don't need fertilizer. After summer's heat, apply some fish emulsion or compost tea to provide the necessary nutrients for a fall crop.

ENJOY IT: Cucumbers usually germinate in five to ten days and are ready to harvest in about 60 days. When they are small (about five to six inches long), cut them off with sharp scissors. Pulling them off can damage the vine.

PROTECT IT: To prevent Birds from eating the emerging sprouts, cover seeds with upside down strawberry baskets until seedlings are two inches high. Plant with Radishes to protect Cukes from cucumber Beetles. Let the Radishes go to seed and dig them back into the soil.

EGGPLANT

ALTHOUGH widely cultivated in the Mediterranean region, Eggplants are actually native to Thailand. They thrive in the heat of the Sonoran desert, but require ample water. Eggplants are members of the Tomato family. They produce beautiful lavender flowers, and the lovely glossy fruit comes in colors ranging from white to lavender to dark purple and there are even striped varieties. These vegetables are perfect additions to the flower garden, adding both diversity and beauty.

CHOOSE IT: There are many varieties ranging from plump, round fruit to long, cylindrical fruit. Among the Asian varieties are Pingtung (70 days from Seedling Transplant) with its long, slender lavender fruit; Farmers Long Eggplant (70 days), producing violet pink fruit; and Ichiban Hybrid (61 days) with 12-inch fruit. You can also plant the miniature Eggplants: Bambino Hybrid (45 days) produces clusters of one-inch bite-sized fruit, while Little Fingers (60 days) bears clusters of plump, seven-inch long, dark purple fruit. For Heirloom gardeners, try Rosa Bianca (75 days), a traditionally shaped Eggplant in shades of lavender and white. Another Heirloom variety is Violette di Firenze. A compact, early producer is Early Bird Hybrid (50 days), producing fruits five to six inches long.

Eggplant is indeterminate, which means it will continue to produce fruit until extreme heat or cold stops it. Once it is planted, Eggplant will be productive for at least two years, if you care for it well.

Factoid
Tarragon and Thyme enhance the flavor of Eggplant

PLANT IT: Plant when soil temperatures are 75-90° (F). That's usually in March. If the soil is too cold, the Eggplant will be stunted. They enjoy their own company, so they should be planted several in a group, about 12 to 18 inches apart. They need good drainage, and the planting bed should contain a lot of organic material, such as compost. After planting, apply a thick (four to six inches) layer of mulch or alfalfa hay over the soil to conserve moisture and help keep the roots cool.

WATER IT: Don't use overhead or sprinkler irrigation, as the water will damage the fruit. Keep the drip system or hose at the soil level for watering. When the top one-half inch of soil is dry, water deeply to about two feet. Always keep soil moist.

CARE FOR IT: Eggplants appreciate the support Tomato cages provide. An added advantage to the cages is that you can to use the frames of the cages to hang shade cloth (use less than 50% shade cloth) to protect the Eggplants from afternoon summer sun. Plant Coriander, Dill, and Parsley and allow them to go to seed to encourage beneficial insects into the garden.

When winter rolls around, dig up the Eggplant and transplant it into a five-gallon container. Put it in a protected area during the cold weather. Or leave it in the ground and protect it from low temperatures. Use a floating row cover (a light, breathable material that lets light in and holds the heat), or provide it with a heat source, such as a lamp. In this way you can get the plant to produce fruit for you the next spring and summer.

FERTILIZE IT: To keep Eggplants producing, fertilize with an organic form of nitrogen such as cottonseed meal every month, or apply a solution of fish emulsion every two weeks.

ENJOY IT: Harvest the fruit when they are shiny and firm for best flavor and texture. If the fruit is dull, it's overripe. Cut fruit from the plant rather than pulling it off, which could damage the plant. To get the plant to keep producing, you must pick the

Companion Plants
Artemisia
Beans
Lavender
Marigold
Tansy

fruit as soon as it ripens. At the end of the second growing season, remove the plants and compost them.

PROTECT IT: Don't plant Potatoes, Onions, or Garlic near Eggplants. Caterpillars will nibble on Eggplant leaves, so handpick them and dispose of them in a bucket of soapy water. To deter Snails and Slugs, sprinkle cayenne pepper around the plants and on damp leaves.

Rotate Eggplant every two years to keep diseases from building up.

GARLIC

THIS pungent member of the Lily family is easy to grow and rewards you with plump bulbs filled with flavorful and healthy cloves. Grow it for its own sake, or use Garlic around your garden as a workhorse companion for other plants. I swear, it has magical powers. The scent from the plant repels Aphids, Crickets, and Grasshoppers (as well as providing vampire protection!).

CHOOSE IT: You can separate the cloves of store-bought bulbs and plant those, or order some of the fancier varieties from seed catalogs. They have Garlic cloves like the purple-skinned Asian varieties, red-skinned Spanish types or the giant-sized and mild-flavored Elephant Garlic. Occasionally, Nursery Stock is available, allowing you to harvest Garlic earlier.

What You Need To Start
Garlic cloves
Narrow trowel
Compost
Mulch

PLANT IT: Always plant Garlic cloves in the fall when soil temperatures are around 80-90° (F) (October is the prime time here in the low desert). Dig one to two inches down into the soil and put the clove in with the flat (base) side down. Keep cloves two to three inches apart in compost-enriched soil with good drainage. Garlic needs five to seven months to mature, so plant it where it won't be disturbed by other garden chores or planting.

Always plant some Garlic when you put Roses in. I have Garlic plants all over my yard, front and back.

Don't plant with Beans, cabbages, Eggplant, Peas, or Strawberries.

WATER IT: When the top one-half inch of soil is dry water 12 inches deep. Garlic grows during the winter months when water needs are less, so be sure to check soil moisture with the Soil Probe (see "TOOLS" chapter) before irrigating.

CARE FOR IT: Put a four to six inches of mulch over the soil to maintain even soil temperatures. The Garlic will grow through it.

FERTILIZE IT: Soil that contains a lot of compost or other organic materials usually won't need additional fertilizer. Hit the area with fish emulsion once a month to supplement some nutrients.

Factoid
Garlic is a rich source of sulfur, so it makes a good natural antiseptic and antibiotic.

ENJOY IT: Leaves grow out the top of Garlic, and when those start to wilt and die off, it's time to harvest the heads. Dig the cloves up, but don't remove the leaves. Tie the leaves together and dry thoroughly. Store in well-ventilated containers or braid together and hang in the kitchen, out of the sunlight.

Companion Plants
Beets
Tomatoes
Lettuce

PROTECT IT: Insects and diseases don't really bother Garlic. In fact, Garlic protects other plants and trees from them. Never plant Roses without also putting in some Garlic to keep Aphids away. For deciduous fruit trees, planting thickly with Garlic discourages Borers and weevils. It also helps perennial shrubs and herbs.

KALE

WITH their lovely ruffled leaves and dark green color, Kale plants are rich in nutrients and make for a tasty winter green. It's a beautiful autumn crop that adds color to a winter garden and gets sweeter as it gets colder. Kale grows best with others of its kind, such as cabbages, but also likes Onions, Lettuce, and early Potatoes. Stay on top of weeding, however, because a few weeds can harbor harmful pests (see "PROTECT IT").

CHOOSE IT: Varieties include Dwarf Blue Curled Vates (70 days from Seedling Transplant) and Dwarf Green Curled (65 days). For a variety of leaf shapes and colors, try Wild Kale Mix (60 days).

PLANT IT: Use Seedling Transplants or Nursery Stock from six-packs as soon as they are available in the nursery, usually October through January when soil temperatures are 40-75° (F). Also plant by seed from mid-August through November when soil temperatures are 50-90° (F). Plant seeds directly into the garden and cover with one-quarter inch of soil. Add an extra couple of weeks to the "days to harvest" if you plant by seed. Keep the seedbed moist until the seeds germinate. Spread a layer of mulch four to six inches thick around the plants once Seedling Transplants or seeds get to be three-four inches tall.

WATER IT: Keep seedbeds moist. When the top one-half inch of the soil gets dry, water deeply to 18 inches.

Companions Plants
cabbage
Lettuce
Onions
Potatoes

CARE FOR IT: This is a plant that would snow ski if it could — it loves the cold. You should feel lucky if frost hits, because this only enhances the flavor of Kale.

FERTILIZE IT: Every two to three weeks, use fish emulsion or compost tea.

What You Need To Start
Seeds or transplants
Shovel
Compost
Manure

ENJOY IT: Begin harvesting the outer leaves as baby greens or let them grow larger. They are most tender when they are picked at about three to five inches long. The leaves will grow as large as two to three feet. For food, it's usually best to pick them before they get that long. You can pluck outer leaves and the plant will keep producing.

PROTECT IT: Keep Kale well weeded. Be especially diligent with mustard and shepherd's purse, which can harbor pests and insects harmful to Kale. Caterpillars might nibble on the leaf edges, but overall, Kale is not prone to diseases or pest damage. In the late winter/early spring, you might have to hose a few Aphids off the succulent new growth.

LEEKS

RARELY does a vegetable provide a dichotomy. Considered elegant (it's the national flower of Wales), it's also called "the poor man's asparagus." Leeks have a delicious flavor of their own, but also enhance the flavor of soups and stews. From the Lily family, Leeks are rich in sulfur and have been used as an antiseptic. They help ward off insects and are heavy feeders that need compost-rich soil to root deeply.

CHOOSE IT: The Broad London (130 days from Seedling Transplants) is a variety found in most nurseries and do-it-yourself stores. Some European varieties found in

Companion Plants
Onions
Carrots

seed catalogues include Ofina (120 days), Albinstar (a baby vegetable variety at 110 days), and King Richard (75 days). From seed, Leeks have a growing season as long as four months.

PLANT IT: For a winter crop, plant by seed from mid-August to mid-October when soil temperatures are 80-95° (F). Plant again in January for a late spring crop when the soil temperature is about 50° (F). Seeds need loose soil, so this is one vegetable that needs tilling — at least four inches of compost or manure tilled into the top eight inches of soil. Or plant in the loose compost of a raised garden. Apply a layer of mulch four to six inches deep over the soil to conserve moisture. Look for Leeks in the nursery and cut the days to harvest by several weeks.

They are grow slow and need ample water. Interplant with cabbage, Lettuce, and herbs such as Borage, Chamomile, and French sorrel.

Leeks also do wonderfully in pots. Try a couple in plastic pots that have good drainage.

WATER IT: Leeks need lots of water. Make sure soil is moist 12 to 18 inches down. Never let it dry out.

CARE FOR IT: They need blanching to keep them white and tender. That means the sun should not reach the plant base. As it grows, push soil up against the stem, or make a little paper collar for it. Be patient. Leeks take a long time to Germinate. Once they do Germinate, though, they are very easy to grow.

Leave them in the ground during cooler months and dig them up as needed. As the weather warms, simply dig up the remaining ones, wash, cut pieces three to five inches long, and freeze for future use.

What You Need To Start
Seeds
Shovel
Compost
Mulch

FERTILIZE IT: Soil that's very rich in organic material is all you need to grow great Leeks.

ENJOY IT: The plant itself will grow two to three feet high. As baby vegetables, harvest any time they reach finger length. You are able to harvest them up to the mature size of three-quarters to one inch in diameter. Trim before cooking.

PROTECT IT: Avoid putting Leeks with Broccoli and Broad Beans.

LETTUCE

WHY don't you Lettuce entertain you? Take my garden, please! I got a million of 'em. But seriously, folks there aren't a million, but there are many types of Lettuce that do extremely well here in the desert. It might not be one of the first things you think of in a garden, but when you go to make your salads, you'll be glad you have it.

CHOOSE IT: Let's start with the baby Romaine (Cos) types. Little Caesar and Little Gem Mini Romaine both produce petite heads the perfect size for individual salads. The regular-sized Romaines (70 to 85 days), Parris Island Cos, Paris White, and Jericho may be harvested leaf-by-leaf or by cutting off the entire head. The Butterhead or Bibb

What You Need To Start
Seeds or transplant
Shovel
Compost
Manure
Mulch

Lettuce (70 days) are both tender and delicate with a butter smooth texture. Buttercrunch, Merveille des Quatre Saisons, and Little Gem are all excellent Bibb varieties. Loose Leaf varieties (45 to 80 days), Crispy Frills, Simpson, and Oak Leaf types all do well. Choose the varieties with the fewest number of days to harvest so you can have several crops before the heat of summer sets in. For Lettuce, the days to harvest measure from Direct Seeding, not Germination.

Companion Plants
Beets
cabbages
Calendula
Carrots
Cucumbers
Chrysanthemum paludosum
Leeks
Marigolds
Onions
Petunias
Strawberries

Make sure to put Lettuce seeds into the refrigerator four to five days before you plant. This will help with germination during warm weather.

PLANT IT: Plant Lettuce seed from mid-August through February when temperatures are 40-90° (F). Plant in soil enriched with compost or manure. Lettuce needs light to germinate, so only cover the seed with one-quarter inch of soil, spacing the seeds about one inch apart. Because it is important to keep the seedbed moist for Germination to occur, cover the seeds with a thin layer of cheesecloth or burlap, and water through that so you won't dislodge the seeds.

Put in Seedling Tranpslants or Nursery Stock from mid-September to mid-February, spacing them about six inches apart for the baby types and 12 inches apart for the regular-sized ones. A transplant will shave 10-15 days off the time to harvest. For Lettuce started in the heat of summer, provide some shade.

WATER IT: Water deeply to 12 inches and keep moist at all times. Don't let the soil dry out, or it can cause Lettuce to grow slowly and become bitter tasting.

CARE FOR IT: To keep the soil evenly moist, apply four to six inches of mulch over the surface, not letting the mulch rest up against the Lettuce stems.

Factoid
For the juiciest Lettuce, pick it in the early morning, rinse, and put right into the refrigerator

FERTILIZE IT: Apply a solution of fish emulsion every two weeks during the late fall, winter, and early spring. Use a solution of liquid seaweed during the warmest months, as it helps promote heat tolerance. Keep the mulch layer thick and replenished to help the soil stay cool.

> Factoid
> Lettuce protects the Radish from the Radish Beetle and the Lettuce seems to make the Radishes juicier.

ENJOY IT: Begin enjoying your Lettuce by tossing the thinnings into the salad bowl. Harvest the outer leaves from several plants at a time. That keeps the head alive and producing more Lettuce. When the head is mature, cut it off about two inches above the soil. What's left will usually regrow into a new head. This way you can get two crops off one Lettuce! For the baby greens and mesclun mixes, also cut off the top of the plants, leaving about two inches to regrow for another harvest.

PROTECT IT: You need to watch out for a host of pests, including Aphids, Caterpillars, Slugs, and Snails (see "Organic Pest Control" for suggestions).

MELONS

THEY don't ship well. Consequently, the stuff in the grocery store won't taste nearly as good as what you can grow. You might be surprised how fantastic they taste when they come out of your own garden. And there are so many types to choose from, you might never tire of fresh Melons!

CHOOSE IT: For low desert area, choose smaller types. Cantaloupes and Muskmelons can be planted by seed from mid-February through July for a spring or summer garden. Watermelons should be planted mid-February through March when soil temperatures are 70-95° (F) for your spring garden. Choose smaller Watermelon varieties unless you have a lot of room for vines to spread. Cantaloupe varieties to try are Ambrosia Hybrid (86 days from Seedling Transplant), Hearts of Gold (90 days), or Sweet and Early (75 days). Watermelon varieties include Sugar Baby (73 days) and Crimson Sweet (85 days). For quicker Melon production, plant Nursery Stock as soon as it's available. Or if planting by seed, add 10-15 days to allow for Germination.

> When I was a kid, my dad would soak the Watermelon seeds in a milk-bath a day before we planted them. Why milk? I still don't know, but we always had the best Watermelon patch in town!

PLANT IT: See the diagram for the best planting technique. All varieties love enriched soil. Dig a large hole, two feet deep and one foot wide. Fill the hole with composted manure to within two to three inches of the top. Finish backfilling with garden soil, forming a mound at the top. Plant six to eight seeds on top, one inch deep and two inches apart. Place these hills four to eight feet apart, as Melons will cover a lot of ground. Do not plant near Potatoes.

WATER IT: Water deeply to 18 inches. Don't let the soil dry out. Irrigate at the base of the plant to direct water to the roots, while also preventing the diseases overhead sprinklers can

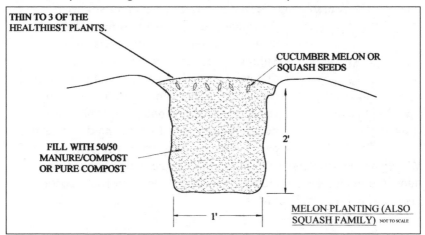

THIN TO 3 OF THE HEALTHIEST PLANTS.

CUCUMBER MELON OR SQUASH SEEDS

FILL WITH 50/50 MANURE/COMPOST OR PURE COMPOST

2'

1'

MELON PLANTING (ALSO SQUASH FAMILY) NOT TO SCALE

cause. Squash and Melons have similar water needs. There's a diagram in the Squash chapter for a great way to plant and water at the same time.

CARE FOR IT: Thin to the strongest three to four plants per hill. Keeping a layer of mulch (compost or alfalfa hay) four to six inches deep over the soil to retain moisture and keep the fruit away from hungry bugs.

Companion Plants
Bachelor's Button
Corn
Lemon Balm
morning glory vine

FERTILIZE IT: Feed every two weeks with fish emulsion solution. Melons are heavy feeders, so follow them with a soil-building vegetable — such as Beans or Peas — to help return nutrients to the soil.

ENJOY IT: Pick Melons when they're fully colored and fragrant ("store-boughts" are usually not fragrant) and "slip" away from the vine. Some varieties do not "slip," but are ready when they smell ripe. The blossom end, where the flower had been, should give a little when gently pressed. For Watermelons, check the underside — the white spot will turn yellow when it's ripe.

PROTECT IT: Keep a lookout for cucumber Beetles that can damage the Melon crop. Sprinkle leaves, vines, and soil with Diatomaceous Earth to control them. Also select varieties that are resistant to Mildew diseases. Don't follow Melons with Cucumbers or Squash, as these vegetables are in the same family and prone to the same pests. Additionally, rotate Melons every three years to prevent diseases and pests from building up in the soil. As Watermelons develop, lift them off the ground to prevent rot and minimize insect damage. Use straw, wood, or even foam board from a do-it-yourself center.

If you've got a small area for gardening, grow your Melons on a trellis and let the fruit hang, supported by lengths of cloth or pantyhose.

OKRA

THIS plant loves the heat and is so robust you might wonder where it gets all of its energy. Okra is a protein-rich vegetable. It was originally from Africa, and was probably introduced into the southern part of the United States by French settlers where it has become an essential component of gumbo.

CHOOSE IT: Dwarf Green Pod is ready for picking in 50 days from Seedling Transplant. Louisiana (58 days) and Clemson Spineless (56 days) are also good selections. Add two weeks for Direct Seeding.

PLANT IT: Plant from mid-March through May when soil temperatures are approximately 60° (F). Soak seeds in water 24 hours, then plant one-half inch deep and five inches apart.

Companion Plants
Alyssum
Marigolds
Nasturtiums

I grow a lot of Okra in 15-gallon buckets. If you do that, remember to water them daily in summer.

WATER IT: Always keep soil moist 18 to 24 inches deep. Apply four to six inches of mulch or alfalfa hay to help keep even moisture.

CARE FOR IT: Thin plants to 20 inches apart. You will notice Okra fruit when the plant is a foot tall. To keep it healthy and producing, harvest fruit daily. When it slows down in mid-summer, prune off the top third of the plant to rejuvenate it enough to put out another flush of new growth and fruit. Remove weeds to reduce competition for water and nutrients.

Okra does best in summer and I love to grow it just to look at the flowers. As a relative of cotton and Hibiscus, Okra just loves the heat and has beautiful yellow flowers.

FERTILIZE IT: Apply a solution of fish emulsion or liquid seaweed every two weeks.

ENJOY IT: The plant will keep producing until frost hits. This veggie is at its best when it grows to between two and three inches long. Pick it every day. If you, your neighbors and co-workers get sick of eating Okra, compost them. Just keep harvesting them.

PROTECT IT: Okra is virtually pest-free. Any Aphids that do get a foothold can be hosed off with a sharp stream of water.

ONIONS

HISTORY has been good to the Onion. It was a favorite food of ancient Egyptians. Before that, it was reputedly used as currency. Introduced to America by Spanish explorers, Onions are still one of the most popular cooking vegetables in the world. They're easily one of the most common garden tenants around.

CHOOSE IT: There are two types of Onions, bunching varieties (like scallions) and bulb types (like steak Onions). Within the bulb types, there are long-day varieties and short-day varieties. The long-day (or northern kind) do well planted north of a line drawn between San Francisco and Washington, D.C. (Check a map. They're at the same latitude!)

Onions Repel
Borers
Caterpillars
Crickets
Grasshoppers
Moths

The short-day (or southern kind) grow in the southern half of the United States. The bunching varieties include Evergreen White Bunching (120 days from Germination) and summer Bunching (75 days). Bulb Onions come in different colors, shapes, and degrees of pungency. In the low desert, short-day Onions will grow the best. Granex Hybrid (80 days) is a sweet Vidalia-type Onion. Red Granex (82 days) is similar and adds color to cooking.

PLANT IT: The green bunching Onions are planted as seed from the first of August through April, when soil temperatures are 50-95° (F). They take two to four months to mature. To get the bulb Onions, you can either plant baby bulbs (Onion sets) the first two weeks of February, or plant by seed from October through mid-November when soil temperatures have cooled to 50-85° (F). Sets will take four to five months to mature. Seed will take seven to eight months to mature. Plant several of each variety, because one of each will never provide enough for culinary use.

Companion Plants
Beets
cabbage family
Chamomile
Leeks
Lettuce
Roses (more fragrance when planted w/Onions)
Strawberries
Tomatoes

For green bunching Onions, plant seeds one-half inch deep and one to two inches apart. Onion sets should be planted one inch deep and four inches apart. Plant seeds for bulbs one inch deep and four inches apart.

To develop fully, Onions require enriched soil and lots of water. Add lots of manure or compost to the soil before planting. Keep in mind that once Onions mature, they require very dry soil, so you must plant them away from other plants that need moisture. Try a raised bed or large pot to keep them separate.

Factoid
Onions planted around the garden or yard will help ward off insects and plant diseases.

WATER IT: Onions have shallow roots, so keep soil moist twelve to eighteen inches deep. While they're growing, don't let the soil dry out between irrigations. Mulch thickly to conserve moisture in the soil. But once the leafy stalks on top flop over and wilt, stop watering.

CARE FOR IT: As the Onion leaves grow, snip off the green tops and use as scallions. New ones will continue to develop. Keep the bed free of weeds to prevent competition for moisture and nutrients. As the Onions grow, apply four to six inches of mulch to keep the soil as cool as possible. Onions become very pungent and spicy when grown in warm areas. As the Onions grow, thin them to four inches apart and enjoy the thinnings as scallions. When the bulbs reach harvest size (three to four inches in diameter) they need to cure for storage. Stop watering so the soil will dry out. Dig up the bulbs and leave them on the soil to dry for four to five days in the sun. Make sure this is not near other plants that require watering, because damp soil can rot Onion bulbs.

> Let some of your Onions flower, because they will attract beneficial insects. Also, the flowers make great seasoning for soups and salads.

FERTILIZE IT: Feed with a solution of fish emulsion or liquid seaweed every two weeks, especially when the plants are young.

ENJOY IT: Harvest Onions when tops wilt and die down. Remove the tops, clean off the dirt, and store them with good air circulation. Onions need to air dry for two weeks in order to properly cure for storage.

PROTECT IT: Don't plant near Peas and Beans because Onions will inhibit the growth of legumes. Thrips attack Onions. To minimize damage, keep the Onions growing as vigorously as possible. Increase vigor by interplanting with Chamomile. Don't plant with Eggplant.

PEAS

SEVERAL varieties of Peas make this an interesting and beautiful member of any garden. They draw a lot of nitrogen into the soil and nitrogen-hungry plants like to be near Peas. They are very nutritious and deserve to grow up and away from the ground to show off their beauty and keep them producing the best yields (see "CARE FOR IT").

CHOOSE IT: The sugar pod varieties are especially delicious. Super Sugar Mel (68 days from Germination) is loaded with sweet, crispy pods with great flavor and crunchiness. Other edible Snap Peas include Sugar Bon (56 days) and Super Snappy (65 days). Snow Peas, the flat-pod varieties used extensively in Asian cooking, include Snow Peas (58 days) and Dwarf White Sugar (50 days). For heat resistance, try the shelling Pea Wando (68 days).

Companion Plants
Beans
cabbage
Carrots
Corn,
Cucumbers
Lettuce
Potatoes
Radishes
Tomatoes
Turnips

PLANT IT: Before planting, soak Peas overnight in water for better germination rates. For most varieties, plant the seed mid-September through the end of February when soil temperatures are 50-75° (F). For Super Sugar Mel, you can extend the planting season to mid-March, as this variety likes a warmer soil to germinate. For higher yields, add ground rock phosphate, cottonseed meal, or bonemeal when planting. Just before planting, mix damp Peas with Pea Inoculant to increase yields. Inoculants are available at most nurseries or by mail order. Plant seeds ½ inch to one inch deep and five inches apart. Peas are deep rooting and appreciate soil with lots of compost or manure added to it. After the seeds germinate add four to six inches of alfalfa hay or mulch over the soil. Don't let the mulch touch the stems. There's no advantage to planting Nursery Stock.

Factoid
The Super Sugar Mel is especially heat and drought tolerant and also resistant to some Mildew.

Potatoes do especially well when companion planted with Peas. Do not plant Peas with Strawberries, Fennel, or members of the Onion family (including Garlic and Shallots).

WATER IT: Water deeply to 18 to 24 inches. Always water at soil level, as overhead sprinkling can promote Mildew diseases.

CARE FOR IT: Train Peas up a trellis or similar device for better yields. Keeping them off the ground also prevents disease. If you don't have a trellis, string untreated twine (because it composts faster) between two stakes placed four or five feet apart. At the end of the season, cut the vines down, leaving the nitrogen-rich roots in the soil. Also, clean up the garden and rotate the beds every couple of years so diseases don't take hold.

FERTILIZE IT: Fertilize with a fish emulsion solution every two weeks to keep Peas growing vigorously and to increase yields.

ENJOY IT: Pick often for greater yields. The edible pod Peas should be picked when they are two to three inches long, and very thin with undeveloped Peas. The edible snap Peas can be harvested as thin pea pods, plump and juicy for Snap Peas, or for shelled Peas when mature. Pick Peas daily to increase production.

PROTECT IT: Hungry Birds can make a wasteland of your Peas, so cover them while they're germinating with a breathable material (row cover) or inverted Strawberry baskets. When the Peas are two inches high, it's safe to uncover. Except for Mildews, Peas are resistant to most pests and diseases. Choose Mildew-resistant varieties and avoid overhead watering. (See "Organic Controls" for Mildew solutions.)

PEPPERS

WHEN it comes to Peppers, you might say, "The hotter, the better." But the plants don't feel the same way. These members of the Tomato family do best in warm, mid-range temperatures. Over 90° (F), and they stop producing fruit. Maintain them through the hottest time of the summer and they'll start producing again in September.

CHOOSE IT: There are lots of different types, ranging in color from red to green to yellow to purple. Peppers go from sweet and mild to fiery hot. They'll add an explosion of color to your garden and taste to your cooking! Peppers mature 65 to 75 days from Seedling

Companion Plants
Flowering herbs
Sage
Tarragon

Transplant into the garden. Gypsy Hybrid, All America Winner and Crispy Hybrid are great sweet Pepper varieties. Big Dipper and California Wonder are bell Peppers you can harvest when they're either green or sweet and red. Then there are the hot chili Pepper varieties such as Anaheim, Habanero, and Jalapeno. You can save additional growing time by planting larger Nursery Stock.

PLANT IT: Plant Seedling Transplants from mid-February through the end of March. A second planting period pops up again for the month of July. Peppers do best planted when soil temperatures range between 65-85° (F). Ideally, plant in an eastern exposure or provide afternoon shade with Sunflowers or tall Corn. Space

Factoid
To keep my Peppers going all year, I transplant them into buckets during winter and keep them in a well protected frost-free area.

the plants about 12 to 18 inches apart. This helps the plants shade their own fruit from sunburn. Plant in soil enriched with compost or manure.

WATER IT: Don't let soil dry out. Water deeply (18 to 24 inches) to keep it moist.

CARE FOR IT: Afternoon shade is important for good fruit production. Plant under Sunflowers or Corn, or use a 50% (or less) shade cloth. Spread a thick layer (four to six inches) of mulch or alfalfa hay under the plants to keep the soil cool and evenly moist. Keep weeded. Pepper plants will overwinter (live through the cold season) if they are protected from frost.

What You Need To Start
Seeds or transplants
Shovel
Compost or manure
Mulch

FERTILIZE IT: Apply fish emulsion every two weeks to keep plants growing vigorously. Three weeks after you plant it, sprinkle a tablespoon of blood meal around each plant. At four weeks, sprinkle a tablespoon of Epsom salts (manganese sulfate) on each plant.

Pest Repellent Recipe
4 Habanero Peppers
1 gallon water
Mix and set in sun for 24 hours. Strain through cheese cloth and spray.

ENJOY IT: Because plants are brittle, cut fruit from the stems rather than pulling it off. Harvest the sweet Peppers when they are green, or allow them to mature to their full color. Fully mature Peppers are the sweetest. Harvest the chili peppers when they have reached full maturity and color.

Dogs and Cats don't like the smell of Peppers, so spread dried plants in places you don't want them to go.

PROTECT IT: Peppers are susceptible to cutworms, Flea Beetles, Slugs, Snails, and Tomato Hornworms. Refer to the "Organic Controls" for solutions. Blossom-end rot can strike if there is uneven soil moisture. A thick mulch layer (four to six inches) will even things out. Don't plant with Onions.

POTATOES

If names are a measure, this one's gotten some travel in. A native of Peru, it's varieties have got such exotic names as Yellow Finn, Gold Rush, Maine Kennebec, Red Sun, and Yukon Gold. There are many others, and the flavors are worth the trip. Firm, sweet flesh bursting with taste. As an added bonus, Potatoes are high in fiber and low in fat.

CHOOSE IT: Potatoes take about 65 to 75 days to develop into "new potatoes" and about 90 to 120 days for full-sized tubers. Many of the Heirloom and new varieties are available as "mini-tubers". These miniature Potatoes grow into full-size plants with exceptional yields. Since each mini-tuber is completely covered with its own skin, it does not need to be chemically treated. There are so many fantastic Potatoes to choose from, check a seed catalog to decide.

What You Need To Start
Mini-tubers
Shovel
Compost
Mulch
Hay

PLANT IT: Here in the low desert, plant Potatoes in January and February when temperatures are 50-70° (F). Other than always avoiding heavy clay soils, Potatoes can be grown several ways. One way is to plant them in well-draining sandy soil four to six inches deep and 12 inches apart in rows spaced 12 to 24 inches apart. Another way is to plant them two inches deep in loosened soil, and then cover with 18 inches of straw, mulch, or compost. They'll develop in the mulch rather than in the soil, making them easy to harvest. An effective alternative garden idea is to plant Potatoes in a stacked tire tower (see "ALTERNATIVE GARDENS"). Stack two tires, plant Potatoes in the ground, fill the tire tower with mulch, alfalfa hay or compost and let the fun begin!

CONCRETE REINFORCEMENT WIRE TRELLIS OR BLOCK WALL WITH REINFORCEMENT WIRE MOUNTED TO WALL.

4" BLACK ABS PLASTIC PIPES

FILL SPOUTS: DRILL HOLES TO FILL EACH LAYER OF TUBES WITH WATER. SEAL HOLES WITH SILICONE.

THE SUN HEATS THE WATER INSIDE THE PIPES. AT NIGHT THE HEAT IS RELEASED THROUGHOUT THE GARDEN BED, PROMOTING GROWTH OF VEGGIES.

SUN'S RAYS HEAT WATER

NORTH
EAST
WEST
SOUTH

RAISED GARDEN

DRIVE 1/2" REBAR OR 2X4'S INTO THE GROUND TO BRACE THE PIPES AND HOLD THE RAISED GARDEN IN PLACE.

SOLAR HEATED WINTER GARDEN

NOT TO SCALE

WATER IT: They need regular irrigation to form good tubers. And when you do water, do it to at least 18 to 24 inches (deeply and infrequently). Let soil dry out between waterings.

CARE FOR IT: A soil enriched with lots of organic material gives the best production.

FERTILIZE IT: Avoid excessive Nitrogen fertilizers. Well-composted soils with four to six inches of mulch will provide the necessary nutrients for proper Potato growth.

Companion Plants
Corn
Beans
cabbage
Peas
Petunias
Strawberries
Nasturtiums
Marigolds

ENJOY IT: If you grow taters in mulch or the tire tower, it'll be easy to find the developing tubers. Harvest them at any size from baby veggies to full-sized. Some vines "die" when Potatoes mature. If the plant seriously wilts, check the Potatoes — they might be ready.

PROTECT IT: Potatoes are susceptible to various diseases and insects. Beetles and Aphids enjoy tender new Potato shoots. Grubs and nematodes will chew on the tubers. The best line of defense is to plant disease-resistant varieties in rich soil with lots of companion plants nearby (especially Peas) and flowering shrubs and herbs throughout the garden. Avoid planting with Cucumbers, Eggplants, Pumpkins, Sunflowers, and Tomatoes which reduces Potatoes' resistance to the blight Phytophthora.

PUMPKINS

JACK-O-LANTERNS are popular at Halloween, but Pumpkins are also great for cooking and decoration. They can last four to six months, if you store them in a cool, dry place and don't pierce the skin. Because they need several months to mature, plant seeds during July. One last thing to remember about Pumpkins for the low desert: the smaller, the better.

CHOOSE IT: The antique French Pumpkin, also known as Cinderella's Carriage (110 days), is a large, thick-fleshed variety that looks just like the old-fashioned pictures of a fairy-tale coach. Other

> For hundreds of years Native Americans have put Corn and Pumpkins together. Their great success prompted settlers to copy the technique.

varieties include a baby Pumpkin, Jack Be Little (95 days), and a white Pumpkin called Lumina (90 days). Pumpkins for carving include Jack-O'-Lantern (110 days) and Big Max (120 days). Triple Treat (110 days) is a triple performing variety — good for carving, seeds, and pies.

PLANT IT: When the soil temperature is in the 70°s (F) in March, plant by seed for a summer-maturing crop. When the soil temperature is around 90°(F) in July, plant again for a Halloween crop. Like Melons, Pumpkins love enriched soil. Dig a hole one foot wide and two feet deep, then fill it with compost or composted manure. But stop when you're two to three inches from the top. Backfill the rest of the way with native soil, and make a mound at

the top. Plant six to eight seeds on top of the mound, one inch deep and two inches apart. Pumpkins can grow to 35 pounds, so prepare the soil with enough nutrition for a major feeding. The vines require a lot of space, therefore consider a Raised Garden. Or plant them on the edges of the garden so they can sprawl. To minimize Mildew, provide good air circulation and don't crowd plants.

Companion Plants
Beans
Corn
Mint
Nasturtiums
Radishes

Factoid
Stored properly, a Pumpkin seed can stay good for three years.

Do not plant Potatoes with Pumpkins.

WATER IT: Pumpkins need a lot of water to produce large fruit. Irrigate deeply to 24 inches. Check the soil daily. Don't let it dry out. During the summer, water deeply at the base of the Pumpkin, channeling the water into the compost-filled hole. Water less often during the spring. Overhead irrigation promotes Mildew, so water at ground level.

CARE FOR IT: Plants germinate in about a week and reach full size in about 110 days. When plants are two inches tall, thin down to the four strongest plants per hill. Grow Corn so the tall stalks will shade the Pumpkins, while the Pumpkins' big leaves keep the soil cool. Put four to six inches of alfalfa hay under Pumpkins to keep the soil cool and evenly moist. The hay also lifts developing Pumpkins off the ground to prevent rot and insect attack. Transplanting Nursery Stock can shorten the time to harvest by a week or two.

FERTILIZE IT: Besides enriched soil, feed the Pumpkins with a solution of fish emulsion or liquid seaweed every two weeks. Apply a thick mulch (four to six inches deep) over the soil to conserve water and to provide a continuous source of nutrients as the mulch slowly decomposes.

What You Need To Start
Seeds or transplants
Trowel
Shovel
Compost or Manure
Mulch

ENJOY IT: Harvest when the Pumpkins are large and the vine begins to die. Leave four to six inches of stem on the Pumpkin. Let the Pumpkin cure in the sun for about ten days, then store in a cool, dry place for up to six months.

PROTECT IT: These seedlings are prime targets for Birds. Cover with upside down Strawberry baskets until they are at least three inches tall. Sometimes Aphids will be attracted to the succulent new growth. Hose them off with a sharp stream of water. Inspect for Slugs. Check for Beetles and handpick or dust the plants with Diatomaceous Earth. Plant lots of flowering herbs and flowers to encourage beneficial insects to enter your garden.

RADISHES

THIS is a wonderful crop for children to plant because they sprout so quickly. The color and size seem to appear as if by magic! Radishes will sprout within five to seven days of planting and they're ready to eat just three weeks after that. Aphids seem to steer clear of Radish plants, as do most pests. This might be a good veggie to plant in all corners of the garden.

CHOOSE IT: There are many different varieties, most maturing in 24 to 28 days. Sow Easter Egg II, French Breakfast, or White Icicle for variety. The Easter Egg II is a rainbow-colored mix in shades of cherry-red, white, dark purple, and Rose pink.

What You Need To Start
Seeds
Shovel
Compost
Mulch

PLANT IT: Plant by seed from the first of September through April, when soil temperatures are 45-90° (F). They thrive in a compost-rich soil. As far as I'm concerned, you can plant them in 100% compost. Every two weeks, put in a new crop to keep a steady harvest. Companion planting with Nasturtiums makes Radishes spicier and more tender.

Companion Plants
Beans
Carrots
Cucumbers
Lettuce
Melons
Nasturtiums
Peas
Squash
Tomatoes

WATER IT: They require frequent irrigation to at least eight inches to keep the flesh crisp and flavorful. Don't let the top of the soil dry out, because it will slow growth.

CARE FOR IT: About ten days after Germination, thin plants to approximately 1½ inches apart. Radishes really prefer cooler weather. If you plant them during the still-hot days of September, keep them well-irrigated and feed weekly with liquid seaweed so they grow quickly. As soon as the

Radishes are marble-size, harvest them and keep in the refrigerator for up to three weeks. Radishes grown during the warmer weather will be hotter and spicier.

Be sure to cover the tops of any exposed Radishes as they grow. Radishes are very aromatic and will deter many pests, including Spider Mites and Beetles.

FERTILIZE IT: During warm fall days, fertilize weekly with liquid seaweed. It helps increase tolerance to heat and promotes vigorous growth. In cooler months, fertilize with fish emulsion, liquid seaweed, or another organic nitrogen fertilizer.

Factoid
Save some seed to plant in your fall garden because Radishes grow well in winter.

ENJOY IT: The warmer the weather, the spicier the Radish. And the flip side is also true — the cooler the weather, the milder the taste.

Harvest when the Radishes are marble sized, or larger, depending on the variety. Some varieties will be ready to harvest within 20 days of seeding. They can be stored in the refrigerator for three weeks.

PROTECT IT: Flea Beetles and root maggots can spoil Radish crops. Dust the leaves with Diatomaceous Earth to combat flea Beetles.

Spray Radishes with a Garlic-Pepper spray (see "Bug Remedies") to deter the root maggots. Otherwise, Radishes are pest-free and are good companion crops to many vegetables. If you let some of the plants flower and go to seed, they'll attract many beneficial insects. Don't plant Radishes with members of the cabbage family.

> My dad always said, "Radishes are the tell-tale sign. If you can grow them, you can grow a great garden in the same place."

SPINACH

SPINACH has come a long way from Popeye's canned stuff. Picked young and used in salads, stir-fries, or lightly steamed, iron-rich Spinach is a gourmet delight and one of my favorite vegetables.

CHOOSE IT: From the time you plant seed in the ground, Spinach is ready to harvest in about 45 days. Two good varieties are Bloomsdale Long-Standing and Melody Hybrid. Being a cool weather crop, it fizzles out during the summer.

One good way to enjoy Spinach-like flavor during the summer is to try New Zealand Spinach or Malabar Spinach. The young leaves and red stems are particularly tasty in salads.

Companion Plants
Onions
Peas
Strawberries

PLANT IT: Spinach does best planted from mid-September to the end of February when soil temperatures reach 45-75° (F). In soil enriched with compost or manure, plant the seed one-half inch to one inch deep and two inches apart. Firmly pat the soil over the seed for better Germination. Plant some seed every two weeks for a continuous harvest.

Plant New Zealand Spinach in March when soil temperature is in the 55-65° (F) range. Two months later you can harvest. Sow seed one-half inch deep and three inches apart.

The other Spinach substitute, Malabar Spinach, grows as a vine and does well on a trellis, fence, or bean tower. From mid-March to mid-April, plant the seed only one-quarter inch deep and three to four inches apart.

Both of these Spinach substitutes will produce better and longer if they have some afternoon shade. So plant them on the east side of Corn or Sunflowers, or put up 50% or less shade cloth to protect them.

WATER IT: Don't let the soil dry out. Water deeply 12-18 inches, and apply a layer of mulch four to six inches over the soil. Be sure not to let the mulch rest against the Spinach stems.

> **Factoid**
> Spinach has been grown in European gardens since the fifteenth century.

Water New Zealand Spinach when the top one-half inch of the soil is dry, and mulch with a four to six inch layer of alfalfa hay or compost.

CARE FOR IT: Thin Spinach to six inches apart. Keep the Spinach bed weeded.

New Zealand Spinach needs to be thinned to at least one foot apart — don't neglect this chore. The plant will spread out over the ground, reaching four feet in diameter. The tops of the plant are the most tender. Pluck tips continually to keep production going.

> **What You Need To Start**
> Seeds
> Shovel
> Compost or manure
> Mulch

For the Malabar, it's important to thin these plants to at least one foot apart. Keep the soil deeply mulched and don't let the soil dry out.

FERTILIZE IT: Every two weeks, fertilize with a solution of liquid seaweed during the warm weather and fish emulsion during the cooler months. This keeps the Spinach growing vigorously with bigger yields.

ENJOY IT: Enjoy the thinnings in salads. Harvest the outer leaves to keep plant producing Spinach and to prolong the harvest. Or you may harvest the entire plant and put something else in the empty place.

PROTECT IT: Insects don't usually bother Spinach. Plant Mildew-resistant varieties and you won't have disease problems, either.

SQUASH

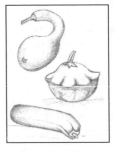

HERE is where you get to practice what you know about the Birds and the bees. This plant needs assistance with pollination (see "CARE FOR IT"). Also, there are two general categories of Squash. Summer Squash, with a soft rind, is harvested and eaten before it matures. Winter Squash, on the other hand, is allowed to ripen on the vine until the rind is hard. You can store winter Squash for several months, but you must eat summer Squash immediately after harvest.

CHOOSE IT: With Squash, the days to harvest are counted from planting. If you use Seedling Transplants, subtract 10-15 days. Summer Squash includes Crookneck, Pattypan, Straightneck, and Zucchini. The Crookneck has varieties such as Dixie (45 days) and Sundance (58 days). Pattypan (scalloped) summer Squash varieties to try are Sunburst (50 days), and Butter Scallop Hybrid (50 days). A Straightneck variety is Butterbar, producing in 49 days. That old standby, Zucchini, is a prolific producer of sweet and tender Squash. Try Raven (42 days) with its tender skin and delicate flesh. Or plant Gold Rush (45 days),

Companion Plants
Alyssum
Beans
Corn
Melons
Mint
Nasturtium
Radishes

a golden-fruited Zucchini. An unusual variety to look out for is Tromboncino, a vining summer Squash that should be trellised so fruit can grow into their distinctive curvy shape.

What You Need To Start
Seeds or transplants
Shovel
Composted manure or compost
Mulch

Winter Squash varieties include Acorn, Butternut, Spaghetti, Hubbard, and Buttercup. All of the winter Squash varieties require 90 to 120 days to mature. They also require a lot of space, so plant them in the corners of the garden or along the back fence.

PLANT IT: Plant summer Squash seed from mid-February through mid-April when soil temperatures range from 60° to 85° (F). Plant again the last two weeks in August when the soil is about 95° (F). For winter Squash, the planting window is much narrower: only the month of March when soil temperatures are 65-70° (F), and then again in July when soil temperatures are 90° (F). Plant the seed one-half to one inch deep in compost rich soil. If planting in hills, dig a well at least 12 inches wide and two feet deep. Fill with compost or composted manure. Cover organic material with several inches of mounded soil. Plant seeds one inch deep in the mound of soil. As plants grow, the roots will reach down into the buried supply of nutrients, water will be channeled and contained in the well and plants will spill over the hill.

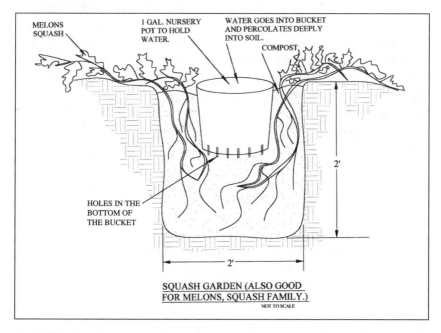

SQUASH GARDEN (ALSO GOOD FOR MELONS, SQUASH FAMILY.)
NOT TO SCALE

WATER IT: Water deeply to at least 24 inches! These are such vigorous growers that they need deep irrigations. Overhead irrigation and sprinklers spread diseases, so water at ground level. Spread four to six inches of mulch (such as alfalfa hay) over the soil to conserve moisture, keep the roots cool, and raise the fruit off the ground.

CARE FOR IT: Squash produce better if you assist with pollination. The male flower (usually first to appear) is upright and has no bulb. The female flower has a small bulb at its base, and does not stand so upright. To pollinate, shake the male flower over the female flower. Or you can use a paintbrush to gently collect the male pollen and brush it inside the female flower. That's it! At the same time you plant your Squash seed, plant some Radish seed. Allow the Radishes to grow and flower to attract many beneficial insects.

> **Factoid**
> Keep developing fruit off the soil with alfalfa hay or compost to prevent rot or insect damage.

Don't squish the Squash! They don't like being overcrowded. Thin them to two to three plants per hill (five feet in diameter), or every 18 to 24 inches apart in rows. The rows should be at least four to five feet apart. Plants that are not properly thinned are very susceptible to mildews and other diseases. The Climbing Tromboncino should be thinned to one foot apart.

Companion Plants
Alyssum
Beans
Corn
Mint
Nasturtiums
Radishes

FERTILIZE IT: The compost or manure-rich soil will release nutrients slowly. Feed every two weeks with a solution of fish emulsion or liquid seaweed (which helps increase heat tolerance). For nitrogen, apply cottonseed meal or alfalfa meal every month. Rabbit food is made of alfalfa meal, but also contains molasses as a binding agent. Scatter a handful under and around each plant.

ENJOY IT: Harvest summer Squash frequently to encourage production. For best flavor pick summer Squash when they are tiny (three to five inches), with the blossoms still attached. The younger, the better when it comes to eating Squash. To tell if winter Squash is mature, give it the fingernail test. If your fingernail cannot puncture the rind, it's ripe. Cut (don't pull) it off the vine, leaving five to six inches of stem. Let it cure in a dry place (such as a garage) for ten days before storing in a cool, dry place. A basement would be another good choice.

PROTECT IT: Proper thinning, deep watering, and good air circulation are the most important cultural practices to keep plants free of disease. If you worry about Aphids, plant Nasturtiums throughout the Squash patch. Squash grows so quickly that you need to plant Nasturtiums several weeks in advance to give them a headstart.

Protect ripening Squash by placing them on a thick layer of alfalfa hay. And plant lots of flowering plants and herbs to bring in the beneficial pollinators and insects.

SWISS CHARD

THINK of it as a Beet-like plant, without the Beet. Swiss Chard has been grown in Europe since the time of the Roman Empire. It tolerates summer heat, making it a good substitute for Spinach.

CHOOSE IT: The red and green varieties are especially prolific. Fordhook Giant (60 days from Direct Seeding) has white stems. Rhubarb Chard (60 days) has red stalks, and the wildly colorful Bright Lights has sunshine yellow, hot pink, crimson, bright orange, purple, white, and green stalks! This is one variety that will really electrify the summer flower bed.

PLANT IT: By seed or transplant, put it in the ground from mid-September through mid-February when soil temperatures are cooling down from 85° to 50° (F). Sow the seed one-half inch deep and six inches apart. Plant transplants 24 to 30 inches apart to allow for mature size. Plant Swiss Chard in soil enriched with compost or manure. If you use Seedling Transplants, knock off 10-15 days.

Factoid
Plant Bright Lights Swiss Chard in with your summer flowers for knock 'em dead color.

WATER IT: Water deeply (18-24 inches deep) when the first one-half inch of soil is dry. Keep a layer of mulch four to six inches thick over the soil to conserve water and keep soil evenly moist.

CARE FOR IT: Thin carefully so that the seedlings are at least one foot apart. Toss the thinnings in the salad bowl or use in stir-fry dishes. Keep the layer of mulch or alfalfa hay four to six inches thick to conserve moisture and cool the soil.

What You Need To Start
Seeds or transplants
Shovel
Compost
Manure
Mulch

FERTILIZE IT: Apply fish emulsion or liquid seaweed every two weeks for nitrogen and other nutrients. It also helps heat tolerance.

ENJOY IT: Begin harvesting the outer leaves as soon as they are several inches long. Keep harvesting the outer leaves because Swiss Chard will keep on producing more. Don't discard the center ribs, as they are delicious braised, grilled, or added to stir-fries and soups. Swiss Chard will keep growing until a hard frost knocks it down. If you provide winter protection with hay bales or frost cloth, you will be able to really prolong the harvest.

Companions
Beets
Onions
Lavender

PROTECT IT: Other than a few nibbles by hungry Caterpillars (which really don't create much damage), Swiss Chard is not troubled by pests or diseases.

TOMATOES

NOTHING, but nothing comes close to the taste of a homegrown Tomato. Pluck it, brush off the dust, and bite into vine-ripened heaven. It's easy to grow juicy, sweet Tomatoes here in the Sonoran Desert, if you keep a few things in mind.

CHOOSE IT: Choose varieties that ripen early. For seed, pick varieties that mature in 70 days or less. Now that might seem a little confusing, because the "70 days" listed on the seed packet refers to the time from *transplant to harvest*. It does not mean you will have Tomatoes 70 days after planting seed. Seeds take about four weeks before they are ready for transplant, then it is another 70 days before you can harvest.

Resistance Symbols
"V" resists Verticillium wilt
"F" resists Fusarium wilt
"N" resists Nematodes
"T" resists Tobacco Mosaic Virus

For transplants, choose varieties that are disease-resistant. Check the accompanying box for more information.

Successful Varieties
Early Girl
Roma VF
Celebrity VF
Pearson
Patio Tomatoes
• Sweet 100
• Yellow Pear
I suggest early-ripening varieties

Tomatoes come in two classes: "indeterminate," and "determinate." The Determinate types give just one crop, and they're done. But the Indeterminates keep producing fruit until extreme heat or cold stop them. Even then, though, if you maintain the plant and soil, tomatoes will start producing fruit again when the temperatures start cooling off at night in late August or early September.

PLANT IT: Choose an area that will get afternoon shade in the summer or plan to provide shade with a fence, a 50% shade cloth, or a row of Corn or Sunflowers. Then transplant as early as possible in February through March when soil temperatures get over 55° (F). Mix lots of compost about four to six inches into the soil. Thoroughly water the bed, but don't plant yet. Digging in wet soil can destroy soil structure. Wait a few days, then dig a shallow trough the same length as the plant. Leave the top leaf-pair, but take off all lower leaves. Don't remove the little white hairs, because they turn into the roots. Lay the plant down in the trough length wise — like you're laying a pen down. Cover it with compost, but fold the leaf tip up so it can get sun. At first, there will not appear to be a lot of growth, but those little hairs are taking root. And soon enough, the plant will get bigger.

Companion Plants
Asparagus
Basil
Corn
Marigolds
Nasturtiums
Peas
Sage
Sunflowers

Don't plant in the same area as Cauliflower, Eggplants, Fennel, Peppers, Potatoes or other members of the Solanaceae family. Rotate Tomato placement every year to keep soil healthy.

What You Need
- Tomato transplant
- Shovel
- Mulch or compost
- Epsom salts
- Frost protection

Temperatures and Tomatoes
- Lower than 55°, Tomatoes will not set
- Provide frost protection
- Provide a soil warming mulch
- Over 90-100°, Tomatoes will not set
- Provide afternoon shade
- Use an organic mulch
- Keep evenly moist

WATER IT: Tomatoes need even moisture. Don't swamp or drought them. While they are establishing, irrigate deeply (to a depth of 24 inches) and frequently. They need to stay on the moist side, so compost goes a long way toward keeping them from getting thirsty.

CARE FOR IT: When it gets hot (over 100 degrees), you'll need to help your plant a few times a week. In the morning, pollinate the plant by gently shaking plants and flowers to distribute pollen. If flowers face downward or there are very few of them, use a small brush to transfer pollen from one flower to another. Do this in the morning, before the pollen has dried out. Or use Tomato Set, a product sold at most nurseries.

Keep a layer of mulch or compost four to six inches thick over the garden bed. It helps retain moisture, keep soil cool, and prevent diseases by keeping fruit up off the ground.

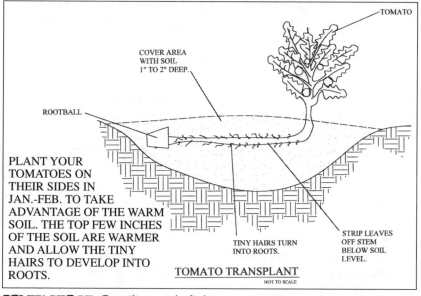

TOMATO

COVER AREA WITH SOIL 1" TO 2" DEEP.

ROOTBALL

PLANT YOUR TOMATOES ON THEIR SIDES IN JAN.-FEB. TO TAKE ADVANTAGE OF THE WARM SOIL. THE TOP FEW INCHES OF THE SOIL ARE WARMER AND ALLOW THE TINY HAIRS TO DEVELOP INTO ROOTS.

TINY HAIRS TURN INTO ROOTS.

STRIP LEAVES OFF STEM BELOW SOIL LEVEL.

TOMATO TRANSPLANT
NOT TO SCALE

FERTILIZE IT: Fertilize with fish emulsion or liquid seaweed every two weeks to increase heat tolerance and feed the soil. If you mulch with compost, it will increase microbiotic activity in the soil and prevent soil-borne diseases from splashing onto Tomatoes. In contrast, nitrogen-based

Harvest Tips
- Red, red, red color
- Taste test
- Pick just before using
- Cut or twist off fruit
- Cut just before using
- If green, ripen in a sack with a Banana or Apple

chemical fertilizers promote more leaf growth, but very few Tomatoes. It also does nothing to promote the microbiotic activity that strengthens plants.

ENJOY IT: Plan to spend about a half hour a week taking care of your Tomato patch. This includes watering, feeding, pest control, and weeding. This is a minimum. Don't let it limit how long you relax in the garden!

PROTECT IT: There are a few diseases and pests that can affect Tomatoes: Aphids, Caterpillars, Spider Mites, Whiteflies, Blossom-end rot, or curly top virus. A couple of gruesome names, but not at all uncommon. There are quick and simple solutions to each of

Beneficial Insects and Critters

Assassin Bugs
- $1/2$-inch long brown bug
- Eats insects like Caterpillars by sucking out their fluids

Braconid Wasps
- Tiny brown or black flying insect
- Lays eggs in Moths and Caterpillars

Lacewings
- Green bodies with fragile wings
- Larvae are voracious Aphid predators

Ladybugs
- Eat Aphids, Thrips, Mealybugs, and Mites
- Larvae can eat 30-40 Aphids per day

Spiders
- Some spin webs to trap insects
- Attract to the garden
- Some hunt insects

Toads
- Will eat 10,000-20,000 insects per year
- Like cool and shady homes
- Provide water

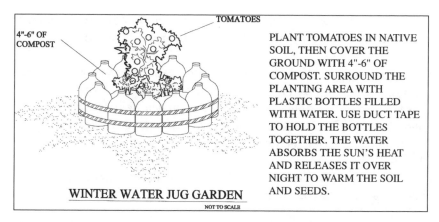

4"-6" OF COMPOST

TOMATOES

PLANT TOMATOES IN NATIVE SOIL, THEN COVER THE GROUND WITH 4"-6" OF COMPOST. SURROUND THE PLANTING AREA WITH PLASTIC BOTTLES FILLED WITH WATER. USE DUCT TAPE TO HOLD THE BOTTLES TOGETHER. THE WATER ABSORBS THE SUN'S HEAT AND RELEASES IT OVER NIGHT TO WARM THE SOIL AND SEEDS.

WINTER WATER JUG GARDEN

NOT TO SCALE

them (see below, or "Organic Controls"). Watch the temperature. If it boils over 100° (F), provide afternoon shade. If it falls below 30° (F), keep things warm with a lamp, insulate with red plastic mulch or with a product called Wall O' Water (check my website).

TURNIPS

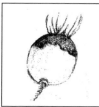

THE new Turnip varieties are full of flavor and very tender. My son and I grow them, cut them into slices, and eat them with a little salt. Yum! Harvest them as a baby veggie to taste a whole new treat.

CHOOSE IT: Turnips can be grown both for the root and for greens. One root variety to try is Purple Top White Globe. A variety specially bred for greens is Seven Top Greens. The Greens will be ready about ten days before the root crop, which takes about two months from Germination to harvest.

PLANT IT: Plant seeds from September through the end of February when soil temperatures are 40-90° (F). In soil enriched with compost or manure, plant the

Companion Plants
Beans
Lettuce
Peas
Radish
Spinach

seed one inch deep and one to two inches apart. Make successive plantings every two weeks to provide a continuous harvest.

What You Need
To Start
Seeds
Shovel
Compost
Mulch

WATER IT: Keep the seedbed evenly moist and don't allow the soil to dry out. A layer of mulch four to six inches deep will help conserve moisture and prevent weeds. Don't let the mulch rest against the stems of the Turnips.

CARE FOR IT: Thin Turnips to three to four inches apart. Use the thinnings in salads or lightly steam them.

FERTILIZE IT: Fertilize every two weeks with a solution of liquid seaweed in the warm weather of early fall and fish emulsion when the weather has cooled down.

ENJOY IT: Harvest the greens when they are a few inches tall. Pick a few leaves from each plant (rather than from one plant). When the Turnips are one to one and one-half inches in diameter, they are ready to harvest.

Factoid
Turnips are Turnips, while rutabagas are a cross between cabbages and Turnips.

PROTECT IT: Turnips are susceptible to many of the same diseases as cabbages; namely Aphids, Beetles, and root maggots. Check out the pest solutions in "Organic Pest Control."

FRUITS AND NUTS

FRUIT and nut trees can do very well here in the desert Southwest. Apples, Guavas, Oranges, Blackberries, and Pecans thrive in the desert and show just how diverse your garden can be.

To grow strong trees that produce a lot of healthy fruit, I want to let you in on a couple of secrets (these secrets don't apply to Citrus). First, the earlier you plant in the season, the better your trees chances of success. Second, there is an area of your yard that is the coolest, and you want to plant there. I'll tell you how to find it.

Bare-root fruit and nut trees usually are available in stores and nurseries starting in mid-December up to early February. Buy and plant as soon as you can, because the sooner bare-root trees go in the ground, the better they grow. However, you can install container-grown plants until mid-March. After that, temperatures are generally too hot for the tree to become established.

In order to produce fruit, deciduous fruits and nuts require a certain number of hours every year where the temperature is below 45° (F). When it's that cool for 60 minutes, you've got yourself a "chill hour." Maricopa County, Arizona, usually has 300 to 400 chill hours per year.

Choose varieties with low minimums, usually 250 chill hours or less. Also choose varieties that ripen early enough to avoid sunburn and insect damage to the fruit. In the following pages, I list the required chill hours for individual varieties of fruits and nuts.

To maximize the cool air, plant trees in the coldest part of the backyard. Cold air is heavy and will linger in low spots, so look for low areas with eastern or northeastern exposure. A backyard with a solid block wall is an ideal place for cold air to collect.

Once you've found the "coolest" area of the yard, figure out which spot will stay the coolest longest (usually a corner). That is where you want to plant the trees that require the highest number of chill hours. Situate trees with the fewest chill hours in more open areas.

To really help the process, dig out a large area of your yard's coldest location. Lowering the ground helps retain cool air and will channel water and rain to the trees for irrigation purposes.

Some homes have fences with drainage holes at the bottom. When it's not raining, close off those holes to keep the cold air from floating away. Use a board or just stuff it with newspaper.

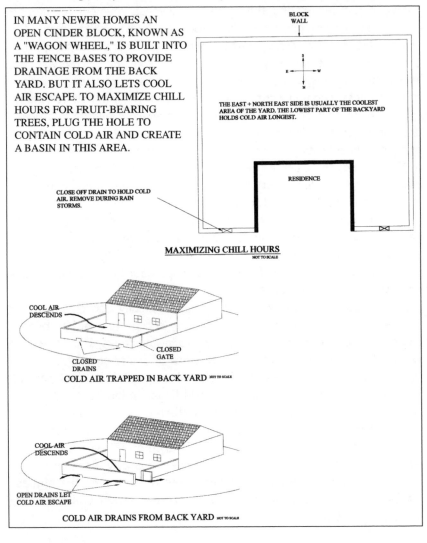

IN MANY NEWER HOMES AN OPEN CINDER BLOCK, KNOWN AS A "WAGON WHEEL," IS BUILT INTO THE FENCE BASES TO PROVIDE DRAINAGE FROM THE BACK YARD. BUT IT ALSO LETS COOL AIR ESCAPE. TO MAXIMIZE CHILL HOURS FOR FRUIT-BEARING TREES, PLUG THE HOLE TO CONTAIN COLD AIR AND CREATE A BASIN IN THIS AREA.

BLOCK WALL

THE EAST + NORTH EAST SIDE IS USUALLY THE COOLEST AREA OF THE YARD. THE LOWEST PART OF THE BACKYARD HOLDS COLD AIR LONGEST.

RESIDENCE

CLOSE OFF DRAIN TO HOLD COLD AIR. REMOVE DURING RAIN STORMS.

MAXIMIZING CHILL HOURS NOT TO SCALE

COOL AIR DESCENDS

CLOSED GATE

CLOSED DRAINS

COLD AIR TRAPPED IN BACK YARD NOT TO SCALE

COOL AIR DESCENDS

OPEN DRAINS LET COLD AIR ESCAPE

COLD AIR DRAINS FROM BACK YARD NOT TO SCALE

In the valley of the Salt River, fruits and nuts grow and produce better when planted away from turf grasses that compete for nutrients and water. These fruit and nut trees are deciduous (they drop their leaves in the fall and go dormant in winter) and should be planted on the eastern side of your yard or home to provide cooling shade in the summer, yet allow the sun to enter in the winter.

Also, some trees listed here do better in higher elevations. Just as a reminder, the elevation ranges in The Valley from about 1100 feet in Phoenix to about 1800 near Apache Junction, and parts of Cave Creek and Carefree are up to 2500 while Casa Grande's elevation is nearly 1400 feet. If you plant and care for the trees well, you can expect them to live for ten to 15 years.

ALMONDS

ADD them to chicken or fish dishes or stir-fry, or just harvest them for a snack. Almond trees live for about 50 years, but I'll be honest with you, it can be tough to grow them in anything but ideal conditions. The beautiful tree and tasty nuts are worth a try, though.

CHOOSE IT: Almonds really do best at elevations over 3,000 feet. Ne Plus Ultra, (250 chill hours) needs a pollinator for nut production; Nonpareil is best. Garden Prince (250 chill hours) is a genetic dwarf tree (ten to 12 feet tall) that is self-fruitful. All-In-One, (500 chill hours) may not be successful in the desert. The semi-dwarf or dwarf varieties are the easiest to harvest. Your chances of bearing fruit increase if you plant more than one to assist in pollination.

PLANT IT: Dig a wide, shallow hole, no deeper than the root system, but five to six times the width of the roots. Fill the hole halfway up with water and let it drain out before planting. Position the tree with the graft (where the rootstock and variety are joined) facing east. Backfill the planting hole with native soil only. Construct a berm around the tree as wide as the planting area. Fill with water. Apply four to six inches of compost over the planting area, being careful not to let the compost touch the trunk. If you are short on space, plant two or three trees in one large hole.

What You Need To Start
Bare-root tree or container-grown plant
Shovel
Sharp pruners
Several bags of compost

WATER IT: Don't let the soil of a newly planted tree dry out. As the tree matures, continue to extend the watering basin. Water longer during each irrigation but space the irrigations more widely apart. Always water to a depth of three feet.

CARE FOR IT: At planting, trim the very tips of the branches back to an outward-facing bud (a swelling on the branch). Outward-facing buds will encourage branching to the outside of the tree, which is more desirable, than to the inside of the tree. Do any pruning from late-December through early January.

FERTILIZE IT: During the first spring and summer, the decomposing compost mulch will provide steady nutrients to the tree. Keep the layer four to six inches deep. In the fall, apply a thick layer of steer manure, chicken manure, or cottonseed meal to provide a readily available source of nitrogen. This fall fertilization is the most crucial, preparing the tree for winter dormancy and allowing the roots to store nutrients for future spring growth and fruit production. Use only organic fertilizers. Synthetic fertilizers could get faster growth, but the tree will be weaker.

ENJOY IT: Harvest Almonds when the hulls split open. Knock them from the trees or gather them off the ground. Remove the hull and spread the nuts in the sun for a day or two to dry. The nuts will rattle in the shells when they are adequately dry. Store in a cool dry place.

Companion Plants
Plant Chives, Garlic Chives, and Onions thickly around trees.

PROTECT IT: Paint the trunks of young trees with a 50/50 mix of water and white latex paint, or wrap them with shade cloth to prevent sunburn. Protect developing nuts from the Birds with bird netting. If you use netting, secure it at the trunk. Inspect the undersides of leaves for mites. If you find any, see Recipe #2 in "Organic Pest Control."

APPLES

PICTURE sinking your teeth into an Apple so juicy that it squirts flavor! There are several varieties that perform so well in the desert, Johnny Appleseed could have a field day.

CHOOSE IT: Choose varieties that require low chill hours and that ripen in the early summer to reduce sunburn and insect damage. Anna (200 chill hours) has a crisp and sweet fruit and ripens in June. Fruit sets in the center of the tree and provides a little protection from Birds. Dorsett Goldens (100 chill hours) were discovered in the Bahamas, and are sweet and firm. Ein Scheimer (100 chill hours) bears sweet Apples that ripen in June.

These three types are all self-fruitful, meaning they will fruit by themselves. But they will produce more fruit if pollinated by another variety.

Companion Plants
Artemisia
Chives
Garlic Chives
Marigolds
Nasturtiums
Onions
Plant thickly around tree

PLANT IT: In the coldest part of your backyard, dig a wide, shallow hole, no deeper than the root system, but five to six times the width of the roots. Fill the planting hole with several inches of water and let it drain the day before planting. Position the tree with the graft (where the rootstock and variety are joined) facing east. Backfill the planting hole with native soil only. Construct a berm around the tree as wide as the planting area. Fill with water. Apply a four to six inch layer of compost over the planting area, being careful not to let the compost touch the trunk.

Plant bare-root apple trees when they are first available, usually mid-December and January. Container-grown plants can be installed until mid-March. After that time, the temperatures are generally too hot for the tree to become established.

WATER IT: Don't let the newly planted tree dry out. Keep soil fairly moist — without drowning the tree — until it gets past its first summer. As the tree matures, wean it to avoid excessive irrigating. Water deeply to three feet (usually every couple of weeks), and then let the top inch of soil dry out. Don't let sprinkler water hit the trunk and leaves, because it can cause salt burn and leaf drop.

CARE FOR IT: Paint the trunks of young trees with white latex paint mixed 50/50 with water, or wrap them with shade cloth to prevent sunburn. At planting, trim the very tips of the branches back to an outward-facing bud (a swelling on the branch). Outward-facing buds encourage growth to the outside of the tree, which is better than growing in toward the tree.

On your new bare-root tree, there can be a tangle of branches. Remove all but three main branches that are eight or nine inches apart and evenly spaced around the trunk. This will form your new scaffold.

What You Need To Start
Bare-root or container-grown plant
Shovel
Several bags of compost
Mulch
Thinning shears

As the tree grows, prune out dead branches, crossing branches, and branches that rub on each other or are growing into the center of the tree. Leave all the spurs (short branches that have grown on second-year wood), as flowers and Apples will form on these spurs. Thin the pea-sized fruit to six to eight inches apart. Thin at least

10% of the fruit. Thinning is important to harvesting quality fruit! And remember — prune only during the dormant season from December through January.

On the Annas and the Dorsets, leave a little top growth to give some shade to the fruit.

FERTILIZE IT: As mulch decomposes during the first spring and summer, it provides a steady supply of nutrients to the tree. Keep the layer four to six inches deep, and keep the mulch four to six inches away from tree trunk. In the fall, apply a thick layer of steer manure, chicken manure, or cottonseed meal as a source of readily available nitrogen. This fall fertilization is crucial, preparing the tree for winter dormancy and allowing the roots to store nutrients for future spring growth and fruit production.

Use only organic fertilizers. Synthetics could get faster growth, but the tree will be weaker. Organic fertilizers help create a richer soil with more microorganisms that will give you healthier, more productive trees.

ENJOY IT: Pick the fruit as it ripens in June. If it stays on the tree, the fruit will sunburn or spoil.

PROTECT IT: Protect developing Apples from the Birds with bird netting. Bring the netting in to the trunk and secure it.

APRICOTS

IMAGINE picking tree-ripened, sun-warmed Apricots right off your backyard tree. One bite and you'll wonder why you haven't grown Apricots before. Velvet texture and rich flavor far surpass store-bought Apricots. Sun-dry the surplus for a flavor treat reminiscent of spring.

CHOOSE IT: Choose early-ripening varieties so you will be able to enjoy the fruit before the green fruit Beetle can harvest them for you! Blenheim or Royal varieties ripen in late May or early June. They bear small tasty fruit and require minimum chilling hours, but they need a pollinator. Gold Kist (300 chill hours) is excellent for backyards. It is self-fruitful, heavy-bearing, and ripens late May to early June. Katy (400 chill hours) is self-fruitful, has large and flavorful fruit, and ripens late May to early June. Royal Rosa (500 chill hours) is a self-fruitful, vigorous, disease-resistant tree whose fruit ripens mid-May. While many Apricots are self-fruitful, yields will be heavier with a second tree as a pollinator.

Companion Plants
Basil
Chives
Garlic
Nasturtiums
Onions
Tansy

PLANT IT: In the coldest part of your backyard, dig a wide, shallow hole no deeper than the root system, but five to six times the width of the roots. Fill the planting hole with several inches of water and let drain the day before planting. Position the tree with the graft (where the rootstock and variety are joined) facing east. Backfill the planting hole with native soil. Construct a berm around the tree as wide as the planting area. Fill with water. Apply a layer of four to six inches of compost over the planting area, being careful not to let the compost touch the trunk.

WATER IT: Don't let the newly planted tree dry out. Keep soil fairly moist (without drowning the tree) until the end of its first summer. As the tree matures, avoid excessive water. Water deeply (to three feet deep) over a wide area and then let the soil dry. Don't let sprinkler water hit trunk and leaves, as it can cause salt burn and leaf drop.

CARE FOR IT: Paint the trunks of young trees with white latex paint mixed 50/50 with water, or wrap them with shade cloth to prevent sunburn. At planting, trim the very tips of the branches back to an outward-facing bud (a swelling on the branch).

Outward-facing buds encourage growth to the outside of the tree, which is better than growing in toward the tree.

When the tree is dormant (not growing and leafless), prune out dead branches, crossing branches, branches that rub on each other, and those growing in toward the center of the tree. Carefully prune the tree so it will be short enough that it can be covered with bird netting as the fruit ripens. When pruning, remove wood that is six years old or older. Leave all the "spurs" (short branches that have grown on second-year wood) as flowers and Apricots will form on the spurs. The spurs will usually bear for three to four years. Then they may be pruned off to encourage new spur growth. Thin the pea-sized fruit to four inches apart. Thinning is important to harvesting quality fruit!

What You Need To Start
Bare-root tree or container-grown plant
Shovel
Couple bags of compost for mulching
Pruning snips

FERTILIZE IT: During the first spring and summer, the decomposing compost mulch will provide steady nutrients to the tree. Keep the layer four to six inches deep. In the fall, apply a thick layer of steer manure, chicken manure, or cottonseed meal to provide a readily available source of nitrogen. This fall fertilization is the most crucial, preparing the tree for winter dormancy and allowing the roots to store nutrients for future spring growth and fruit production. Use organic fertilizers like those listed above. Synthetic fertilizers could get faster growth, but the tree will be weaker. Organic fertilizers help create a richer soil with more microorganisms that will give you healthier, more productive trees.

Spread dried grass over the Apricot tree's root zone to improve yields.

ENJOY IT: If Birds are a problem, harvest Apricots when they are nearly ripe, and let them finish ripening indoors. Place the green fruit in a paper bag with a Banana or Apple for a day or two. If you're lucky and have a bumper crop of

Apricots, slice the fruit in half, remove the pits, and place on cheesecloth lined racks. Cover with another layer of cheesecloth and dry in the sun for several days until dried and chewy. Bring them under cover each evening so they will not get damp.

PROTECT IT: Protect developing Apricots from the Birds with bird netting. Bring the netting in to the trunk and secure it.

BLACKBERRIES

PICKING Blackberries on a summer day is a cherished event for kids visiting friends or family on Nantucket Island. Whether it actually happened to you or not, you can relive childhood memories or create them for your own kids, by planting a Blackberry patch. They grow well here in the low desert. You might not get the sound of seagulls, but you will get fruit for pies or just for snacking.

CHOOSE IT: Three varieties do best: Brazos Blackberries have a flavor that is great for making pies; Brisons are the hardiest and prolific with sweet, tart berries and low acids; Womacks are the most prolific with more, smaller berries per plant. A Womack is not quite as hardy as a Brison, though. Depending on which variety you choose, berries start to ripen in late to early June. All of these varieties require 200-700 chill hours.

What You Need To Start
Cuttings to transplant
Shovel
Cottonseed Meal
Peat Moss

PLANT IT: From December to January, put cuttings in compost enriched soil. Plant in an eastern exposure so plants get afternoon shade. To lower pH in the soil, add cottonseed meal or maybe some peat moss. Blackberries also need a little nitrogen, so add fish emulsion, blood meal, or cottonseed meal. Make sure soil drains well, adding gravel, sand, or a chimney at the bottom of the hole if necessary to facilitate water dispersion.

WATER IT: Keep the soil moist until plant is established. But then cut watering back to a minimum amount. I suggest doing it once every week to ten days. A couple friends of mine in the Mesa area get away with irrigating every two weeks to a depth of two to three feet. It might not be often, but they do a very deep watering to wash away salt deposits and really give the roots a drink. It's another example of deep and infrequent irrigation.

CARE FOR IT: There are two types of canes or stems growing from a Blackberry bush: primocanes and floricanes. A primocane grows this year, without producing fruit. A floricane is last year's growth that produces fruit this year. So the stems that are primocanes this year are the same ones that will give you berries next year. Right after you have harvest berries (usually in June) from the floricanes, immediately prune them down. Leave the primocanes alone so they can get sunlight to grow and develop for next year's production. The more chill hours, the higher the berry production. Note: fruit burns at 105° (F). After that, berry production falls off quickly.

Factoid
Watch your Blackberry bushes. They are invasive and can take over areas of your yard.

With baskets or wires, you can force lateral growth and let the plant gradually grow to the height you want.

FERTILIZE IT: Twice a year (in spring and fall), fertilize with an organic fertilizer such as cottonseed meal or blood meal.

ENJOY IT: The secret to the best Blackberries is time of production. The earlier they pop out, the better the fruit. When berries are dark and plump, harvest them by hand. Taste them

Companion Plant
Apple trees help Blackberry bushes by providing afternoon shade.

straight from the bush to see if they're ready. Pluck gently from the stem so as not to damage fruit. Because you'll be cutting the canes back almost immediately, there's not much danger of damaging the stem. Blackberries are wonderful additions to breakfast and lunches, and make a refreshing desert. If you'll be using them for pies, consider the Brazos variety.

PROTECT IT: Blackberry bushes prefer as many chill hours as they can get, but watch out for frost. Protect the plant with a frost cloth, newspaper, or heat source during frosts.

FIGS

WEALTHY folks in ancient times loved Figs of all types. Valued for the variety of tastes — from naturally sweet to dark and oily — Figs have remained popular throughout the ages. As the United States grew toward the Pacific, slips of prized trees traveled with pioneers and settlers to be planted as soon as they arrived at their new homes in the West. They have grown well here ever since.

CHOOSE IT: Several varieties of Figs do well here in the low desert and they require fewer than 100 chill hours. Look for varieties that have a tightly closed "eye" (the opening at the end of the Fig. The eye needs to be tightly closed to prevent insects from entering the Fig and spoiling it. Black Mission (a deep purple-black Fig) and Conadria (a white Fig) do well in the valley of the Salt River. Another white variety that does well is White Kadota. Brown Turkey is another variety that will grow satisfactorily; however, it performs better at slightly higher elevations.

What You Need To Start
Bare-root tree or
Container-grown tree
Shovel
Compost
Mulch

PLANT IT: Plant bare-root trees as soon as they become available in December or January. Container-grown plants may be set out in late winter, spring, or fall in the low desert. Loosen the soil in a wide diameter and dig the planting hole only as deep as the root ball or bare roots. Fill halfway with water and let it drain out, providing a reservoir of water in the soil. Backfill the planting hole with native soil, and construct a berm around the outermost edge of the loosened soil. Water well. Add a layer of mulch, six to eight inches thick, to conserve moisture and to keep the soil cooler.

WATER IT: Don't let the Fig tree dry out for the first two years. Young Fig trees, with their shallow root system, are not drought-tolerant and will drop their crop if stressed for water. Water to a depth of two to three feet at least once a week during the growing season. After the Figs have been harvested and the leaves drop off in the fall, water every two weeks. Mature trees can tolerate some drought, but wilting leaves is a signal that you must irrigate. The trees will need approximately one inch of water a week over the entire root zone — not just next to the trunk.

Companion Plants
Chives
Garlic
Lavender
Nasturtiums
Onions
Tansy

CARE FOR IT: In areas where the temperatures dip below 32° (F), young trees may be killed. Mature trees may be killed at 28° (F). Provide a thick layer of mulch over the soil during the winter, and be prepared to provide frost protection, such as frost cloth, burlap, or other non-plastic covering.

FERTILIZE IT: Fig trees will require some additional nitrogen to produce a large crop. The trick is to apply just enough for fruiting, but not so much that the tree only produces leaves. A thick layer of slowly decomposing compost will provide a steady amount of nutrients. Manure applied over the soil in fall, winter, and spring will provide nitrogen as will cottonseed meal.

ENJOY IT: Sometimes, you might get two Fig crops — one in June and the main crop in late summer and fall. Figs generally will ripen and be ready for harvest as early as August, and sometimes as late as October. Pick Figs off the tree when they're ripe for eating fresh. You can tell when the Figs are ripe, because they will detach easily when they are bent back towards the branch. Once Figs begin to ripen, harvest them daily.

Factoid
The Fig is not truly a fruit but actually a "fleshy" flower.

PROTECT IT: The greatest problem facing Fig growers is to keep the fruit Beetle out of the ripening Fig. Other than choosing varieties that have a closed end, there is not much you can do. Keep the fruit picked up off the ground or pavement and compost any that you cannot eat or dry.

PEACHES

PROBABLY nothing shouts "summer!" as loudly as picking ripe Peaches off the tree. Homegrown Peaches are so much more flavorful than their store-bought cousins that you'll wonder why you waited so long to grow them! And since there are so many varieties that do well in the desert, it's tough to choose just one or two.

CHOOSE IT: Babcock (250 to 300 chill hours) is the quintessential white-fleshed freestone Peach, sweet and juicy. It's self-fruitful (meaning it will fruit by itself), ripens in June, and has done well in the Salt River Valley. Protect it from the green fruit Beetle. Bonanza (250 chill hours) is a five to six-foot dwarf tree with sweet yellow flesh. Desert Gold (250 to 300 chill hours) has sweet flavor and ripens mid-May.

What You Need To Start
Bare-root tree or container-grown plant
Shovel
Couple of bags of compost to use as mulch

Earligrande (275 chill hours) ripens in May, and does well in the low desert. Floridaprince (150 chill hours) ripens in late April to early May. It is very tasty when allowed to ripen on the tree.

PLANT IT: In the coldest part of your backyard, dig a wide, shallow hole no deeper than the root system, but five to six times the width of the roots. Fill planting hole with several inches of water and let drain before planting. Position the tree with the graft (where the rootstock and variety are joined) facing east. Backfill the planting hole with native soil. Construct a berm around the tree as wide as the planting area. Fill with water. Apply a thick layer of compost four to six inches deep over the planting area, being careful not to let the compost touch the trunk.

WATER IT: Don't let the newly planted tree dry out. Irrigate regularly during fruit formation. Peaches require good drainage. As the tree matures, avoid excessive irrigation. Water deeply (to three feet) over a wide area, then let the soil dry. Don't let sprinkler water hit trunk and leaves, as salt burn and leaf drop can occur.

Companion Plants
Basil
Chives
Garlic Chives
Nasturtiums
Onions
Strawberries
Tansy
Plant these thickly around trees

CARE FOR IT: Paint the trunks of young trees with a 50/50 mix of white latex paint and water, or wrap them with shade cloth to prevent sunburn. At planting, trim the very tips of the branches back to an outward-facing bud (a swelling on the branch). Outward-facing buds encourage branching to the outside of the tree.

When the tree is dormant (not growing and leafless), prune out dead branches, crossing branches, branches that rub each other, and branches that grow to the center of the tree. When pruning Peach trees, remove approximately one-third to two-thirds of the previous year's growth. Remove entire branches, or cut back at least one-third of each branch. On remaining wood, leave all the spurs (short branches that have grown on second-year wood), as flowers and Peaches will form on the spurs. The spurs will usually bear for three to four years. Then they may be pruned off to encourage new spur growth. If you plan to use bird netting, carefully prune the tree so it will be short enough that it can be covered with the net. For quality fruit production, it is critical to thin the one inch diameter fruit to six to eight inches apart, or no more than two Peaches per spur.

FERTILIZE IT: As the mulch decomposes during the first spring and summer, it will provide a steady supply of nutrients to the tree. Keep the layer four to six inches deep. A fall fertilization is crucial for preparing the tree for winter dormancy and allowing the roots to store nutrients for future spring growth and fruit production. Apply a thick layer of steer manure, chicken manure, or cottonseed meal to provide a readily available source of nitrogen. Synthetic fertilizers could generate faster growth but the tree will be weaker. Organic fertilizers help create richer soil with more microorganisms that will give you to healthier, more productive trees.

ENJOY IT: Let the Peaches ripen on the tree for the very best flavor. If Birds or the green fruit Beetle become too great a nuisance, pick the fruit green, and ripen indoors or in a paper bag with a Banana or Apple.

PROTECT IT: Protect developing Peaches from the Birds with bird netting. Bring the netting in to the trunk and secure it.

PEARS

ALTHOUGH Pears usually require more chill hours than we normally have in the low desert, there are a couple of varieties to try. See the list below to choose which you'll plant. A fresh Pear combined with a flavorsome cheese makes a great picnic addition. Or try one gently baked with sugar and cinnamon syrup-ambrosia!

CHOOSE IT: On the whole, Pears do best at elevations above 3,000 feet because those areas have more cool days – Pears require up to 600 chill hours. Bartlett generally needs to be grown above 1,200 feet to consistently bear fruit good quality fruit that ripens September through October. Keifer usually produce crops at elevations of 1,200 to 3,000 feet that ripen October to November. But I know a few people in Phoenix who get plenty of great fruit every year. See if your love for Pears helps your tree thrive.

Companion Plants
Alyssum
Bachelor's button
Catmint
Chamomile
Coriander
Coreopsis
Dill
Feverfew
Marigolds
Marjoram

PLANT IT: Definitely needs to be planted in the very coldest part of the backyard in an area where cold air sinks and collects. Dig a wide, shallow hole no deeper than the root system, but five to six times the width of the roots. Fill planting hole with several inches of water and let drain before planting. Position the tree with the graft (where the rootstock and variety are joined) facing east. Backfill the planting hole with native soil. Construct a berm around the tree as wide as the planting area. Fill with water. Apply four to six inches of compost over the planting area, being careful not to let the compost touch the trunk.

WATER IT: Don't let the newly planted tree dry out. Irrigate regularly during fruit formation. Pears require good drainage. As the tree matures, avoid excessive irrigation. Water deeply (to three feet) over a wide area, and then let the soil dry. Don't let sprinkler water hit trunk and leaves, as salt burn and leaf drop can occur.

What You Need To Start
Bare-root tree or Container-grown tree
Shovel
Compost
Mulch
Lots of flowering herbs

CARE FOR IT: Paint the trunks of young trees with a 50/50 mixture of white latex paint and water, or wrap them with shade cloth to prevent sunburn. At planting, trim the very tips of the branches back to an outward-facing bud (a swelling on the branch). Outward-facing buds will encourage branching to the outside of the tree, which is more desirable, than to the inside of the tree, which should be kept open. Once mature, Pears require very light pruning. Do any pruning when the tree is dormant (not growing and leafless). Prune out dead branches, crossing branches and branches that rub on each other or are growing into the center of the tree. Pear spurs will usually bear for ten to twelve years. Thin small Pears to six to eight inches apart. If you plan to use bird netting, carefully prune the tree so it will be short enough that it can be covered with the netting.

FERTILIZE IT: As the mulch decomposes during the first spring and summer, it will provide a steady supply of nutrients to the tree. Keep the layer four to six inches deep. In the fall, apply a thick layer of steer manure or chicken manure to provide a slow but readily available source of nitrogen. The fall fertilization is the most crucial, preparing the tree for winter dormancy and allowing the roots to store nutrients for future spring growth and fruit production. Use organic fertilizers like those listed above. Synthetic fertilizers can get faster growth but the tree will be weaker. Also, avoid high nitrogen fertilizers with Pears. Organic fertilizers help create a richer soil with more microorganisms that will give you to healthier, more productive trees.

ENJOY IT: Pears should not be allowed to ripen on the tree. Harvest while still hard and pale green or golden green. Wrap Pears individually in sheets of newspaper and store in a cool place for ten days to ripen. Pears may be kept in cold storage for several weeks or longer before ripening. Place them in paper bags in the refrigerator. Remove and allow Pears to finish ripening at room temperature.

PROTECT IT: Keep Bermuda grass well away from the trunks of Pear trees (at least five feet in all directions). Grass roots aggressively compete for water and nutrients. To prevent the spread of fire blight which attacks members of the Rose family, choose resistant varieties and do not plant Pears near Roses, pyracantha, or Apple trees. Fire blight appears as a blackening of the branch ends. If this occurs, cut off the branch six to eight inches below the blackening. Dispose of the branch (but not in the compost pile or left on the ground). For more than a single pruning cut, dip the pruners in a 10% household bleach solution between each cut.

Sometimes, Pears are attacked by psylla, a small insect that sucks the juice from the leaves. Their sugary honeydew lands on leaves and can promote the growth of sooty molds. Spray Recipe #2 (from "Organic Pest Control") before the buds open, then again when flower petals fall off.

PECANS

PECANS have long been associated with older homes in the Salt River Valley homes, their towering size and lush greenness promising coolness in the hot desert summers. Once the nuts are ripe and ready to harvest, their buttery-rich nutmeats can be enjoyed all winter long.

CHOOSE IT: Western Schley (250 chill hours) is widely planted for both commercial and home orchard production. This variety produces early and requires cross-pollination to bear thin-shelled nuts of good quality. Western Schley is not as zinc-dependent as other varieties. Wichita requires cross-pollination to produce its distinctive flavored nuts and is prone to zinc deficiency. Burkett also has a distinctive flavor and does very well at elevations of 2,000 to 3,000 feet. In the low desert, however, the nuts might split before they are ripe. Cheyenne, a slow-growing dwarf type nut tree needs cross-pollination to produce an early and heavy crop. Limb breakage is a factor associated with Cheyennes. Success, Mohawk, Barton, and Bradley are other varieties that will produce nut crops in the low desert.

Along with regular roots that anchor a tree, Pecans have a tap root which shoots straight down from the tree into the soil. So plant in a place where the soil is deep. Avoid extra sandy or rocky areas.

PLANT IT: Pecans should be planted 30 feet from buildings and other trees. For best growth, they require a deep soil without caliche or hardpan (a compacted, almost impenetrable soil). Dig a wide, shallow hole no deeper than the root system, but five to six times the width of the roots. Fill planting hole with several inches of water and let drain before planting. If the tree is bare-root, trim off any broken or damaged roots

Companion Plants
Mints
Peanuts
Tansy

prior to planting. Position the tree with the graft (where the rootstock and variety are joined) facing east. Backfill the planting hole with native soil. Construct a berm around the tree as wide as the planting area. Fill with water. Apply four to six inches of compost over the planting area, being careful not to let the compost touch the trunk. Select three branches as the scaffold branches (these branches will provide the structure of the future tree). These branches need to have wide angles (greater than 45 degrees) and be positioned around the tree. Remove any remaining branches. Prune the scaffold branches back to an outward-facing bud.

WATER IT: Don't let the newly planted tree dry out. Water deeply (to three feet) every week during the first year, more often if needed. When the tree begins producing, water deeply and consistently in August and September to ensure proper development of the nut. Pecans require good drainage. Apply a deep irrigation after the nuts have matured, usually mid-October to mid-November. Pecans generally will not need irrigation again until the buds start to swell in the spring. As the temperatures climb, water deeply over a wide area. When the trees begin to produce nuts, plan to deep irrigate them every two weeks during the summer months. Don't let sprinkler water hit trunk and leaves, as severe salt burn on leaves and subsequent leaf drop can occur which will reduce photosynthetic energy available to the roots, lowering nut quality and yield.

What You Need To Start
Bare-root or container-grown tree
Shovel
Sharp pruners
Bags of compost to spread as mulch

CARE FOR IT: The area around Pecan trees, as with other fruits and nuts, needs to be kept free of Bermuda grass for the first three years. Watch for Aphid infestations. Severe infestations can weaken the tree, lower fruit quality, and allow Aphid "honeydew" to cause you more headaches. Plant a wide diversity of flowering shrubs and herbs to attract beneficial Aphid-eating insects.

FERTILIZE IT: Additional nitrogen and zinc are required for quality nut production. Apply extra nitrogen (such as cottonseed meal) in the spring and early summer when the nuts are developing. Spread the fertilizer over the entire root zone, from one foot beyond the trunk outward to beyond the leaf canopy. Always water well before and after fertilizer applications. Fall fertilization is not necessary. However, a layer of manure one to two inches deep will supply a slow release of nutrients during the fall and winter months. Zinc, critical to quality nut production, is most efficiently utilized if it is applied as a foliar spray. Apply zinc at bud break and twice during leaf growth.

ENJOY IT: In the fall, the Pecan husks will split open. Allowing the Pecans to continue to dry for three or four more days on the tree (or spread them on trays) will result in tastier nuts. Pecans in the shell may be frozen for six months. For eating or cooking, store in airtight containers in the refrigerator.

PROTECT IT: Pecans are cold hardy in the low desert. Careful pruning is necessary to prevent major wind damage during storms. Paint the trunks of young trees with a 50/50 mixture of water and white paint, or wrap them with shade cloth to prevent sunburn.

PINEAPPLE GUAVAS

THIS lovely plant may be used in the landscape as a large shrub or small tree, and as an added bonus, the beautiful pink and white flower petals are edible, as are the small fleshy fruits.

CHOOSE IT: While Pineapple Guava is not a true Guava, it is a very decorative plant requiring more than 300 chill hours to set fruit. They generally produce tasty fruit beginning in about 10 years.

PLANT IT: This versatile fruit is best planted in fall (September to January). You can try to plant in spring or winter, but you're reducing your chances of success. Because nurseries don't often have the plants available until they're blooming in February, ask them to special order them for you. Summer planting can work if you provide lots of afternoon shade for the first few weeks and water enough to keep the root ball from drying out. Pineapple Guavas can be planted in full sun to part shade, but does best on an eastern exposure.

What You Need To Start
Container-grown plant
Shovel
Mulch

WATER IT: This plant is also very versatile in its irrigation requirements. Pineapple Guavas tolerates lawn irrigation, deep watering, and even dry situations once it is established. On the deep watering schedule, water the root zone under the entire canopy and to a depth of three feet. This may be as often as every five days in the summer, and once every two weeks in the winter.

CARE FOR IT: Prune selectively as needed. Pineapple Guavas may also be trained as an espalier or sheared into various shapes. Flower and fruit production will be nearly eliminated with the more extreme forms of pruning.

FERTILIZE IT: Generally, Pineapple Guavas do not require additional fertilizer. Keep a thick layer (six to eight inches) of mulch over the soil. Well-mulched soil will provide a steady amount of slowly released nutrients, conserve moisture and cool the soil.

Companion Plants
Alyssum
Bachelor's Button
Coreopsis
Calendula
Feverfew
Marigold
Nasturtium
Rosemary

ENJOY IT: For best flavor, harvest the fruits when they drop from the plant. They will keep for about a week. Compost any uneaten fruit, and don't leave any on the ground where they will attract insect pests.

PROTECT IT: Pineapple Guavas can tolerate temperatures ranging from summer highs of 115° (F) to lows of 15° (F) in the winters.

PLUMS

DEEP dark purple to soft green, Plums have been a favorite for centuries. Luckily, Plums grow well here in the Valley of the Sun, and their lovely foliage and flowers are a bonus in the landscape.

CHOOSE IT: Santa Rosa is the variety most often planted. Other varieties include Gulf Gold and Gulf Ruby.

PLANT IT: Because Plums need good drainage, avoid planting in low spots of the yard. Also, don't put these trees in the lawn, because grass is getting wet all the time. Plant bare-root trees when they become available in late December or in January. Early spring or fall is a good time to put in container-grown plants.

> **Factoid**
>
> Prunes, a European Plum, can be dried because the extra sugar content keeps them from rotting around the pit.

WATER IT: Plums need to be deep watered under the entire leaf canopy to a depth of three feet. Irrigate when the top two to three inches of soil is dry.

What You Need To Start

Bare-root tree
Container-grown tree
Shovel
Mulch
Compost

CARE FOR IT: Keeping a layer of mulch or alfalfa hay six to eight inches deep over the soil will conserve moisture, provide nutrients and cool the soil. Plum trees do not need to be protected from the cold weather or frosts. In the Salt River Valley, Plum trees and other "stone" fruit trees have a life expectancy of ten to fifteen years, even with the very best of care. To foil Birds, cover with bird netting and bring into the trunk and secure. Thin the fruit to four to six inches apart when they are about one to one and one-half inches in diameter. When the trees are dormant, in the late fall and early winter (December to the end of January), prune out any crossing branches and remove some of the shoots. Don't prune off all the fruiting spurs (short branches where the fruit grows).

FERTILIZE IT: Plums benefit from some additional nitrogen to produce bumper crops. Spread manure over the root zone in the fall, winter, and spring to provide nitrogen. Other good organic fertilizers include cottonseed meal, blood meal, or Milorganite. Spread these over the root zone September through March.

Companion Plants
Alyssum
Chamomile
Chives
Garlic
Nasturtiums
Onions
Strawberries
Tansy

ENJOY IT: Harvest the fruit when it's ripe and sweet. The Santa Rosa Plum has a thicker skin, so it may not be damaged by the Birds as much as other varieties.

PROTECT IT: Here in the Southwest, Aphids, Spider Mites, Scale, and Borers will all try to have a bite of the Plum tree. Hose off Aphids and Spider Mites with a strong stream of water. Plant a diversity of flowering herbs to entice predatory beneficial insects into the garden to keep the Aphids, Spider Mites, and Scale under control. Keep your Plum tree growing vigorously. A healthy tree is the best defense against insect attacks. In spring, use netting to protect fruit from Birds.

POMEGRANATES

SINCE biblical times, Pomegranate shapes have influenced the decorative arts, adorning ancient temples as well as influencing contemporary Native American art. Along with the flowing, sensuous shape of the Pomegranate, the fruit itself has a legendary past appearing in the magical tales of folklore.

CHOOSE IT: The variety Wonderful does very well here in the low desert, producing plump, juicy fruit with fewer than 200 chill hours. This variety may be grown as a large, bushy shrub or as a small tree with corrective pruning. Wonderful accepts the desert's heat and soil and is drought tolerant when established.

Companion Plants
Coreopsis
Garlic
Marigold
Nasturtium
Onion
Rosemary
Tansy

PLANT IT: From late December to the end of January, plant as a bare-root tree. In the spring and fall, container-grown trees may be planted. Choose a full sun location. Morning sun with afternoon shade is also acceptable, although the tree will not be as dense. As with other fruiting trees, loosen the soil in a wide area, three to four feet in diameter. Dig the actual planting hole just as deep at the root mass or root ball. Fill the hole halfway with water. It should drain within five to ten hours.

Plant the tree, backfilling with native soil. Construct a four to eight inch high berm on the outer edge of the planting area as an irrigation basin.

What You Need To Start
Bare-root tree or
Container-grown tree
Shovel
Compost
Mulch

Apply a layer of compost or mulch (alfalfa hay works well) six to eight inches thick over the soil surface, keeping it one foot away from the trunk.

WATER IT: Water newly planted trees several times a week. Water young trees at least once a week the first summer, and then once every two weeks in the winter. Established plants are quite drought tolerant and prefer deep irrigations (to three foot depth) every ten to fourteen days. While fruit is developing, maintain a regular irrigation schedule to keep the soil consistently moist. During the winter months when Pomegranates are deciduous, water deeply each month.

CARE FOR IT: Do any corrective pruning when the tree is dormant in December and January. Remove crossing branches and clean out some of the twiggy interior growth. To encourage a tree form, do any shaping at this time.

FERTILIZE IT: Other than a thick layer of compost or mulch that is replaced as it decomposes, Pomegranates do not need to be fertilized.

ENJOY IT: Harvest Pomegranates when the rind is a deep burnished red and the fruit inside is a deep ruby color.

Factoid
The Pomegranate shape is actually the model for the Navajo "Squash Blossom" necklace

PROTECT IT: The one insect pest that can cause damage to the Pomegranate fruit is the flat-footed plant bug. This annoying insect pierces the developing fruit to sip on the juices, leaving the way open for fungus to enter and spoil the fruit. The best organic defense is to attract Birds and beneficial insects by planting a wide diversity of flowering herbs and shrubs.

STRAWBERRIES

YOU'VE got your Strawberries and cream, your chocolate-covered Strawberries, your Strawberry jams and preserves. So how do you want your Strawberry today? Maybe you long for the little red devil, but don't like the high prices in the grocery store. Plant it yourself and take care of your cravings. They are simple to grow and Strawberries like to be the first fruit of the season. They also don't follow the Fruit rules described on the introduction page at the beginning of this chapter. So follow these rules of planting.

In the wild, Strawberries often grow near pine trees, happily rooting down under a bed of pine needles. If you don't have pine trees, see if you can at least get some pine needles. Spread a thick layer (four to eight inches) around your Strawberry bushes. As the pine needle mulch decomposes, helpful nutrients blend into the soil.

CHOOSE IT: Strawberries come in two types: plants that will bear one crop (usually in June), and the ever-bearing type. For the low desert, go with the June-bearing type because it works better in the heat. Varieties include the Sequoia, Tioga, Lassen, Shasta, and Tufts. Both the Chandler and the Camerosa varieties give big sweet berries from February/March all the way until it gets too hot in June.

PLANT IT: Transplant from late August to early November. As soon as transplants become available, put them in. My friend Arnott Duncan, the great Strawberry farmer, says, "The sooner you plant, the better. It gets the plant growing a little before it starts to fruit."

Companion Plants
Beans
Borage
Lavender
Lettuce
Marigolds
Onions
Spinach
Tansy

A month before you plant, add compost and a little soft rock phosphate to soil to lower pH. Soil needs to drain very well, as roots need to get fairly dry after each watering. Add sand, gravel, or a drain to help if necessary. Mix steer fertilizer, a little soil sulfur, and cottonseed meal 10 to 12 inches into the soil. The plant needs loose soil to grow roots. Transplant Strawberries in fall between mid-September and mid-November for a spring harvest. Put in ground so crown (where leaves attach) is level with surface of soil. Keep plants 12 inches apart. Immediately water after planting.

Tip
Do not plant Strawberries with Cauliflower, Mint, Rosemary, or Thyme. And don't plant with gladioli, or the Strawberries will die.

WATER IT: Strawberries are highly sensitive to salts, so make sure you water deeply. New plants need water every day for a week. After that, keep soil moist, watering deeply (to 12-18 inches) and infrequently.

CARE FOR IT: Strawberries need a little afternoon shade, so consider planting them under a grape arbor and keep them warm in the winter.

FERTILIZE IT: If you add compost and phosphorus before you plant, you won't need to add fertilizer later.

ENJOY IT: Come late spring and early summer, you will get to harvest big, luscious berries. Wait until they're ripe before cutting them off the plant. Leave an inch or so of stem on the berry.

What You Need To Start
Transplants
Shovel
Compost
Mulch
Alfalfa hay or pine needles make good mulch for Strawberries

PROTECT IT: Chlorosis of leaves is a problem that shows up once in a while. You might see leaves turn light green, then fade to yellow. As things get worse, the leaves turn white. The likely culprit is water. So before things get bad, water less often or check to see water is draining properly. You might also need to increase the plant's iron intake. Add chelated iron to the soil, but be careful because it can stain concrete and pool decks.

SUBTROPICAL FRUIT

In Arizona?! The usual response is, "No way." However, with proper sun exposure, wind protection, and ample water, many subtropical and tropical plants are vigorous growers and bear delicious and unusual fruits.

There are many different types to choose from and they should all be planted in warm weather, usually March to October. I'll list the types for you first. Then at the bottom of this chapter, I'll tell you how to plant and care for them.

All Spice
- Easiest of all spices to grow
- A weed from Jamaica that can take all our desert conditions
- Planting
    - Landscape shrub will grow to be four feet wide by eight feet high
    - Very fragrant leaves, but berries are used as spice
    - Cold hardy to mid-20°s (F)
    - Evergreen

Avocados
- Varieties
    - Choose grafted and named varieties
    - Grafted varieties produce more quickly, often as soon as two years from planting
    - Seedlings may not produce for ten years and the flavor quality is extremely variable
    - Pollen is produced at different times of the day; therefore, plant two varieties for pollination
    - The trees are beautiful and large
- Planting
    - Need humidity during flowering for fruit set. Misters work well to supply necessary moisture
    - Plant as a grove. As plants grow, they create their own microclimate, adding shade and humidity
    - Needs filtered sun, such as from trees

- Needs good drainage and a well-composted soil mix
- Plant with an east or southeast exposure
- Or plant against a south-facing wall

Bananas

There are over 1,700 varieties of fruiting Bananas. A fraction of those work well in Arizona.

- Varieties for the Phoenix area
  - Orinoco
  - Apple Banana is a tall variety that does well
  - Brazilian Banana
  - Ice Cream
  - Dwarf varieties work well. They reach six to eight feet, and have stout trunks that withstand the wind better than taller ones
    - Orinoco Dwarf
    - Gold Finger
    - Raja Puri #1 variety for the desert. A stout tree that is a heavy producer
- Planting
  - Plant on southeast side of home for wind protection
  - Will lose leaves at 32° (F)
  - Put four inches of steer manure in the bottom of the planting hole. Cover with several inches of soil. Backfill planting hole with a 50/50 mixture of mulch and soil. This will cover fertilizing needs for one year
  - After plant is established, fertilize one time per month with a solution of fish emulsion or liquid seaweed
  - Water only after new leaves appear
  - <u>Don't water in the winter</u>, or when temps are below 50° (F)

- Production
  - Will produce in two to three years
  - A mature Banana tree will produce mini-trees (called mats or pups) at its base. Remove all but two of them. They will eventually form a clump of Banana trees

Blood Orange
- Varieties
  - Moro has darkest red fruit and grows best in the desert. Bears fruit in clusters
- Corsica produces a lot of juice
- Sanguinelli produces the most delicious juice, however, it's difficult to find

Blue Elderberry (Sambuscus Mexicana)
- Elderberry often grows along streams
- Needs ample water
- Need afternoon shade
- Small edible, blue berries following white flowers in April to August
- Will grow as small shrub, four to ten feet tall, or as a tree, depending on area and growing conditions

Carambola
Also known as Star Fruit
- Variety
  - Carrie is best for low desert
- Carambola have better wind resistance than other tropical fruits

Indian Fig (Opuntia Ficus Indica)
- This Prickly Pear Cactus becomes tree-like with age
- This variety has no thorns, but it does have sharp glochids that are difficult to remove. (Glochids are tiny little spines that look like freckles on the cactus.) Watch out for these sharpies!
- The fruits are prized in Mexico, the Middle East, and some parts of the United States for their use in cuisine

Guava
- Easiest to grow of all subtropical fruits
- Guavas do not travel well, which is why they rarely taste good from the grocery. For the best tasting fruit, grow your own
- Varieties
  - Bangkok Apple Guava #2
    - Pick when still green and crunchy. Add a little salt. Delicious!
  - Tropic White
  - Tropic Pink
    - Pick both tropic varieties when they turn yellow
  - Strawberry Guava
  - Lemon-Strawberry Guava
    - Both Strawberry varieties need full shade, ample water (up to four irrigations per week)
- Planting
  - Although foliage dies back at 25° (F), it regrows quickly in warm weather
  - Will grow to 12 feet tall in eight to nine years

Jujube
- This is a good plant for beginning tropical fruit gardeners
- Varieties
  - Ling
  - Lang
  - Also seedlings produce tasty fruit
- Large (can get 20 to 30 feet tall) deciduous tree is very tolerant of desert conditions
- Fruit produced in the fall
- Tastes like blend of date and apple

Lime
- See "Citrus" chapter

Subtropical Companion Plants
Alyssum
Calendulas
Coriander
Lantana
Marigolds
Nasturtiums
Pennyroyal

Limequats
- Grow in the coldest areas
- Cross between Mexican Lime and Kumquats
- Beautiful tree
- Does well in containers
- Bears fruit nearly all year. Good substitute for Limes in colder areas

Longan
- Very flavorful. Small, one-inch diameter fruits are juicy and tart
- Very easy to grow
- The evergreen tree is hardy to 24° (F), and more resistant to wind than many tropical fruits

Loquat
- Variety
  - Big Jim
- Planting
  - Flowers have a beautiful fragrance.
  - Good plant for beginning tropical fruit growers
  - Fruit production starts early (January or February)
  - When deciding between grafted varieties and seedlings, consider two things
    - Grafted varieties produce fruit at a younger age
    - Grafted varieties top out at eight feet, while seedlings get to 18 feet and are prone to sun, wind and frost damage
  - Grow in part shade or full sun
  - Plant is underutilized in garden designs

Mangos
- Varieties
  - Choose grafted varieties with early production
  - Kent is Indian variety with fruit weighing up to four pounds
  - Nan Doc Mai, from Indonesia, is most flavorful

- Planting
  - Very sensitive to cold, damaged at 25° (F)
  - Plant on southeast, east, or northeast side
  - Plant about five feet away from house, wall, or outbuilding to protect from cold
  - Okay to plant under a tree with filtered shade
  - Don't use fertilizer for first two years
- Production
  - Arid-loving plant
  - Don't over water
  - Humidity prevents fruit set

Papaya
- Sweet, large, wonderful fruit
- Very easy to grow
- Varieties
  - Grafts of Hawaiian or Mexican Papaya do well
  - With seedlings, plant Mexican variety. The seed of the Hawaiian variety is often killed by the required processing prior to shipping
    - Will fruit in nine months from seed
  - To pollinate, use one male tree for several females
- Planting
  - Dies when temperatures drop below 28° (F)
  - Plant in groups for successful pollination
  - Pollinated by sphinx Moths in evening, early morning
  - Thin fruit to avoid bruising from over crowding

  > Papayas grown from seed will bear fruit in nine months.

  - Overhangs of home protect from cold weather, wind
  - Papayas love sun and heat
  - Don't water in winter. Roots die in cold weather
  - Don't add fertilizer

Pineapple
- Does well here in low desert
- Cuttings perform the best, though you can grow Pineapples by planting the tops
- Protect from frost
- Provide afternoon shade

Purple Passion Vine
- For fruiting, plant edible variety Frederick
- Delicious fruit
- Requires a strong trellis for support
- Plant needs afternoon shade

Surinam Cherry
- Does well here in low desert, growing into a bush shape
- Varieties
  - Surinam Cherry
  - Barbados Cherry
    - Known as the Vitamin C Cherry
    - An excellent variety for low desert
    - Use Fruit Set to ensure good crop
  - Grumi Chana Cherry

White Sapote
- Means "sweet fruit"
- Technically, not a true Sapote
  - Native to Mexico
  - Resistant to drought
  - Beautiful tree
- Heavy fruit production and vigorous root system, so plant away from walkways
- Varieties
  - Plant grafted varieties
  - Suebelle
  - Macdill

For Subtropicals...
CHOOSE IT: First of all, choose a warm location that is protected from the wind and cold winter air. This is normally under a roof

overhang or against a southern wall. Plant either an offshoot from the parent plant (known as a "pup"), or a container-grown variety. Named varieties usually produce superior quality fruit, bear fruit at an earlier age and stay more compact than seed-planted specimens.

PLANT IT: Subtropical and tropical fruit trees need to be planted in the warm spring weather. Once nighttime temperatures hit 60° to 65° (F), you can safely plant these delicate fruits. The planting season generally extends from March through October. Loosen the soil in a wide, four to five-foot diameter circle. Dig the planting hole only as deep as the actual root ball. Fill halfway with water and let drain out. This not only ensures adequate drainage, but also provides a reservoir of water in the soil that the plant can use later. Carefully plant the fruit tree, keeping the top of the root ball at grade level. Backfill with soil, and water well. Build a four to eight-inch berm around the outer edge of the planting area. Fill with water, let drain, and then apply a layer of compost four to eight inches thick over the soil, keeping the compost about twelve inches from the trunk.

WATER IT: When your tropical or subtropical fruit is established, usually after the first summer, water deeply (to three feet) and infrequently. Until then, keep the soil consistently moist. You may need to water newly planted fruit trees two to three times a day to keep the rootball moist. Subtropical and tropical fruit require deep watering that moves salts down away from the roots and gives the sweetest fruit possible.

What You Need To Start
Container-grown plant or Offshoot (pup) from parent
Shovel
Compost or mulch

Once established, water twice weekly in the hot months and once every month when the temperatures are below 50° (F). There are some specialized requirements for growing tropical and subtropical fruit in the low desert. Check separate listings for specific information.

CARE FOR IT: Wind and cold weather are the two most dangerous (and potentially deadly) limitations to successfully growing tropical and subtropical fruit. Choose a warm location, plant in the spring, water consistently, and enjoy these exotics. When cool weather arrives, reduce the number of times you irrigate. Some varieties should not be watered at all during the winter months. Refer to individual listings for specific information.

During frost days, cover your tropical fruit trees with cardboard, blankets, frost fabric, or burlap and add a heat source such as electric lights to keep the air moving. When cold air settles, more damage can occur. Some gardeners will even dig up fruit trees, such as Bananas, and store them in the garage all winter, wrapped in burlap. Come spring, the Bananas are replanted in the garden. This delays fruiting, but in very cold areas, it keeps the plant from dying.

FERTILIZE IT: <u>Never</u> use chemical fertilizers on subtropical and tropical fruit the first year they're planted. And some varieties should not be fertilized at all for the first two years from planting. Organic fertilizers, such as compost and mulch, will slowly decay, providing a gradual, steady stream of organic material that enriches the soil, encourages the growth of beneficial microbes, maintains consistent soil moisture, and is also low maintenance.

ENJOY IT: Pick most fruit when they are ripe, then eat immediately.

PROTECT IT: Frost is the most common enemy of subtropicals. Watch the temperatures, and have a ready supply of cold-weather protection for your trees and shrubs. In a highly diverse garden with many flowering herbs and bushes, insect pests and diseases are not usually a problem. However, since most tropical and subtropical fruit are not native to the low desert, you will need to keep a careful eye on your investment, protecting them from excessive heat, high winds, and cold winters.

CITRUS

Citrus is one of the best fruit trees to grow in the Valley. At one time, Citrus orchards covered a lot of ground in the Phoenix area and were a major source of income for original settlers. With deep watering, occasional fertilizing, and very little pruning, you'll have a friend for life. They're easy to grow, but unlike most fruit trees, Citrus thrives in the heat. So don't follow the instructions under the Fruit and Nut introduction page. Plant Citrus in warm aras of your yard.

Companion Plants
Lavender
Marigolds
Tansy

CHOOSE IT: When you buy a Citrus tree, you'll see a swelling on the trunk, usually near the bottom. That's called the graft, or bud union. It is where two trees were joined to provide a tree that will produce delicious sweet fruit on a disease-resistant rootstock. You want Citrus that's been grafted onto Seville Sour Orange rootstock for its resistance to frost damage and most diseases. This information should be listed on the tree tag. Ask your nursery to guarantee the rootstock, if you don't find it written on the tag.

There are several different varieties and types of Citrus that do well here. Most do not start producing fruit for two to four years.

Types of Citrus

I've got these listed in order of hardiness for the low desert area, Kumquats being most hardy and Limes the most sensitive to frost.

Kumquat
- Meiwa — the fruit is spicy sweet. Eat the rind or pulp
- Nagami — good container plant or use as small, decorative landscape tree

Grapefruit

Acid content diminishes as fruit are left to sweeten on the tree. What's technically ripe in November, could stay on until April.

- Redblush is popular here. Leave on tree until spring
- Marsh white is most widely planted Grapefruit in low desert. Ripens in November, but is sweeter if picked in April and May
- Pummelo are huge, thick-skinned Citrus that look like large Grapefruit without the acidity. The Troyer or Carrizo rootstocks produce the most flavorful fruit. Two popular hybrids of pummelo and white Grapefruit include:
  - Oro Blanco is more like Grapefruit in flavor, acidity
  - Melogold is more like pummelo in sweetness, low acidity

Tangerines (also known as Mandarins)

These Citrus are easy to peel, have few to many seeds and ripen mostly November through January. They also bear more fruit when they're cross-pollinated.

- Fairchild ripens in November. The fruit has more seeds if it is cross-pollinated. This variety might have heavy fruit production one year, then bear a light crop the next (called alternate bearing)
- Clementine, also known as Algerian. Cross-pollination increases fruit production, but can increase number of seeds
- Kinnow matures late in the season and can be alternate bearing. It tends to have more seeds

Tangelo

It's a cross between a Tangerine and Grapefruit.

- Minneola has few seeds and can be harvested in January
- Orlando can be harvested in November, and might have lots of seeds, depending on cross-pollination

Oranges

- Navel Oranges are excellent right from the tree. Drink the juice of navel Oranges immediately. The chemical limonin causes the juice to quickly turn bitter
  - Parent Washington Navel is the most popular Navel Orange in the low desert. It ripens in late November

- - Other varieties, many from Australia, are being evaluated in the low desert
- Arizona Sweets are a group of sweet Oranges that do well here. They're good for juice and eating from right from the tree
  - Trovita ripens in early spring
  - Diller ripens in November and December, and consistently produces large yields of excellent juice Oranges
  - Marrs ripens October to November
  - Valencia varieties do well here, ripening about March

Lemons

These are the fastest growing Citrus, especially if grafted to Volkameriana or rough Lemon.

- Lisbon Lemons have a smooth rind and ripen in the fall. They also are more cold (frost) tolerant
- Eureka produces Lemons throughout the year. You can harvest while fruit is still green (commercial growers gas them with ethylene to bring on a yellow color)
- Ponderosa produces thick, bumpy fruit

Lime

They're very frost-tender and need to be placed in a warm area for protection.

- Mexican/Key/West Indian Lime has small fruit that ripens in September. Tree stays small, and is very frost-tender
- Tahiti/Bearss/Persian, is hardier of the two varieties. Fruit ripen in June and are larger than the Mexican variety
- Sweet Lime is used extensively in Southwestern cooking
- Kafir Lime is used in Thai cooking

PLANT IT: March and April are the best months to plant Citrus, but I also like to plant in September and October. Be careful about over watering and possible frost danger later in the winter. Make sure soil has excellent drainage. Choose the warmest part of your yard to avoid frost. If you have a pool, plant Citrus around

> **Factoid**
> Citrus don't like wet feet and need to dry out between irrigations. So don't plant things around them that require damp soil.

it because the water keeps the surrounding air warm for the tree.

And when you choose the site, make sure you've got a good 20 feet of room — the trees could get that big. Plant in an area where they'll get eight hours of sun a day, but avoid late afternoon summer sun. The leaves and trunk can get sunburned and become a possible site for diseases and insects to enter.

You can dig a wide hole, but don't dig any deeper than the root ball. Partially fill the hole with water prior to planting and let drain. This technique adds necessary moisture to the bottom of the planting hole. Citrus roots are very fragile and easily damaged. Remove the bottom of the container and gently place the tree into the hole. Then cut the sides of the container to remove it. Backfill around

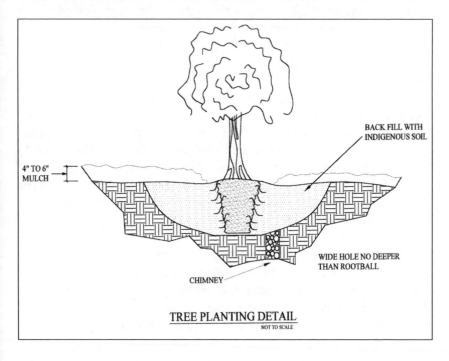

BACK FILL WITH INDIGENOUS SOIL

4" TO 6" MULCH

WIDE HOLE NO DEEPER THAN ROOTBALL

CHIMNEY

TREE PLANTING DETAIL
NOT TO SCALE

the roots with the same soil that was removed from the hole. If you have very rocky soil, use no more than 20% organic material mixed into the backfill. With regular soil, you don't need to do anything.

Construct a berm under the drip line (the widest part of the branches, also known as the canopy) for irrigating. Make sure every tree has its own well. This prevents diseases from traveling through the water from one tree to another.

WATER IT: Irrigate moderately, being careful not to over water. Citrus trees prefer a schedule that allows them dry out between deep waterings. Water every three to five days to establish. Once the trees have gone through their first summer, irrigate every 15 to 20 days in winter, and every seven to ten days in summer. Use your Soil Probe to make sure water penetrates two to three feet into the soil. As the tree grows, move the berm outward to the drip line.

CARE FOR IT: Prune in March after frost danger has passed — but don't wait too long. Pruning after April opens the tree to bark damage from sunburn. Don't remove the long, angular shoots that grow upward from within the canopy. They provide shade protection. Prune suckers (branches below the graft) at any time.

FERTILIZE IT: Do NOT fertilize Citrus the first year. The salts can burn young trees. After the first year, use only organic fertilizers such as fish emulsion, liquid seaweed, compost tea, compost, or chicken and steer manure. (I use chicken manure.)

The trees need nitrogen from the fertilizer source. Regardless of what type you use, figure your fertilizer amounts based on actual amounts of nitrogen. For the first few years, only put two to six tablespoons of actual nitrogen down per year. In the fourth year, go up to one-half pound of nitrogen for the year. After that, the system breaks down to this:

- Grapefruit gets one pound nitrogen per year
- Oranges, Tangerines and Tangelos get one and one-half to two pounds nitrogen per year
- Lemons and Limes get between two and two and one-half pounds nitrogen per year

Fertilizing Schedule For Established Citrus
- Late February for spring growth
- Late May, after first fruit drop, to help fruit survive summer
- Late August to help enlarge fruit
- Winter, apply several inches of well-composted manure or compost under tree canopy. Don't let compost touch tree trunk

ENJOY IT: After all the hard work of caring for Citrus trees, it's satisfying to know the rewards are so delicious! The type of Citrus and the time of year determine what's harvested. For sweeter fruit, keep it on the tree a little longer.

PROTECT IT: Citrus are VERY sun-sensitive, so protect trunks and branches. Paint the trunk with a 50/50 mixture of white latex paint and water, or wrap exposed trunk with shade cloth or burlap.

You might have guessed by driving around the Valley or walking through your neighborhood that Citrus trees are very popular. But they're also susceptible to various diseases and pests. I've listed those at the bottom of the chapter.

Potential Problems
Fungal Diseases
- Gummosis (Phytophthora citrophthora and P. parasitica)
  - Appears as a brown gummy oozing at the crown (base) and trunk of the tree. You might see cracks in the bark at or just below the soil level. Foliage becomes thin and yellow. During summer rains, infected soil can splash up onto fruit, causing "Brown Rot"

- It's caused by too much water at the tree's crown
- Allow soil to dry out between irrigations
- Build a dike four inches high and 18 to 24 inches out from the trunk, to keep water away from the crown
- Pull soil away from infected area, remove discolored bark, and apply a paste made from Bordeaux mixture (copper fungicide) thinned with water
- Mix three tablespoons of Bordeaux with a gallon of water. Pour the drench over roots near the trunk
- Don't let water flood from one tree to another

- Sooty canker (hendersolula toruloides)
  - The fungus enters the tree only through a wound in the bark
  - Leaves become sparse and small, and bark becomes dry and thin (the bark eventually splits open and reveals a black mass of fungal spores)
  - Treat the disease by removing infected branches in spring. Cut the branch off AT LEAST four inches (12 inches is better) beyond the infection. Clean the tools by dipping them into a 10% bleach solution AFTER EACH CUT; otherwise, you will keep on spreading the disease. Spread a paste of Bordeaux mixture over each cut.
  - CONTROL the disease by protecting bark from sunburn and wounds.

Bacterial Disease
- Stubborn Disease (Spiroplasma citri)
  - The leaves become smaller and are yellow or mottled with yellow. The branches become bushy due to abnormal branching. The fruits are odd-shaped and have dry and granular flesh.
  - This disease is most commonly transmitted by leafhoppers which feed on the sap of infected trees and then move on to healthy ones

- There is no chemical control. Diseased trees should be removed
- Note: Vincas (Vinca Rosea) can host the virus

Citrus Pests
Aphids
- Appear on growing tips of Citrus
  - Hose off with a stream of water. If the tree is in bloom, be careful you don't knock off blossoms
  - See Recipe #2 in "Organic Pest Control." Don't use if the tree is in bloom. See above

Orange Dogs
- Look like black and white bird droppings
- These are larval stage of Giant Swallowtail Butterfly, the largest Butterfly in Arizona
- Don't destroy them. They don't eat much, and they eventually pupate and become beautiful Butterflies

Spider Mites
- Look for webbing, or shake leaves over a white piece of paper (you'll see them as little dots moving across the paper)
- Hose off leaves in the <u>early</u> morning, especially the undersides of the leaves. Do this weekly through May

Thrips
- Thrips are tiny insects that cause scarring of fruit and curling of Citrus leaves
- Damage is cosmetic only. No need to treat in home garden

Extra Citrus tips
- Grapefruit, Kumquats, and Tangerines can tolerate cooler temperatures
- Every cut is a wound, so prune as little as possible
- Citrus roots are very fragile and easily damaged. When planting, cut bottom of bucket off, gently place in hole, and then cut sides of bucket to remove

- For existing trees, small yellow and stunted leaves indicate lack of nutrients in the soil
- Place six to eight inches of organic mulch on root zone to add micronutrients to soil. Keep 18 to 20 inches away from trunk
- Feed with a nitrogen-rich organic fertilizer
  - Blood meal, cottonseed meal, fish emulsion, liquid seaweed
- Common signs of previous Thrips damage include scarring at blossom or stem end of fruit, and curled and yellowing leaves. It's cosmetic and will not affect fruit. No control is necessary
- Holes in fruit are from Birds, not insects. But insects will enter holes to dine on fruit. Discard damaged, fallen fruit
- Expect fruit drop in March/April. This thinning process is natural. Water moderately, but don't over water
- Navel Oranges have heavy fruit drop in May to June. It's normal
- There are periods of fruit drop during summer months. This thinning process is natural. High temperatures and winds aggravate the occurrence
- A sudden wilt or drop of Citrus leaves in late summer/early fall is called Mesophyll collapse. Sudden weather changes usually provoke it. The east side of trees (often Grapefruit trees) usually have the most collapse. No control or treatment is necessary. Don't over water
- Volkameriana rootstock is exceptionally vigorous; therefore, the variety to which it is grafted will grow very quickly. This fast growth may affect fruit quality in some varieties
- Lemons can be grafted to rough Lemon rootstock
- Dwarf trees should be grafted onto "Flying Dragon" rootstock
- Only plant Citrus in areas with excellent drainage
  - If necessary, break up or remove caliche

FLOWERS

FLOWERS are an important part of Arizona gardens, from petite Alyssum to stately Zinnias. Using flowers in your garden has all kinds of benefits: flowers please the senses, enrich the soil, and attract pollinators and other beneficial insects. Flowers that grow, bloom, set seed, and die in one season are considered annuals. You can grow annuals from seed or nursery containers.

Generally, annuals are divided into two categories, cool weather or warm weather flowers. Annual flowers usually are replaced a couple times a year, so you'll always have colorful flowers in bloom.

Perennial flowering plants live from year to year and can flower several times a year. Perennial beds are usually permanent, and can include Artemesias, Lavenders, Roses, and Society Garlics, to name just a few.

Alyssum
- Annual
- Plant from October through April
- Available as seed or Nursery Stock
- Low growing (six inches high), reseeding white, pink, and lavender flower for the edges of all your garden areas
- Especially happy with Roses and Bulbs (hides the drying foliage)
- Sweet honey scent
- Easily reseeds several times a year
- Except summertime, Alyssum likes full sun and alkaline soil
- Provide afternoon shade in the summertime to prolong bloom
- Attracts many beneficial insects
- Butterflies love Alyssum

Artemisia (Artemisia)
- Perennial shrub grown for its aromatic foliage
- Plant in full sun

- Beautiful and fragrant gray to silvery foliage
- Attracts beneficial insects
- The strongly aromatic foliage discourages insect pests, including Ants, Aphids, Caterpillars and Moths

Bachelor's Buttons (Centaurea cyanus)
- Annual
- Plant in full sun from September through November
- Available as seed or Nursery Stock
- Attracts bees and other beneficial pollinators
- Benefit rye and wheat crops
- Traditionally blue-flowered, now available in shades of pinks and purples
- Very long blooming
- Good cut flower
- Also known as Cornflowers, because they once grew along the edges of cornfields

Begonias (Begonia)
- Perennial (can be grown as annual)
- Plant from September to May
- Available as Nursery Stock
- Does best if given filtered sun
- Plant in compost-rich soil
- Keep well-watered and fertilize with a fish emulsion solution every two weeks

Black-eyed Susan (Rudbeckia hirta)
- Perennial (can be grown as annual)
- Plant seeds from October to January
- Available as seed or Nursery Stock
- Thrives in sun and is drought tolerant
- Attracts beneficial pollinators
- Easily spreads by seed in the garden, and can become invasive

Bougainvillea (Bougainvillea)
- Perennial flowering vine
- Many colorful varieties. Barbara Karst is hardiest
- A favorite, except around pools (they're a little messy)

- Handle root ball carefully; a broken one spells death to the plant
- Protect plants from frost
- Evergreen, unless hit by frost
- Don't need much water or fertilizer after established

> Those spots of color you see on a Bougainvillea are not really flowers. They are actually colored "leaves" (called bracts). They protect the flowers, small white or yellow blooms, and attract pollinators to the bush.

Chrysanthemum paludosum
- Annual
- Plant from October through April
- Available as seed or Nursery Stock
- Low-growing (eight to ten inches tall), with tiny flowers that have white petals (rays) and yellow centers
- Attracts Butterflies, pollinators and other beneficial insects
- Good companion to Lettuce
- It is free of diseases and pests
- Plant with bulbs and as edgings throughout the garden

Cockscomb (Celosia)
- Annual
- Plant from April to June
- Available as seed or Nursery Stock
- Full sun
- Mass for best effect
- Many different shapes
- Color ranges from sunshine yellow to deep, dark red, and even pink

Coreopsis (Coreopsis sp.)
- Annual and perennial varieties
- Plant in full sun October to April
- Available as seed or Nursery Stock
- Member of the Sunflower family
- Cheerfully bright flowers in shades of yellow, orange and maroon colors
- Remove the spent blossoms with hedge shears to trigger repeat bloom
- Will reseed in the garden

- The seed attracts Birds into the garden
- The bright flowers attract Butterflies and other beneficial insects

Cosmos (Cosmos sp.)
- Annuals and perennials
- Native to Mexico
- One of my favorites. Easier to grow by seed than by transplant in low desert. Plant March through August
- Drought-tolerant, but water deeply when needed
- Flowers attract Birds, Butterflies, and other beneficial insects
- Comes in a wide range of color from yellows, to pinks, purples, and oranges
- The pink, Rose, and magenta varieties benefit from afternoon shade, especially in the summer
- Non-stop bloomers, summer and fall
- Excellent cut flowers
- Will reseed

Dianthus or Pinks (Dianthus sp.)
- Annual and perennial varieties (will last from year to year, if they get afternoon shade)
- Full sun to afternoon shade
- Plant mid-August through February
- Available as seed or Nursery Stock
- Needs good drainage
- Perfect as a low-growing border plant in front of taller plants in the garden
- Pop these little charmers throughout the garden to attract the eye and beneficial insects
- Compost all clippings and spent flowers, because they release a lot of minerals as they decompose
- Old-fashioned flower loved for its spicy scent and long bloom period
- Considered to be one of the "cottage garden" plants of European and British folklore; the blossoms were once used to flavor wine, vinegar, and various jellies

Fleabane (Erigeron)
- Annual
- Easy to grow by seed. Plant in October, November
- Attracts many beneficial insects, so plant freely throughout your garden
- Plant in full sun
- Charming reseeding member of the aster family with lavender flowers

Four-o'clock (Mirabilis jalapa)
- Perennial, however tops will die back in cold weather
- Will reseed in the garden
- Plant in full sun March to June (it loves the heat!)
- Pink and white, and pink and yellow color combinations
- Very bushy plants that grow to three feet tall
- Fragrant flowers, especially in the afternoon

Gallardia (Gallardia)
- Perennial
- Easy to grow from seed. Plant in full sun from mid-September to April
- Reseeding wildflower in the low desert
- Available as seed or Nursery Stock
- Attracts beneficial pollinators and other insects
- Very hardy. Will flower until frost if the old blooms are removed
- Also known as Blanket Flower

Geraniums (Pelargonium)
- Perennial
- Plant in full sun September through January
- Plant in filtered sun or afternoon shade February through May
- Geraniums are frost-tender
- Available as seed or Nursery Stock
- Grown for their scented foliage which ranges from ginger through Citrus and on to Apple and Rose fragrances
- Plant with cabbages to deter Moths. Also deters Ants

- The flowers and leaves of scented Geraniums are edible (use in cakes, jams, jellies and punches
- Prefers afternoon shade or dappled shade
- Needs soil that drains well. Let the soil dry between waterings
- Don't use overhead irrigation
- Fertilize with a solution of fish emulsion every two weeks, and apply a thick layer of compost over the soil

Hibiscus (Rosa-sinensis)
- Perennial flowering shrub, plant mid-February through April
- Likes afternoon shade in low desert
- Grows five to six feet tall and requires ample water
- Wonderful trap plant, attracting Aphids, Spider Mites, Whiteflies. This in turn attracts predaceous insects such as Green Lacewing and Encarsia formosa wasp

Hollyhock (Alcea Rosea)
- Annuals and biennials
- Full sun
- Try cutting back in June or July (you might get lucky and see some new growth in the fall)
- Available as seed or Nursery Stock
- Plant seeds from March to October
- Plant seedlings from October to March
- The annuals will bloom the first year from seed, biennials the second year
- Will grow four to seven feet tall
- Will provide some shade to shorter plants

Johnny-Jump-Up (Viola tricolor)
- Annual
- Low-growing edging plant with miniature purple and yellow flowers similar to Pansies
- Plant in a shady spot mid-October through January
- Available as seed or Nursery Stock
- Needs rich, moist soil

- Interplant with chamomile for a lovely effect that will attract beneficial insects, Moths, Butterflies
- Use the edible flower petals in salads and as garnishes
- The old-fashioned name is Heart's Ease

Lantana (Lantana camera and L. Montevidensis)
- Perennial
- Plant in full sun with good drainage from mid-February through September
- Attracts Butterflies
- Use as a trap crop to protect other plants. Whiteflies love Lantana and will choose it as a food source. Once you see them, spray plants with water. The little suckers drown easily!

Mexican Sunflower (Tithonia)
- Annual
- Native to Central America
- Plant in full sun from March to June
- Grows to six feet tall and will bloom until frost
- Brilliant red-orange bloom color and velvety green leaves
- Pest free
- Attracts Butterflies

Pansy (Violacea)
- Annual
- Available as seed or Nursery Stock
- Plant nursery packs (in well drained soil) as early in the fall as they are available, usually from October through January
- Grows best when temperatures are below 85° (F)
- Plant in partial shade to prolong bloom
- Edible flower petals

Petunia (Petunia)
- Annual
- Plant in full sun in September through April
- Available as seed or Nursery Stock
- Interplant with many flowers and with Beans, Broccoli, Lettuce, Potatoes, Squash, Tomatoes

- Companion plant with Beans and Potatoes because they repel Beetles
- Petunias are in the same family as Tomatoes, Eggplants, Peppers (Solanaceae)
- Fragrant flowers will tolerate alkaline soil (perfect for the low desert!)
- Except for the occasional Caterpillar, Petunias are not usually bothered by pests
- To encourage new flowers, pinch off old flowers at least one-half inch behind flower base
- Water in the morning so the leaves will dry during the day
- Fertilize every two weeks with fish emulsion

Poppy (Papaver sp.)
- Annual
- Plant in full sun October through March (California Poppy, October and November)
- Available as seed or Nursery Stock
- The colorful flowers will attract beneficial insects into the garden and will reseed easily
- Keep the flowers cut to prolong bloom
- The seed has been used as a flavoring and as a bread topping for centuries
- Poppies are heavy feeders, so fertilize with fish emulsion or compost tea every two weeks
- After the poppies have finished blooming, replant the area with a light feeder or a soil-builder such as clover or Peas

Portulaca (Portulaca)
- Annual
- Available as seed or Nursery Stock
- Keep the flowers cut to prolong bloom
- Plant in full sun from March to mid-July
- Blooms all summer and into the fall until frost
- Will reseed
- The flowers are open in the sun, partially closed in the afternoon shade

- Don't over water
- Also known as Moss Rose

Rain Lily (Zephranthes)
- Bulb
- Plant in full sun to afternoon shade from Aug.-Oct.
- Plant the bulbs one inch deep and three inches apart
- Keep the plants alternately wet and dry to trigger bloom
- Yellow and white varieties go dormant in the summer and die back to the soil
- Pink varieties bloom in the summer

Rose (Rosa sp.)
- Perennial
- A favorite shrub for centuries
- See next chapter for detailed Rose information

Snapdragon
- Annuals
- Once known as Toad's Mouth
- Available as seed or Nursery Stock
- Plant from mid-October to mid-February
- Full sun to light shade in soil that drains well
- Choose disease-resistant plants, and don't crowd them close together
- Plant in compost-rich, well-draining soil
- Cover seed <u>very</u> lightly with soil as Snapdragons need light to germinate
- Pinch back (remove the tips of the branches) to encourage bushy growth
- Support tall flowers, especially from the wind
- Keep old flowers picked to encourage new bloom
- Snapdragons do well in large containers

Society Garlic (Tulbaghia violacea)
- Perennial
- Landscape plant about 18 inches wide and 18 inches tall, with narrow strap-like leaves and familiar Garlic scent
- Plant from October through April
- Provide afternoon shade

- Will protect plants, like other members of the Onion family
- Lavender-pink flowers may be used as seasoning

Stock (Matthiola incana)
- Annual
- Many varieties available as seed or Nursery Stock
- Sow the seed in fall for winter bloom (prefers cooler weather)
- Wonderful sweet spicy fragrance
- Plant in full sun to part shade in compost-rich, well-draining soil from October to January
- Evening Scented variety is very fragrant after the sun sets, but isn't very showy
- Trysomic is a very early variety that is good for warmer areas

Sunflower (Helianthus)
- Annuals, some perennial
- Attracts many Birds to the garden, often they will stay to feast on a few insects
- Detailed Sunflower information in following chapter

Sweet Pea (Lathyrus odoratus)
- Annual
- The Sweet Pea is poisonous! It is an excellent companion addition to any garden — vegetable, flower, etc. — but do not eat the pods. They resemble other Pea bean pods, but you must not eat them
- Plant from the first of October to the first of March
- Available as seed or Nursery Stock
- Will reseed each year
- Provide support for the twining types
- Plant with Beans, Carrots, Corn, Cucumbers, Potatoes, and Radishes
- Avoid planting with members of the Onion family
- Attracts many beneficial pollinators into the garden
- Plant Sweet Peas throughout the garden to trail on the ground or over the edge of the raised beds

- Wonderfully fragrant flowers in shades of blue, pink, white, lavender, purple, rose, salmon, maroon
- Discovered growing wild in Sicily in the late 1600s
- The varieties with Italian heritage have very good heat tolerance
- Popular with gardeners since first hybridized in 1723
- As with all members of the pea family, when the flowering period is finished, cut the plants off at ground level so the roots remain in the soil providing nutrients for other plants
- Compost the vines or use as a mulch around other garden plants (don't let any of this plant go to waste)

Vinca (Vinca Rosea)
- Perennial, usually grown as an annual
- Plant from March through September
- Blooms through the summer and into the fall until frost
- Available in shades of white, pink, rose
- Rotate each year

Zinnia (Zinnia sp.)
- Annual
- Plant from mid-March to mid-July
- Available as seed or Nursery Stock
- Brightly colored flowers are a fiesta by themselves
- There are short varieties and tall varieties, but they're all brilliantly colored
- To prolong bloom, cut flowers — they'll bloom again and again
- Grow them in full sun anywhere in the garden, as they will attract a myriad of pollinators and other beneficial insects
- They will also tolerate light shade
- To prevent disease, only water at ground-level, not overhead

For Flowers...

CHOOSE IT: There's an art to picking out flowers at the nursery or garden center. First of all, bypass all the Nursery Stock that is in full bloom. Really! The plant expends so much energy producing the bloom that it's exhausted before it even gets into the ground.

What You Need To Start
Seeds or transplants
Shovel
Compost
Soft rock phosphorus

Purchase the smallest plants with the least amount of color showing. Ignore the dry and wilted specimens. Next, check the roots. Avoid those that have masses of roots hanging out of the container holes. Pop out a plant and look at the bottom. White roots are good, yellowish or brownish roots are not (those plants are too old). Skip the plants whose roots have circled around and around the bottom of the container (they've been in the pot too long). Pass by the tallest plants (they've been starved for sunshine, and probably have weak stems). Once you've made your careful choice, take the plants home — don't leave them shut up in the car while you do other shopping.

PLANT IT: Prepare your planting area before you go shopping. Bedding plants need to go into the ground or into containers as quickly as possible. With containers, use a good potting soil or compost only. No native soil, please; it's very heavy and compacts too tightly for container gardening. For in-ground planting, loosen the soil of the entire bed, and work in lots of compost and soft-rock phosphorus. Installing an in-ground drip irrigation system makes watering easier. Plant the flowers at the same level as they were in the containers. Firm the soil around the root balls to remove any air pockets. Water well and apply mulch over the soil to conserve moisture and add slow-release nutrients. If you can, plant in raised beds directly into compost.

Companion Plants
Plant a diversity of these flowers; they all combine well together and attract a variety of beneficial insects into the garden

WATER IT: Keep the soil moist (12-18 inches deep) for the first week to ten days, depending on the season. After the plants are growing, water every second or third day in the summer and every third to fifth day in the winter. As flower beds are fairly high water users, a thick layer of mulch certainly helps to keep the soil evenly moist for optimum root growth and to conserve soil moisture.

CARE FOR IT: For bushy plants, pinch out the growing tip of each branch. Tip pinching will also increase the number of flowers. Remove the faded and dead blossoms to promote new flowers and prolong the blooming season. Some varieties of flowers can be cut back to about one-half their size to rejuvenate them for another bloom period.

FERTILIZE IT: Flowers require a lot of nutrition to produce lots of blooms. Keep the plants healthy and happy in the summer by applying a solution of fish emulsion or liquid seaweed every two weeks.

ENJOY IT: Cut the flowers early in the day when they contain the most water and are the least stressed. Cut each stem as long as possible and immediately plunge it into tepid water all the way to the bloom. Leave the flowers in the water for several hours before arranging. Be sure to remove all leaves that will be under water in the arrangement.

Factoid
Flowers please the senses, enrich the soil, and encourage beneficial insects.

PROTECT IT: Most annual flowers are planted in the fall for winter and spring color, or in the late winter for spring and summer color. Some heat-tolerant varieties can be planted in the spring for summer and fall color. Plan on replacing the plants in your annual flower beds at least twice a year. Watch out for Aphids, Caterpillars, Slugs, and Snails on your flowers. Remember to plant a wide variety of flowering plants so you'll attract beneficial pollinators and hungry predaceous insects into your garden. Your flowers will benefit greatly!

ROSES

FOR thousands of years, Roses have been a gardening favorite. They are so entwined in our culture that they have come to represent the highest ideals of beauty, fragrance, and love. You can have great success with Roses here in the low desert. In fact, Maricopa County is one of the most important Rose-growing areas in the United States. West of Litchfield Park and Waddell, there are acres and acres of this incredible bloom.

CHOOSE IT: In December and January, bare-root Roses are available that have been grown on Arizona rootstock. This is a distinct advantage because the plants are accustomed to our desert soils, water, and extreme temperatures.

Purchasing Roses

Bare-root Roses

They are sold by grade (No. 1, No. 1^1/$_2$, and No. 2). Choose only No. 1 grade Roses, as they are usually two to three years old and have the most canes (branches). The No. 1^1/$_2$ grades are younger, have fewer canes, and will take longer to establish. Avoid the No. 2 grade. They're too young and too small.

CHECK Stems: Choose Roses with plump green stems. Avoid those with brown or shriveled stems (those indicate that the plant has dried out).

CHECK Roots: Do not buy Roses with dried out roots. They should be plump and pliable.

> TIP: Before planting soak the entire Rose in a bucket of water for 12 to 48 hours to plump up the roots and canes.

Container-grown Roses
When they become available in spring and fall, buy plants that have sturdy leaves. Wilted or limp leaves indicate a lack of water. Also, stay away from those that show any sign of Mildew.

Popular Rose Types

An asterisk (*) by a variety name indicates a mild to strong scent.

Climbing Roses and Ramblers
These Roses can be hybrid teas, hybrid perpetuals, and ramblers or floribundas. Due to their potentially large size, space them eight to ten feet apart. To force more blooms, bend the canes of climbers horizontally and attach to a trellis, porch, or pergola.

Varieties for the Low Desert

Blaze (red, blooms in second year)
Chrysler Imperial (red, hybrid tea type)*
Don Juan (red, blooms second year)
Golden Showers (yellow, hybrid tea type)*
Joseph's Coat (multicolor, hybrid tea type)
Wenlock (red English Rose, grows to ten feet and may be used as hedge or vine)*
Queen Elizabeth (pink, grandiflora type)

TIP: Use a tree as a support for a Rose and let it grow up and through the tree.

Floribunda

This class was originally developed from hybrid teas and polyanthas. The flowers are borne in large clusters, on compact and vigorous plants. Space these Roses three to four feet apart.

Varieties for the Low Desert

Gene Boerner (pink)
Heat Wave (orange-red)
Iceberg (white)*

Showbiz (red, guaranteed to bloom with no work)

Grandiflora

These are vigorous plants, usually growing eight to ten feet, but you can find many bushes in the three to five-foot range. The flower shape is very similar to the hybrid tea; however, the blooms can be borne singly or in clusters. These Roses may be grown for cut flowers and as mass plantings for background screens and thorny barriers. One dependable variety for the low desert is the pink Queen Elizabeth.

Hybrid Tea

The most popular class of Rose, Hybrid Teas are prized for their high-centered buds and large blooms, usually one to a stem. The bush will be two to six feet high, and needs three to six feet of space across.

Varieties for the Low Desert

Chicago Peace (pink, multicolor)
Chrysler Imperial (red)*
Double Delight (pink-red)*
First Prize (pink)*
Mr. Lincoln (red)*

Oregold (yellow, short-lived)
Peace (multicolor)
Perfume Delight (pink)*
Tropicana (orange-red, does well in the desert)*

Polyantha

This vigorous bush rarely gets more than four feet high. It is almost everblooming and very disease-resistant. The flowers, usually less than two inches across, are borne in large sprays. For a mass planting, space every two to three feet apart. Margo Koster, with coral-orange double flowers, is the choice for the low desert.

Shrub Rose

Old-fashioned Rugosa Roses, Species Roses, Moss Roses, Damask Roses, and Cabbage Roses are included in this class. For the most part, they are very resistant to disease and are cold hardy.

Varieties for the Low Desert

Carefree Delight (pink; cut back with hedge shears when the majority of blossoms are dead)
Graham Thomas (yellow, English Rose)
Heritage (pink, English Rose)
Pink or Red Simplicity (can plant on 18-inch centers)

Tree Rose

These are a bit tricky. Plant on the north or east side so they get afternoon sun protection, especially in the summer. Put Tree Roses where they can take advantage of landscaped yards, cooler microclimates of lawns, and/or more established trees.

Varieties for the Low Desert

Chrysler Imperial*	French Lace	Showbiz

TIP: Sunburn protection is crucial. Shade the trunk, either with shade cloth, cardboard, or a 50/50 mixture of white latex paint and water.

PLANT IT: Good drainage is the difference between health and death. In areas with heavy clay soils, drainage is vital.

Site location is extremely important. Choose an area with at least six hours of sun daily. Don't plant near a reflective surface, especially on the west side of buildings or walls. Plant at least two feet away from any wall or fence to ensure good air circulation. Afternoon shade works great.

Companions
Artemisia
Garlic
Nasturtium
Onions
Spearmint

Allow proper spacing for a Rose's mature size. If you have a five-foot space, don't buy a bush that will grow six to eight feet. Also, Roses thrive when their roots don't compete with trees and large shrubs.

Dig a hole at least 18 inches deep by 18 inches wide. Fill the hole half full of water to check drainage. It should drain at least one inch per hour. If there's slow drainage, check for caliche. This cement-like soil needs to be broken up so water can drain. Ideally, remove the caliche and replace with topsoil mixed with compost.

Look for a knob or slight swelling at the base of the trunk that shows where the variety was joined to the rootstock. This is the bud union, and must face east.

In the bottom of the planting hole, add:
> 1 cups rock phosphate
> 1 cup soil sulfur
> 1 cup gypsum
> $^1/_2$ cup bonemeal

Mix with two shovels full of soil and proceed either for bare-root planting or container planting. For extra insurance, drench the hole in liquid seaweed.

Planting Bare-root Roses

I like to soak my bare-root Roses overnight in water mixed with a dash of liquid seaweed. As soon as Roses arrive at nurseries in mid-December to February, plant them. In the center of the planting hole, mound the soil into a cone shape.

Spread the Rose's roots (remove all the packing sawdust and snip off any broken roots) over the cone. Backfill with a 50/50 mix of soil and compost. Keep the bud union about two inches above the soil level, and facing east.

Stick the end of your garden hose end all the way to the bottom of the planting hole (now filled with Rose and soil), and water slowly and thoroughly. If the Rose settles too deeply, gently lift the Rose, add backfill, and continue to water.

Planting Container Roses

Prepare the planting hole as described above. Measure the depth of the Rose in the container. Backfill the hole to two inches higher than the measured depth (this allows the soil to settle during the first watering). Remove the container and carefully plant the Rose with the bud union facing east. Don't disturb the roots. Water slowly and carefully.

Plant container-grown Roses any time; however, spring and fall are best. The high heat and temperatures of summer require extra diligence at planting time.

Transplanting Roses
- Do it in December
- Cut back one-half of top area before transplanting
- Small shrubs can be transplanted bare-root, while larger shrubs should be moved with as large a root ball as practical
- Plant as suggested above

TIP: Prepare planting hole before digging up the Rose!

WATER IT: Drainage is vital. The next most important thing is to maintain soil moisture to a depth of two to three feet. Water slowly and deeply to leach salts below the root zone.

In winter/spring, water weekly after bud break (new leaves sprout).

In summer, water every four to seven days in loam soil, and every three to five days in sandy soil.

In extreme heat or windy conditions, water more frequently (daily if necessary).

In late fall/winter, irrigate established Roses (in ground nine months or more) every 21 days in loam soil, and 14 days in sandy soil.

CARE FOR IT: Rose plants are hardy, but when it comes to pruning, there are a few guidelines to keeping the plant healthy and producing beautiful blooms. There are some general rules, which I list first. Then below that, I list varieties that need specific pruning techniques in addition to the general rules.

Pruning
General Rules
- Prune when they're dormant, usually in January or February
- If possible, remove old canes at crown (base of the plant). This allows new canes to grow, providing flowering wood for next season's bloom
- Removing dead or diseased wood is the main reason to prune
  - Next reason: to rejuvenate bush by removing weak, old, and crossing canes
  - Final reason: to remove canes that are too vigorous. This shapes bush, and creates balance. Healthy canes produce for four to six years. Remove suckers (canes growing below bud union) anytime

- Remove canes that don't produce good blooms
- To reduce the height of the cane, make a slanting cut within $1/2$ to $1/4$ inch of an outward-facing bud (those buds on the outward side of the Rose cane). Seal cuts with lipstick, wood or white glue
- After pruning, strip all the leaves off the canes. This tricks the bush into thinking it's dormant, allowing it to rest
- At this time spray the rosebushes with a homemade dormant spray to kill over-wintering insects. Mix one-third cup of vegetable oil (canola, soybean, corn, sunflower, cottonseed, or olive oil) with one gallon of water and one teaspoon liquid dishwashing soap (not the lemon kind, which contains a petroleum byproduct)

Climbers
- Prune during the dormant season, December or January, or after the spring bloom
- Remove the gray canes that are three to five years old, and leave the newer green canes which will produce most of the next season's bloom
- Bend the canes into a horizontal position to trigger bloom along the length of the cane
- Attach the canes to fences, trellises, pergolas, or even trees

Floribundas
- Since these plants usually produce clusters of blooms, leave more canes on the bush when pruning. Remove about one-third of the plant mass
- For hedges, prune the plants to the same height

Grandifloras
- Prune the same as hybrid teas
- Prune when the Roses are dormant, in January or February

Hybrid Tea
- In January/February, remove all leaves to prevent spread of insects and diseases like rust and Black spot
- Keep plant balanced, removing approximately two-thirds of old canes to encourage new canes to develop and become the next season's flowering wood

- Prune suckers (shoots sprouting from below the bud union) anytime

Shrub Roses
- There are essentially three degrees of pruning: heavy, moderate, and light
  - Heavy pruning — thin to three to four canes, each six to eight inches high. Prune this way to produce a few very large blooms. In the desert, this type of extreme pruning shortens the life of the Rose
  - Moderate pruning — leave five to 12 canes, each 18 to 24 inches high. The bush is larger, and summer sun and heat don't do as much severe damage
  - Light pruning — remove tops of branches with hedge trimmers to produce many short-stemmed blossoms. This is effective for shrub and hedge Roses

FERTILIZE IT: Don't fertilize newly planted Roses until new leaves appear. Because our soils are usually low in nitrogen (N) and phosphorus (P), you need to add them every few weeks during the growing season.

Good sources of organic nitrogen include alfalfa, compost, fish emulsion, liquid seaweed, composted manure, bonemeal, blood meal, and cottonseed meal. Choose one.

Ground rock phosphorus and bonemeal are organic sources of phosphorus.

A good rule of thumb is to apply lower doses of fertilizer more frequently.
- Apply fish emulsion every two weeks during the growing season. It's an excellent fertilizer, and supplies organic material

- Dissolve one-third cup of Epsom salts in one gallon of water; spray on leaves, top and bottom, and around base of plant to encourage flower production

Fertilize with composted manure right after you prune to give the plant a little shot in the arm. Apply a layer three to four inches deep, but don't let it touch the trunk, branches, or cover the bud union.

In addition to fertilizing, maintain a layer of mulch two to three inches thick over the root zone. Keep it a couple inches away from the trunk.

Organic mulches
- Compost
- Dried grass clippings (spread thinly, and don't use fresh mown grass clippings)
- Ground bark
- Peat moss (Put mulch over it to keep it from blowing away)
- Pine needles
- Straw (Alfalfa hay is also recommended as mulch)
- Well-shredded brush or leaves (if not shredded, they can mat down and seal off soil)

ENJOY IT: Cut flowers add color and life to any interior (or exterior for that matter). To keep the bush producing more, cut the cane (stem) at a 45-degree angle just above a set of five leaves. That allows the Rose to keep producing more flowers on that cane. Put your flowers in water immediately.

To make cut Roses stay fresh longer, add a tablespoon of vinegar to the vase's water.

With fragrant varieties, use Rose petals to make the house smell good. Just drop petals into a pan of water. Boil for 10 minutes and remove from heat. The oil from the petals sticks to the steam, carrying the smell of fresh Roses throughout your home.

PROTECT IT: Seal all cuts, one-quarter inch or larger, with lipstick, wood or white glue to prevent Borers from entering. If they get in, Borers eat the inside pith of the canes, leaving a hole down the center. It hurts and eventually kills the cane. Carefully cut off the stem, an inch or two at a time, until undamaged pith is found. Seal the cut.

Not too many diseases or pests plague Roses in the low desert; however, there are a couple of potential problems.

Disease

Powdery Mildew

- This fungus shows up as whitish, powdery coating usually on top of leaves and on stems. It looks like tiny cotton balls
- It loves warm days and cool nights of spring
- To prevent it
    - Choose disease-resistant plants
    - Provide good air circulation
    - Water at ground level and don't get leaves wet
    - Make sure leaves dry between irrigations
- To fix it
    - With hose, power wash leaves before 9 A.M.
    - Fix-it recipe
        - Mix $1/3$ cup baking soda, a squirt of blue dishwashing liquid, and 12 ounces water
        - Spray leaves and stems every three to four days

Pests

Aphids

- Preventing Aphids
    - Companion plant Garlic or Onions around the Roses
    - Chives, Society Garlic, flowering Onions also work well
- Fixing Aphid problems
    - With hose, power wash leaves before 9 A.M.

- See Recipe #2 in "Organic Pest Control." Spray every three to four days
- Be patient. Wait for Ladybugs, Green Lacewings to build up (their larvae eat Aphids and Spider Mites)

Leafcutter bees

- If Leafcutter bees munch on Rose leaves, they leave nearly perfect circles. Don't kill them, because the damage is minimal. This beneficial bee is very helpful to your garden

Stem Borers

- These insects enter cut stems and eat the pith of the cane. The cane gets weak, produces fewer flowers, and eventually dies
- Seal cuts (one-quarter inch or larger) with wood, white glue or lipstick.

Companion plants

Put flowers and herbs around the base of Roses. Keep them about 12 to 15 inches from the trunks so as not to disturb Rose roots.

Garlic, Onions, Chives, or Garlic Chives all contribute a lot to Roses.

- Alyssum (reseeds readily)
- Artemisia ("Silver Mound" stays small. Prune other varieties)
- Catmint
- Chrysanthemum paludosum
- Daylilies
- Dianthus
- Garlic
- Mass plantings of fibrous Begonias
- Mass plantings of Thyme
- Mexican Bush Sage
- Moss Rose (portulaca)
- Nasturtium
- Onions
- Scented Geraniums
- Society Garlic
- Spearmint

SUNFLOWERS

LOOK for them in artistic masterpieces of the past and in popular culture today. Sunflowers are also a wonderful way to get the little ones interested in helping plants grow. The size of Sunflowers and their beauty make them fun for gardeners of all and ages. They look great and provide shade in the garden. I love to watch finches outside my window munch away on my Sunflowers.

CHOOSE IT: Sunflowers are fast growing and produce a joyful flower. You and your children can grow tall varieties for seeds. The midsize types are great for cutting or for seed. Short varieties can be planted right in the flower garden, as well as in the vegetable garden. Choose the large-headed seeding varieties to keep shade in your garden spring through summer.

What You Need To Start
Seeds
Shovel
Compost
Mulch

PLANT IT: Plant from early February through July. For a continuous supply of cut Sunflowers, plant seeds every two weeks.

Planted as companions, Sunflowers sweeten Cucumbers, offer shade, and attract beneficial insects and pollinators to help other crops in the garden. As the seeds ripen, Sunflowers attract Birds which will also eat a few bugs.

Companion Plants
Beans
Cucumbers
Melons
Squash

WATER IT: Sunflowers require a lot of water. Plant them where they can receive runoff from rain, extra moisture from lawn irrigation, or low spots in the garden where water accumulates. Otherwise, plan to irrigate them deeply (18 inches deep) and frequently. A thick layer (four to six inches) of mulch helps conserve and maintain even soil moisture.

CARE FOR IT: When Sunflowers get to be one foot high, plant Squash and Melon on the east side of them. They will keep the soil cool, while the Sunflowers provide afternoon shade to the fruit. It's a great relationship. As seeds ripen, cover flower heads with mesh or paper bags or to protect them from Birds.

> **Factoid**
>
> In the 16th century, Spanish Conquistadors returned to Europe with Sunflowers, hybridized them to fit their needs, and made the yellow flower popular in the Old World.

FERTILIZE IT: It's not necessary to fertilize Sunflowers. Regular garden soil and a thick layer of mulch provide all the nutrients Sunflowers require.

ENJOY IT: When seeds are ripe and start falling out, gather Sunflower heads and harvest. Eat them toasted, sprinkled with salt or plain.

PROTECT IT: Other than sharing the Sunflower harvest with the Birds, no protection is necessary.

HERBS

YOU can get a history lesson each time you plant an Herb. Some have been used for centuries in medicine, kitchens, and medieval potpourri. They'll add beauty to your landscape, but they'll usually do something else for you, too. You can plant Herbs that will provide you with an insect repellent, a flower centerpiece, or tasty pasta sauce. There's almost no end to the combinations.

There are different kinds of herbs, though, with very different needs. So be sure to read up on how to PLANT IT at the bottom of each little section.

Annuals for Sunny Gardens
Basil (Ocimum basilicum)
- Plant April to June, and again in September
- Varieties range in color from green to purple and in flavor from mild to clove-cinnamon
- Keep it pinched back for bushy type growth (don't forget to add a little to your pasta!)
- Remove most flowers to increase leaf production
- I grow Basil in the ground or in pots almost year-round. In winter, I find them a sunny location inside. They need protection from frost. I have some in my garden that have been there more than two years
- Plant with Tomato, summer savory, Apricot and Peach trees
- Don't plant near Rue
- Attracts beneficial insects to garden
- Doorway plant, warding off Mosquitoes and flies. Plant near patios and other outdoor rooms
- Provide frost protection to Basil in cold weather
- For Mosquito repellent, liquefy leaves with water in a blender, strain and use as a spray

- Originated in India, where it's used to ward off evil
- Could be most widely used herb in the world
- You can never have too many Basil plants
- Strewn on floors of Mediaeval European homes for scent
- Used in traditional food from Italian dishes to spicy Thai cuisine and beyond
- Use flowers as edible decoration in salads

Borage (Borago officinalis)
- Plant September to February
- Needs some afternoon shade to prolong bloom. Plant as early as possible
- Will reseed
- Strawberries have more flavor and a higher yield when planted with Borage
- The blue flowers bloom in summer, attract bees
- Combine with Tomatoes to repel Tomato Hornworms
- When plants die back, compost them for nutrients
- Freeze the flowers in ice cubes to add to summer drinks
- Historical uses: cheer people up, emblem of courage

Calendula (Calendula officinalis)
- Plant September to March
- Reseeds itself. Also grown from seed or Nursery Stock
- Thick plantings keep weeds from spreading
- Plant with Beans to deter Mexican Bean Beetles
- Plant with Tomatoes to deter Whiteflies
- The bright flowers attract many beneficial insects
- Has antifungal and antibacterial properties
- Wrap a leaf around a minor cut to stop the bleeding
- Known as Herb of the Sun. Flower opens in morning, follows sun's path, closes in evening
- Also known as Pot Marigold. Europeans believed flower petals in soups, stews provided health during long winters

Chamomile (Matricaria recutita)
- Plant September to March (March is best for seeds)
- Prefers afternoon shade, or it goes quickly to seed in summer

- Grow with cabbages, Onions, Mints, wheat
- Gives vigor and strength to nearby plants
- Fragrant foliage deters insects
- Put dried flowers in your pet's bedding to deter Fleas
- Use a spray of chamomile tea to combat fungal diseases (the tea is also good for house plants)
- Valuable as a good source of organic material for compost
- Has anti-inflammatory properties
- Derived from the Greek words for apple (referring to its luscious apple-like fragrance) and Earth

Coriander, also known as Cilantro (Coriandrum sativum)
- Plant in February, and from September to December
- Plant seeds every one to two weeks for constant supply
- Grow near Dill, Anise, chervil
- Keep away from Fennel
- Repels Aphids
- Attracts bees and beneficial insects such as Trichogramma wasps
- One of the oldest cultivated spices (seeds)
- Seeds used in many Middle Eastern and Oriental dishes
- Has aromatic foliage and is used extensively in Southwestern and Mexican cooking

Dill (Anethum graveolens)
- Plant September to February
- Plant seeds every one to two weeks for constant supply
- This member of the Parsley family will bolt when weather warms (bolt means plant flowers, sets seed and starts to die)
- Grow with cabbage, Carrots, Corn, Lettuce, Tomatoes
- Don't plant near Fennel
- Attracts pollinators and many beneficial insects, including Trichogramma wasps
- Grown for seeds and foliage
- Used by Greeks and Romans to honor heroes

Epazote (Chenopodium ambrosioides)
- Plant March to April
- Full sun to afternoon shade

- Aromatic foliage
- Used as seasoning for Native American and Mexican dishes

Fennel (Foeniculum vulgare)
- Plant in February, and from September to December
- Don't plant near Tomatoes, Beans, Kohlrabi, Coriander, Wormwood (Artemisia)
- Helps repel Fleas
- Attracts beneficial insects, including Butterflies (especially Swallowtail)
- A Mediterranean native, Fennel is grown for its lacy, aromatic foliage, anise-flavored seed, and tasty bulbs
- Bronze Fennel is grown for foliage, seeds
- Florence Fennel is grown for bulbs

Marigold (Tagetes)
- Plant February to May, and from August to October in full sun. Soil must be 70° to 75° (F) for germination to occur
- Available as seed or Nursery Stock
- Plant with Vincas
- Thick plantings keep weeds from spreading. Let go to seed for great show next year
- Attracts Butterflies, Hoverflies
- Use throughout garden. Strong scent repels pests
- Deters cabbage worm, Slugs, Whiteflies. Root secretions deter insects such as fungus, black fly, Aphids, as well as various wilts
- Mass plantings deter nematodes in the soil
  - Heavily interplant with Potatoes and cabbages
- Marigold tea will kill Mosquito larvae
- Native to Mexico
- Edible, but strong tasting flowers

Nasturtium (Tropaeolum majus)
- Plant September to February in full sun or afternoon shade
- Thrives in poor soil
- Excellent companion to cabbages, Squash, Zucchini, Fruit Trees

- Needs a headstart. Plant several weeks before Squash
- Repels Aphids, pests of Cucumber family
- Bedding plant or trap crop to attract Aphids, Whiteflies
- Very fragrant. Bright flowers attract beneficials
- Young edible leaves (rich in vitamin C), flowers, unripe seeds have a peppery flavor for salads and garnishes
- Leaves have antibiotic property
- Originally from Peru

Parsley (Petroselinum crispum)
- Plant February to March, and from October to December
- Biennial, although usually grown as an annual
- Likes afternoon shade in the low desert
- Grow with asparagus, Carrots, Roses, Tomatoes to protect them from insect pests
- In the second year, let it set seed to attract these beneficial insects:
  - Predators of Scale, Spider Mites, Thrips
  - True bugs, some of which are predaceous
  - Trichogramma wasps that destroy Caterpillars
  - Hoverflies whose larvae eat Aphids
- Rich in Vitamins A, B, and C and iron
- Loaded with chlorophyll, it's a natural breath freshener
- From Charlemagne to the de Medicis, Parsley has been grown in royal gardens
- Used by the Greeks to adorn graves and heroes' foreheads

For Annual Herbs (sunny gardens)...
CHOOSE IT: Grow any of these from seed, cuttings, or from Nursery Stock. Choose a mix of varieties to see which one you like best for next year. Plant them all around the garden for looks, as kitchen herbs, and as insect pest deterrents. Don't stop at just one, plant several or many of each kind. It's okay for plants to grow together. They'll shade out weeds and create such a diversity of plant life that insect pests will flee.

PLANT IT: In summer, these sun-loving plants can use a little afternoon shade. They also require excellent drainage. Plant them in native soil, then mulch with a thick layer of compost. Keep the compost away from the plant stems to prevent insect damage or disease.

WATER IT: For the first ten days to two weeks, water these plants daily. As they mature, water deeply when the top one-half inch of the soil is dry. For Direct Seeding, keep the bed moist until Germination. If seeds dry out, they might not germinate at all. As seedlings grow, continue to water deeply to a depth of 12 to 18 inches to encourage deep rooting (shallow watering promotes unhealthy shallow rooting).

CARE FOR IT: All of these beauties are low maintenance. Pinch out the growing tips to encourage bushiness. Use the tips for cooking, or dry them to use in sachets for linens and woolens. Being annuals, these plants will need to be replaced each season or even each year, if they cannot tolerate cooler weather. Many of these herbs will reseed for another round of utilitarian beauty.

FERTILIZE IT: Except for Basil (which likes a twice-monthly treat of fish emulsion or liquid seaweed), don't fertilize these herbs. A thick layer of mulch over the soil is all that's necessary.

ENJOY IT: Fragrance, beauty, insect control, culinary delights, and above all, a profusion of harmony and well-being. C'mon, what more could you want?

PROTECT IT: These hardy herbs hardly need protection. Once planted and growing, just enjoy them.

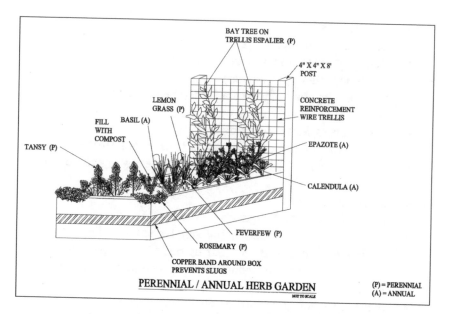

PERENNIAL / ANNUAL HERB GARDEN
NOT TO SCALE

(P) = PERENNIAL
(A) = ANNUAL

Perennials for Sunny Gardens

Artemisia (Artemisia sp.)

- Plant year-round
- Varieties as diverse as French Tarragon, Southernwood, Artemisia shrubs
  - Grow French Tarragon from a container-grown plant, as it does not germinate from seed
  - Southernwood hedge repels Mosquitoes. Plant at patio border
  - Plant with Eggplants, sweet Peppers
  - Good companion to other plants
- Other Artemisias attract beneficial insects
- Strong scent disrupts insect pests' sensory organs
  - Use dried leaves as deterrent to Ants, Moths
  - Plant near Roses to repel Aphids
  - Companion plant with cabbages, Carrots

Catnip (Nepeta cataria)

- Plant September to November
- Plant near pet areas to deter Fleas and Ants

- Repels rats
- Cats adore catnip. Protect young seedlings if necessary
- Becomes quite lush if given extra water

Feverfew (Tanacetum parthenium)
- Plant in October, and from December to April
- Strongly scented foliage
- Plant repels Moths outside
- Inside, put dried leaves in sachets to repel Moths
- Steep in tea or eat fresh leaf on buttered bread to relieve migraines

Lavender (Lavandula sp.)
- Plant September to March
- Put throughout garden in full sun. Needs excellent drainage. Harvest stems just as buds begin opening
- To rejuvenate plant, remove one to two inches of leafy stem when cutting flowers
- Plant with Roses and other flowering shrubs
- Deters Ants, Mosquitoes, Moths, silverfish, and other insects
- Deters Fleas and Ticks. Use flowers and leaves in animal area
- Mice and Rabbits avoid lavender
- Attracts Butterflies and bees
- Used medicinally to treat headaches, reduce stress, and promote sleep
- Fragrant leaves were strewn about medieval floors for scent, and they're still used in potpourri and sachets
- Loved through the centuries and very popular today
- Lavender named after Latin *lavare* (to bathe), and was once used in baths

Lemon Grass (Cymbopogon citratus)
- Plant February to June, and from August to October in full sun to afternoon shade. Frost-tender
- Can grow as accent plant in the garden
- Flavors iced teas
- Used extensively in Southeast Asian cooking

Rosemary (Rosemarinus officinalis)
- Plant year-round
- Companion crop to Beans, cabbages, Carrots, Sage
- Avoid planting with Potatoes
- Attracts bees, other essential pollinators
- Fragrant foliage repels bean Beetles, cabbage Butterflies, Mosquitoes, Moths, Slugs, Snails
- Trailing Rosemary repels Moths, and is a good ground cover
- Upright Rosemary repels Moths, and looks good as a hedge (I surround my vegetable garden with it)
  - Both types of Rosemary have a dark green color that looks good in contrast with the light grays of Artemisia, Santolina
- Use fresh or dried Rosemary in sachets to deter Moths in the home
- A longtime culinary favorite

Rue (Ruta graveolens)
- Plant February to April, and from September to October
- Every garden should have aromatic Rue
- Plant with Roses, Raspberries
- Don't plant with Sage, Basil, cabbage
- Attracts beneficial insects
- Wards off Mosquitoes and flies
- Rub on your pet's fur to deter Fleas
- Also, rub Rue on furniture to prevent Cat scratching

Sage (Salvia officinalis)
- Annual or perennial
- Plant February to March, and from September to November with full sun or afternoon shade (depends on variety)
- A member of Mint family with green to gray aromatic foliage
- Sage is available as seed or Nursery Stock
- Plant with Rosemary, Tomato, Carrot, cabbage family
- Don't plant with Cucumber
- Spread leaves to deter mice, insect pests, Moths
- Red, pink, lavender, and blue flowers attract bees and Hummingbirds

- Long ago used as medicinal herb
- The family name, Salvia, means "to save"

Santolina (Santolina chamaecyparissus)

- Plant year-round
- Aromatic foliage deters insect pests
- The dried foliage also deters wool Moths
- Popular in England since 1500s

Tansy (Tanacetum vulgare)

- Plant March and October
- Has yellow, button-like flowers and aromatic leaves that grow three feet tall
- Plant near Roses to repel insect pests
- Plant near Fruit Trees and Berries to repel Aphids, Ants, Beetles, fruit flies, Moths, squash bugs
- Attracts Ladybugs
- Foliage has a strong scent and was strewn over medieval floors for the aroma

Thyme (Thymus vulgaris)

- Plant January to April, and from September to October in afternoon shade
- Grows to be two to six inches high
- Grow under tall plants that will provide filtered shade
- Water when top one-half inch of soil is dry
- Shown to kill Mosquito larvae
- Thyme deters the cabbage worm
- Use in linen closets to deter bugs
- Small leaves with an amazing fragrance
- Good for planting among stepping stones and pathways
- Ancient Mediterranean herb used in food and medicine
- Has been used to wrap cheese to deter flies and other insects
- Anti-Mildew properties. Egyptians used it as medicine and in embalming. The Romans burned it to deter insects
- In Medieval France, some believed garden fairies danced on a bed of Thyme on Midsummer's Eve

For Perennial Herbs (sunny gardens)...

CHOOSE IT: Choose varieties of each herb that you like, but try to incorporate as many of them into your garden as possible. Plant several of each kind, tucking them here and there in the garden. Being perennials, these plants live for several years.

PLANT IT: Provide good drainage, especially for those that come from the Mediterranean region. The herbs from that area are not used to summer rains. So when monsoon season hits, they can rot if they don't have excellent drainage. In these circumstances, rocky soil is a benefit. But if you're concerned about drainage, dig your planting hole an inch or so less than the depth of the root ball. It raises the plant up and keeps the crown out of the water. Backfill with native soil. Put down thick layer of mulch (four to six inches). Most of our herbs require some afternoon shade.

WATER IT: Water daily for the first ten days to two weeks. Then let the top one to two inches of the soil dry out before irrigating deeply again. Your probe should go at least 12 inches deep. Water less in winter months, but remember to always water deeply.

CARE FOR IT: Snip off faded flowers to prolong the bloom season (most herbs will produce new flowers if the old ones are removed).

FERTILIZE IT: These herbs don't need much fertilizer. Hit them with fish emulsion in late August to boost them for the fall season. Do it again in March when the weather warms up and the bloom season begins. A thick layer of mulch will provide a slow but steady stream of nutrients. And that's all they need.

ENJOY IT: Keep blossoms picked. Use them in wreaths and sachets, and add them to salads, teas, and vinegars. Compost clippings.

PROTECT IT: With their aromatic foliage and flowers, these herbs are remarkably free of pests. Their beautiful blooms attract beneficial insects and pollinators, Butterflies and Hummingbirds. The seeds also draw various other Birds, which are also great insect eaters.

Perennials for Afternoon Shade

Bay (Laurus nobilis)

- Plant March to April, and from September to October in a sheltered location with afternoon shade
- Large shrub or small tree
- Good drainage is essential. Dig planting hole one inch shorter than root ball to keep crown from rotting in too much water
- When you water, water deeply (two to three feet)
- Fresh or dried leaves in the pantry deter Ants, Caterpillars, Moths
- Used as an antiseptic
- Leaves are an essential ingredient in soup, stews, Tomato sauces, veal dishes
- When cooking, the difference between fresh and dried Bay leaves is amazing — go for the fresh every time
- Esteemed in Greece since ancient times
- Used in victory crowns
- Belief that lightning would never strike a Bay tree led people to wear sprigs of Bay during storms

Dutch White Clover (Trifolium repens)

- Plant October to March, with afternoon shade in the low desert
- Plant by seed under perennial shrubs, in the garden, or wherever there is unused space
- Has the ability to "fix" nitrogen in the soil and make it available to roots
- Good "cover crop" (when clover sprouts and gets two to three inches tall, turn it under the soil and let it decompose)
    - Allow a few to flower, as the blossoms attract pollinators

Lemon Balm (Melissa officinalis)

- Plant March, and from October to December (needs afternoon shade in low desert)

- Flowers attract pollinators for Stone fruit trees, Cucumbers, Tomatoes
- Attracts insects that eat Scale, Spider Mites, Thrips
- Lemon-scented leaves used in drinks, salads, and fish dishes, and use dried leaves in potpourris and sachets

Mint (Mentha)
- Tender perennial
- Plant May, and from September to December
- Plant in shady, damp areas of the garden and protect from frost
- Includes Spearmint (Mentha spicata), Peppermint (M. piperita), Pennyroyal (below), Apple Mint, Chocolate Mint, Orange Mint, Corsican Mint, and many others
- Grow mints in a bottomless pot in the garden or plant in a container to limit aggressive spread
- Protects the cabbage family from cabbage worms
- Let it flower to attract bees and other beneficial insects
- Used to flavor teas, sauces, and jellies
- The fragrance is considered energizing
- Spearmint believed to be the oldest of all mints

Pennyroyal (Mentha pulegium)
- Plant May, and from September to December
- A tender perennial, protect from frost
- Deters Ants, Mosquitoes
- Sometimes causes skin rashes if handled
- Fragrant, low-growing herb used for pathways and stepping stones because of its spreading nature
- Has a spreading habit. Plant in bottomless pots in the garden or in containers
- Brought to America by the Pilgrims

For Perennial Herbs (afternoon shade)...
CHOOSE IT: Choose different varieties that you like, but try to incorporate as many herbs into your garden as possible. Plant several of each kind, tucking them here and there in the garden. Being perennials, these plants will live for several years.

PLANT IT: These plants want afternoon shade during our hot summers. Make sure there's good drainage. Although these plants will thrive in pure compost, you can plant them in native soil. Add a thick layer of mulch (four to six inches) to keep soil cool and evenly moist.

WATER IT: Water daily for the first ten days to two weeks. After that, water when top one-half inch of soil dries out. Water less during winter months, but always water deeply to 12 to 18 inches.

CARE FOR IT: Snip off faded flowers to prolong the bloom season. Most herbs continue to produce new flowers if old ones are removed.

FERTILIZE IT: These time-honored herbs do not need fertilizer often. Apply fish emulsion in late August to give them a boost for the fall season. It's also helpful to do another application in March when the weather warms and the bloom season starts. A thick layer of mulch will provide a slow but steady stream of nutrients.

ENJOY IT: Keep blossoms picked. Enjoy them in wreaths and sachets, and add them to salads, teas, and vinegars. Compost the clippings to recycle the nutrients.

PROTECT IT: Aromatic foliage and flowers keep these herbs remarkably free of pests. Their beautiful blooms attract beneficial insects and pollinators, Butterflies and Hummingbirds. Their seeds will also draw various Birds into the garden to eat insects.

GRASS AND LAWN

HAVING a healthy lawn is a matter of having healthy soil. You create healthy soil by encouraging microbiotic activity and nurturing all the soil, including insects, earthworms, microbes, and beneficial nematodes that live there. Avoid synthetic fertilizers, pesticides, and fungicides. OKAY, so your grass might not be as green as your neighbor's, but it sure will be a whole lot healthier for your children and pets. And that's what we're after — the healthiest environment possible!

There are two kinds of lawns: summer and winter. Bermuda grass (Common or hybrid) is the permanent lawn that goes dormant to make way for the winter perennial rye. To get a winter lawn, you have to overseed. But to get your summer Bermuda lawn back, all you have to do is water. All grass needs six to eight inches of moist soil and six to eight hours of sunlight each day. Everything else you need to know revolves around that.

CHOOSE IT:
- Grass Types
  - Summer Bermuda

    Ignore common Bermuda grass and go with hybrid or hybridized types, because they require less water, less fertilizer, and some can be more shade tolerant. The dense, nearly pollen-free grass also has a higher quality blade.
    - Get hybrid sod or hybridized seed
  - Winter

    Choose only perennial rye varieties. They are more expensive to buy, but they require less water, less fertilizer, and less care. In the long run, they're less expensive. The deeper green color doesn't stain clothes. Perennial rye is also more resistant to disease. There are many varieties, but a few do very well here in the low desert.

- Cardinal Sports Blend
- Desert Green II
- Short Cut
- Signature
- Village Green

WATER IT: There are too many variables (season, temperature, wind, soil content, sprinkler head size, etc.) for me to give you a set schedule for irrigating. What I can tell you is that, if you can't push your Soil Probe (see "TOOLS" chapter) six to eight inches into the soil, you need to water deeper. Do whatever testing you need with your sprinklers and timers to do this: get water six to eight inches deep, then let the soil dry a bit, then get it wet again six to eight inches down (don't keep soil wet ALL the time).

80% of the lawn's roots are in the top eight inches of soil. Encourage deep roots with deep watering. This allows you to use less water and fertilizer overall, and reduces insect problems. If you're installing seed, don't let it dry out even once or it will die. For established grass, finish watering by 9 A.M. to avoid fungus problems.

Dry soil indicators:
- Walk across grass, and if your footprints don't spring back up, irrigate
- If grass has slight bluish tinge, it probably needs water

CARE FOR IT: Don't mow wet grass. It's bad for the mower and the grass. Let lawn dry at least 24 hours before mowing, and never remove more than one-third of the leaf blade at each mowing. Mow frequently when grass is actively growing, and alternate the direction (go up and back one week, left to right next, diagonal next, etc.) to eliminate wear patterns and tendency of grass blades to lean in one direction. Also, mow in the evenings when it's cooler and the grass is more likely to be shaded.

Always, but *always,* use a sharp mower. Get your blades sharpened once or twice a year.

It's a good idea to use a mulching mower. And to do that, you must use organic fertilizers. (The natural contents of organic fertilizers help grass clippings break down and provide nutrition to the soil and lawn roots.) You need to mow more than once a week, though, or else you're dumping a big clump of clippings on the lawn and potentially blocking sunlight. Mow two or three times a week, cutting off less grass blade. Keep the lawn taller (one and a half to two inches) so that it develops deep roots. Remember to feed the soil, not the plant! If you've used synthetic fertilizers, don't use a mulcher; instead, discard your grass clippings.

FERTILIZE IT: Use an organic fertilizer once a month. Spread a thin layer (one-quarter inch) right on top of the grass. Water in well. Over-fertilized lawns grow too fast, use too much water, and require more mowings.

Use only organic fertilizers such as compost, blood meal, Grow Power, Milorganite, Renew, or Replenish. (Note: you must use these fertilizers to encourage microorganisms that help break down clippings.) One of my favorite grass fertilizers is liquid seaweed. It helps grass build tolerance to extreme heat and cold.

Also, topdress the lawn twice a year with three-eights an inch of compost.

When Bermuda is actively growing (between June and August), use a core aerator and dethatcher. Core aerators bring little plugs of microbe-active soil to the surface. As the plugs disintegrate, microbes digest grass clippings and thatch and return nutrients to the soil. This contributes to healthy soil and vigorous grass.

If your summer lawn gets a little yellow around August or September, it could have chlorosis. If so, apply a chelated iron foliar spray. It makes grass green without applying more fertilizer; but be careful, because it stains concrete and cool deck surfaces.

One last thing about keeping an organic lawn: expect to have a few weeds. It's okay. You can pick them, or better yet, use a natural spray to get rid of them – vinegar. Kill weeds by spraying vinegar (100% works best) on them at the hottest time of the day.

ORGANIC CONTROLS

ONLY in the last hundred years or so have chemicals been available for use in gardening and farming. For the thousands of years before that, gardeners and farmers used natural means to control the things that ail plants. Those organic control methods didn't change much in those centuries, because the pests and diseases had not changed. Since we started using synthetic pesticides, fungicides and herbicides, however, those pests and diseases have developed a resistance to the chemical controls. That forces scientists to continually come up with new, more powerful chemicals.

We're seeing where all of this science has serious downfalls. They kill everyone (bad bugs AND good bugs) in sight, and recent studies have shown they might be killing us, too.

Now that we know this stuff, we need to stop using things that can hurt us. The bug killers in aerosol cans, the synthetic weed killers, and the chemical fertilizers are all serious potential health risks.

To substitute the bad stuff with good stuff, just ask your old friend for help. No, not me. I'm talking about Nature. She provides organic controls for everything. Every bug, every weed, every disease is prey for something or someone else. All I'm doing is listing her combat-ready warriors for you.

The solutions I offer might not give you results as fast as a chemical might, but that's okay. Fast is not always better. Safe and effective is! Follow the rules and tips I've got for you, and you'll go a long way toward making your home healthy.

ORGANIC PEST CONTROL

When you find Crickets in the laundry room or Ants making highways on the stoop, often times the first reaction is to call the pest control guy. STOP! After you've spent months planting and caring for your Tomatoes, you might get angry to find worms in the fruit. Do you want to reach for chemical insecticides to level the score? WAIT!

Before you start spreading dangerous chemicals around your home, decide if the insect is actually hurting anything. Okay, the worm ruined a few Tomatoes, but if you've planted well, there's a whole crop left. And if you can reroute the Ant trail away from the front door, you'll find they can actually be very helpful in the yard. So long as they aren't hurting much, I'm asking you to put up with some of the bugs around you.

And I have a good reason. You see, we need insects.

Bugs and other critters are the foundation for a big part of the food chain. But more importantly, they help ecosystem's digestion. They process organic stuff, making it useful again to plants and the soil. Of the thousands of insect species in the area, only three to five percent damage food crops and ornamental plantings. The rest are working for you; or at the very least, they're not hurting anything. I'll help you figure out the difference between the bad bugs and the beneficial ones.

For those causing problems, nature has its own warriors. Predator insects hunt and gobble up the bad guys before they can grow to dangerous populations. When you use these predaceous foes (great name, huh?), you avoid using chemicals and losing the advantages of insect work.

Forget the saying, "the only good bug is a dead bug." The bugs you see make up just a tiny percentage of the insect world. There are tiny, even microscopic, battles being fought right now in all the nooks and crannies of your garden and home. That's a good thing. Insecticides disrupt this process of natural checks and balances and can actually increase your problems. By killing all bugs, good and bad, you leave the garden undefended and open to attack from new pests.

Predator insects are not your only defense, though. Birds, Toads, and Lizards are fantastic bug eaters. We'll attract them to your garden. We'll also put certain plants in places that will keep bugs from ever getting into your garden. There are organic concoctions you can whip up in the kitchen and put in the yard and garden to repel or kill pests. There are all types of choices. And none of them involve dangerous chemical products.

There are three parts to this chapter. How do you tell the difference between a Flea and a gnat? What is the white powdery stuff on your Roses? Why are your grape leaves skeletonized? In "Part One," you'll learn how to identify the insect that ails you and expel it.

In "Part Two," I'll tell you how to assess a plant problem and fix it. So what's the best way to combat insects? The best way to keep bugs out is to never let them in. Healthy plants in the right combinations and in the right locations are powerful weapons for fighting bugs.

In "Part Three," I list plants that repel insects and prevent them from ever entering your garden.

Organic control is the way to go, but that doesn't mean it's 100% harmless. Use common sense and care when applying any pest control.

Part One-Insect Identification

If you think you've got insect pests, you need a positive ID. You don't want to mistakenly kill beneficial insects (the good guys that are your allies in the garden). Under each pest in this section, I list three types of controls: organic, insect/other, and plants.

The "organic" controls will include simple solutions and recipes you can make yourself. You'll find the ingredients and instructions near the end of this section under "Bug Remedies."

"Insect/other controls" is a roster of critters that are your allies in the garden. To find out how to obtain and use these, see the list of "Beneficial Insects." For the other animals listed, see "Organic Animal Control."

"Plants" comprise the third type of control. Find out what plant repels your pest, then refer back to Section II to find out how to plant it. For more information, look at Part Three of this section and at "Companion Plants" back in Section I.

Pests and Their Foes

Ants
- Organic controls
  - Pour vinegar into the anthill
  - Pour boiling water into the anthill
  - Blend three to five Lemon peels with water and immediately pour it into the anthill
  - Try Recipe #3, Recipe #4, or Recipe #6 below
- Other Ant controls
  - Encourage Birds, Lizards, Toads, in the garden
- Plants that repel Ants
  - Artemisia
  - Bay leaves keep them out of the pantry
  - Catnip
  - Citrus juice, especially Lemon
  - Lavender
  - Mints, including Peppermint and Pennyroyal
  - Onions
  - Tansy (plant by doorways to discourage Ants from entering your home)

Aphids

As sap suckers, these soft-bodied insects pierce new growth, and can transmit disease from plant to plant. They secrete a sugary substance known as honeydew, that can encourage sooty fungus. Ants will protect Aphids from predators in order to harvest the honeydew. Aphids come in many colors.

- Organic controls
  - Plant Mexican Primrose to act as a trap crop
  - First, spray the plants, and undersides of the leaves, with a stream of water to knock them off
  - Try Recipe #2 until predator population builds up, but then stop. This recipe kills beneficials, too
  - For heavier infestations, use Recipe #1. Spray in the morning
  - As an alternative for heavier infestations, use Recipe #3 on a small portion of the plant. The next day, check plant for damage; if there's none, continue to spray as needed
- Insect controls of Aphids
  - The Big-eyed Bug and larvae
  - Braconid wasps
  - Damselflies
  - Green Lacewings and nymphs
  - Hoverfly larvae
  - Ladybugs and nymphs
  - Praying Mantis
  - Syrphid fly larvae
- Plants that repel Aphids
  - Artemisia
  - Basil
  - Chives
  - Coriander
  - Garlic, including Society Garlic (does excellent job repelling Aphids)
  - Lavender
  - Marigolds
  - Mint
  - Onions
  - Nasturtiums
  - Parsley
  - Petunias
  - Radishes

- ○ Tansy
- ○ Thyme

Beet Leafhoppers

Wedge-shaped insects about one-eighth inch long. They suck the juices out of the plant, often spreading diseases as they move from an infected plant to a healthy plant. They frequently attack Tomatoes. Control of leafhoppers is difficult.

- Organic control
  - ○ Cover crops with shade cloth
  - ○ Dust leaves lightly with Diatomaceous Earth
- Insect/other controls
  - ○ Big-eyed Bugs
  - ○ Parasitizing flies and wasps (see Beneficial Insects)

Beetles

Determine that it's actually a Beetle causing plant damage, as many Beetles eat other leaf-chewing insects. Natural enemies such as Birds, reptiles, Spiders, and parasitic insects often control Beetles. The larvae of the Palo Verde Beetle feed on the roots of Palo Verde trees. The adults, four to six inches in length, emerge in July and fly about in quest of a mate. No control is effective beyond keeping the trees in the best possible health. The larvae of a Beetle is known as a grub.

- Organic controls
  - ○ Sprinkle the surrounding soil with garden or food grade Diatomaceous Earth
  - ○ Dust the plants with Diatomaceous Earth or use spray from Recipe #4
- Insect/other controls
  - ○ The Big-eyed Bug and larvae
  - ○ Birds
  - ○ Praying Mantis
  - ○ Reptiles
  - ○ The Robber fly
  - ○ Spiders
  - ○ Tachnid flies

- Plants that repel Beetles
  - Beans
  - Calendula
  - Catnip
  - Catmint
  - Nasturtiums
  - Parsley
  - Petunias
  - Radishes
  - Rosemary
  - Tansy

Borers

If you notice holes in trunks and branches of trees and shrubs or find small piles of sawdust on the ground or branches, you might be looking at Borer damage. The larval stage of the Borer, (which is a grub or a Caterpillar) usually causes the damage. Since it lives deep inside the tree branch or trunk or down within the roots, control is very difficult.

Flatheaded Borers are about one-half to three-quarters of an inch long. They are usually host specific, feeding on one particular type of plant. They bore into sunburned or damaged bark.

Round-headed Borers have antennae as long as their bodies. The larvae bore into solid wood of plants including locust and mesquite; usually attacking weakened or stressed trees.

Be careful — you could be looking at woodpecker damage.

Another, the squash vine Borer, attacks Squash, Melons, and Cucumbers. In this case, mound some compost over the damaged vine to trigger rooting and renewed growth. Keep the plant healthy and growing vigorously to combat these critters.

- Organic control
  - First priority is to keep your plant healthy
  - If there are holes, probe them with a thin, flexible wire to destroy the grubs
  - Prune off and dispose of infected branches

- ○ Protect trunks from weed-eater and lawn mower damage
- ○ Keep the garden clean. Dispose of vines and plant debris. Rotate crops
- ○ Seal cuts of Roses with drop of wood or white glue
- ○ Don't use pruning sprays
- • Insect/other control
  - ○ Ants, Birds, Predatory Beetles, Wasps
  - ○ Cultivate soil in late fall to expose grubs and larvae to attract hungry Birds
- • Plants that repel Borers
  - ○ Chives, Garlic, or Onions around base of trees

Caterpillars

Depending on how many Moths or Caterpillars you have, you might consider letting some of these guys pupate and emerge as beautiful Butterflies. Remember, the smaller the Caterpillar, the less damage it causes. If there's a lot of damage, however, don't be afraid to dispose of them.

The Cutworm can be gray or brown. It feeds at night right at or near the soil surface. Put a collar around seedlings for protection. Sections of milk carton work well.

The Green Cabbage Looper is pale green. To find him, check the undersides of the leaves, handpick and dispose. Trichogramma wasps will parasitize (devour from the inside out) loopers.

The Corn Earworm can range in color from green to brown to red. To confirm ID, look for stripes that run the length of its body. This Caterpillar feeds on the silks and leaves of ears of Corn. Control the Earworm by applying a drop of mineral oil to the inside tip of each ear after the silk has wilted.

The Orange Dog doesn't live up to its name. It's actually a mottled gray and brown color and looks like a bird dropping. Unless they do severe damage, allow a few to mature on Citrus trees. They become beautiful giant swallowtail Butterflies. The Black Swallowtail Butterfly is also beautiful. It comes from the green and black Caterpillar with white spots. You might see it on Carrots or Parsley.

The Grape Leaf Skeletonizer can ravage grapes during the summer. It's a small worm with yellow and black bands running across its body.

The Tomato Hornworm is lime green with white stripes. The Trichogramma wasp frequently parasitizes (devours from the inside out) the Tomato Hornworm, so little control is necessary. Otherwise, handpick and dispose of them. If one lives, though, it becomes the Whitelined Sphinx Moth, an important pollinator. Consider letting a few survive.

- Organic control of Caterpillars
    - Check undersides of leaves for Caterpillar eggs if you notice Butterfly or Moth activity. Rub off the eggs or remove the leaf
    - If you miss the egg leaf, inspect new, tender growth for Caterpillar damage
    - Handpick the Caterpillars and drop into soapy water
    - For severe infestations, spray with Bacillus thuringiensis (see Bug Remedies)
    - Place sections of milk cartons around seedlings to protect them from night-feeding cutworms
- Insect/other controls
    - Assassin Bugs
    - Big-eyed Bugs and larvae
    - Birds
    - Braconid wasps
    - Praying Mantis
    - Tachinid flies
    - Trichogramma wasps
- Plants that repel Moths and Caterpillars
    - Artemisia
    - Basils
    - Bay
    - Borage
    - Calendula
    - Lavender
    - Marigolds
    - Mints

- ○ Nasturtiums
- ○ Onions
- ○ Pennyroyal
- ○ Rosemary
- ○ Sage
- ○ Tansy
- ○ Thyme

Cockroaches
They will eat most anything. Keep them out of the house with a good caulking. Remove All cardboard boxes. They like to hide in the miles of tunnels cardboard provides. They also love the glue.

- • Organic controls
  - ○ Spread lots of Boric Acid in cracks and crevices, and along edges of kitchens and bathrooms
  - ○ Try Recipe #4 or Recipe #5 (place these recipes away from children and pets)

Crickets
They'll feed on roots, leaves, and anything else that might be available. Scorpions and Spiders are attracted to them. Cover with a light, breathable material (row cover) if infestations are severe. Attract Birds to your garden to eat Crickets.

- • Organic controls
  - ○ Keep the area clean of weeds, cardboard boxes, boards, plant parts, fallen branches, etc.
  - ○ Dust pathways, cracks, and crevices with Diatomaceous Earth. See Recipe #4
- • Insect/other controls
  - ○ Encourage Birds, Geckos, Lizards, Snakes, Spiders, Toads
  - ○ Turn the soil to expose eggs for Birds and insects to eat
- • Sensory-distracting plants that repel Crickets
  - ○ Chives
  - ○ Garlic
  - ○ Lavenders
  - ○ Marigolds
  - ○ Onions

- Pennyroyal
- Rosemary
- Sage
- Santolina

Fleas

- Organic controls
  - Remove trash such as boards, tools etc. from yard
  - Vacuum all cracks and crevices, then treat with a DE or Boric Acid recipe
  - Add one tablespoon vinegar to pet's water dish daily
  - Spread citrus bark around pet areas
  - Give pets regular baths and lots of exercise
  - Chop up Lemon or Orange peels and boil in water for a few minutes. Let cool and rub into pet's fur
  - Stuff pet beds with Eucalyptus leaves and cedar shavings (change leaves and shavings frequently)
  - Recipe #4 — use sock to dust Dog and bedding with Diatomaceous Earth or Boric Acid
  - Every other day, dust carpets with DE, then vacuum
  - Dust Dog and bedding with a 50/50 mix of Diatomaceous Earth and non-systemic Pyrethrin
  - Add one-half teaspoon each of brewers yeast, bee pollen, and Garlic powder to your Dog's food weekly
  - Add one teaspoon of food grade Diatomaceous Earth to Dog's food daily (it won't hurt your Dog, and it actually cleans digestive track)
- Plants that repel Fleas
  - Catnip
  - Chamomile
  - Citrus bark
  - Eucalyptus leaves
  - Fennel
  - Fleabane
  - Lavender
  - Rosemary
  - Rue
  - Santolina
  - Tansy

Grasshoppers

They'll feed on roots, leaves, and anything else that may be available. Birds and Spiders will eat Grasshoppers. Cover with a light, breathable material (row cover) if infestations are severe. Attract Birds to your garden.

- Organic controls
  - Keep the area clean of weeds, cardboard boxes, boards, plant parts, fallen branches, etc.
  - Dust pathways with Diatomaceous Earth
  - Puff Diatomaceous Earth into cracks and crevices with turkey baster used *exclusively* for insect control. See Recipe #4
  - Fill jars partway with molasses and water and bury them halfway in the ground to trap Grasshoppers
- Insect/other controls
  - Encourage Birds, Geckos, Lizards, Nocema Locusta (beneficial fungus), Snakes, Spiders, Toads
  - Turn the soil to expose eggs for Birds and insects to eat
- Sensory-distracting plants for Grasshoppers
  - Chives
  - Garlic
  - Lavenders
  - Marigolds
  - Onions
  - Pennyroyal
  - Rosemary
  - Sage
  - Santolina

Leafcutter bees

They cut circles out of the leaves of landscape plants, such as Roses, jasmine, and Bougainvillea. The bees use the leaf circles to line their nests. There isn't enough damage to the plant to warrant any control measures. Don't worry, be happy.

  - Leafcutter bees are excellent pollinators and should be encouraged to come into the garden.

Mealybugs

You'll find these insects clustered on the stems of houseplants and some landscape plants where they will pierce the stems, leaves, and fruits to suck sap. They can spread diseases from plant to plant. Mealybugs also secrete honeydew, which attracts sooty fungus. They have soft bodies that are usually covered with white, powdery wax.

- Organic control
  - First, hose off plants with a stream of water
  - If the bug population isn't too bad, dip a cotton swab into rubbing alcohol and rub off the Mealybugs
  - For heavier infestations, use Recipe #2 or Recipe #3
- Insect/other controls
  - Green Lacewing nymphs
  - Ladybugs
  - The Mealybug destroyer, Cryptolaemus montrouzieri, also known as Crypts
- Encourage Mealybug-eating beneficial insects by planting
  - Alyssum
  - Coreopsis
  - Coriander
  - Cosmos
  - Dill
  - Parsley

Mosquitoes

- Organic control
  - Blend one and one-half cups of Basil leaves with one quart of water. Strain thoroughly. Spray in a room to repel Mosquitoes
  - Sprinkle instant coffee or spray mineral oil over standing water (a little goes a long way)
  - Use Bacillus thuringiensis israelensis (B.t.i.) to control Mosquito larvae (see Recipe #8)
- Plants that repel Mosquitoes
  - Artemisia
  - Bachelor's-Button
  - Basil

- ○ Lavender
- ○ Pennyroyal
- ○ Rosemary

Moths

- Organic control (in the home)
  - ○ Use the dried flowers and stems of the flowering shrubs listed below in sachets, and place them in drawers and closets
  - ○ Use cedar shavings, cedar chips, and cedar blocks to deter Moths
  - ○ Clean items before storing
- Plants that repel Moths (outside)
  - ○ Artemisia
  - ○ Basil
  - ○ Bay
  - ○ Calendula
  - ○ Lavender
  - ○ Mints
  - ○ Onions
  - ○ Rosemary
  - ○ Santolina
  - ○ Tansy
  - ○ Thyme

Scale insects

Scales are difficult to recognize because they are tiny, flattened oval shapes, usually on the undersides of leaves and along the branches and stems. As Scales mature they secrete a waxy substance that coats their bodies, making control difficult.

The Cottony-Cushion Scale attacks shade plants such as pittosporum and euonymus. This Scale looks like a tiny wad of cotton.

The Cochineal Scale grows on prickly pear cactus. White globs can multiply and cover the plant. At one time, the insect was cultivated and used as a red dye by the Spanish.

- Organic control
  - ○ Inspect plants often, especially the undersides of the leaves and the stems, and rub off the Scale
  - ○ Hose off Scale you find
  - ○ For heavier infestations, use Recipe #2 or Recipe #3

- Insect/other control
  - Green Lacewing nymphs
- Plants that attract Scale-eating beneficial insects
  - Alyssum
  - Bachelor's button
  - Coreopsis
  - Coriander
  - Dill
  - Feverfew
  - Fleabane
  - Lemon balm
  - Nasturtiums
  - Parsley

Scorpions

There are several types of Scorpion, but the only one you should worry about in your home is the Bark Scorpion. It has a slender, almost translucent, yellow-beige body with large pinchers. Unlike other Scorpions, it can climb vertical surfaces. They range in size from one-half inch to three inches in length. They are usually attracted to new homes. This peculiarity is thought to stem from the fact that new homes have a higher humidity level.

If you see types other than Bark Scorpions outside the house, leave them alone. They are eating insects for you and are unable to get inside.

Scorpion activity falls off when nighttime temperatures drop below 70°.

- Organic Controls
  - Hunt for Bark Scorpions on moonless nights with a black light (you can find black lights at most home improvement stores). They'll glow green. I use a fly swatter or step on them
  - Try a product called Tangle Foot on all your door stoops. Scorpions get tangled in the gooey mess
  - Pesticides have a hard time killing these guys
- Insect/other controls
  - Cats and Toads eat Scorpions

Snails and Slugs

A mucous trail indicates the presence of these leaf-chewing mollusks. They feed at night and hide during the day.

- Organic controls
    - Handpick and drop into soapy water
    - Lay a board or piece of carpet in garden; Snails and Slugs will gather there during the day. At daybreak, lift the carpet or board and dispose of the creatures
    - Plant Onions, Rosemary to distract Snails and Slugs
    - Snails and Slugs love to drink beer. At night, put some in a pie plate. Bury it to the rim and you'll find Snails and Slugs hungover in the morning. Throw them away

Spider Mites

They are very small and you might need magnifying glass to see them. They live in colonies on the undersides of leaves, building webbing and sucking sap from the plant, causing leaves to yellow and stipple.

You can identify Spider Mite infestation when a plant or tree takes on a dusty-like appearance.

- Organic control
    - First, hose the Spider Mites off with a stream of water every three to five days
    - For heavier infestations, use Recipe #2 or Recipe #3
- Insect/other controls
    - Green Lacewing
    - Ladybugs
    - Mite Predator
    - Minute Pirate Bug
    - Praying Mantis
- Plant a diversity of flowering shrubs and herbs to attract predaceous insects
    - Alyssum
    - Bachelor's button
    - Basil
    - Coreopsis
    - Coriander

- Dill
- Feverfew
- Lemon balm
- Nasturtiums
- Parsley
- Radishes

Termites

The bane of the homeowner, a termite can literally eat you out of house and home. In the deserts, they have a climate they like and with all of the new homes, they have an excellent food source.

- Organic controls
  - Use 00 grit sand-blasting sand and spread around base of home
  - Break up any termite tubes
  - Encourage ants to take up residence
  - Introduce beneficial nematodes
  - Paint wood with Boric Acid products or shellac
  - Do not plant anything within four feet of your home
  - Move all hose spigots and bibs, and air conditioner bleed-offs away from home to prevent moisture buildup

Thrips

Thrips cause scarring on the blossom end of fruit, and leaves to curl. This is cosmetic and does not affect the quality of the fruit. Thrips are often found on Citrus. Control is difficult for the home gardener.

- Insect/other controls
  - Green Lacewing nymphs
  - Minute Pirate Bugs
- Plant a wide diversity of flowering plants to attract predaceous insects
  - Alyssum
  - Bachelor's button
  - Coreopsis
  - Coriander
  - Dill
  - Feverfew

- o Lemon balm
- o Nasturtiums
- o Parsley

Ticks
- Organic control
  - o To remove Ticks, place a drop of hydrogen peroxide on the Tick
- Plants that repel (these are effective around pet dishes)
  - o Lavender
  - o Santolina
  - o Artemisia
  - o Cedar, Citrus, and Eucalyptus bark work great in flower beds

True Bugs
True Bugs can be good guys or bad guys. Be certain damage is occurring before disposing of them. A distinguishing characteristic of True Bugs is a shield or triangular-shaped plate on their backs.
- The Leaf-footed plant bug is a bad guy (the one-inch long adult has flat back legs, resembling a leaf). Commonly attacks Pomegranates, other fruit. Birds are best predators
- Nasturtiums repel squash bugs
- Plant a variety of seed-producing and flowering plants to attract Birds — they'll often stay around to eat a few insects
- See "Beneficial Insects" for the good guys

Whiteflies
The nymphs hatch from eggs laid on the undersides of leaves. Here they attach themselves, pierce the leaf, and suck juices from the plant. The adult Whiteflies don't cause nearly the amount of damage as the nymphs. Control of the adults is usually not necessary.
- Organic control
  - o Check the undersides of plants, especially Cantaloupe, Hibiscus, Lantana, Tomato for nymphs
  - o Lantana, Hibiscus are great trap crops
  - o Whiteflies drown easily. Use strong stream of water to dislodge nymphs (adults do not damage plants)
  - o For heavier infestations, use Recipe #2 or Recipe #3

- Insect/other controls
  - Encarsia Formosa wasp
  - Green Lacewing nymphs
- Plant a diversity of flowering shrubs and herbs to attract predaceous insects
  - Alyssum
  - Bachelor's-Button
  - Calendula
  - Coreopsis
  - Coriander
  - Dill
  - Feverfew
  - Lemon balm
  - Lantana as a trap crop
  - Marigold
  - Mints
  - Nasturtiums
  - Parsley

Beneficial Insects

If there's a pest in your garden, chances are there is another insect that feeds on it. You won't find a better army to fight your bug battles than the predaceous foes of your insect pests. Beneficials are one of the most effective ways to control insects.

Dragonfly and damselfly
- Usually associated with ponds, lakes, etc.
- These winged acrobats catch flying insects such as Mosquitoes, flies, Moths
- The damselfly is often bright blue and will eat Aphids
- Dragonfly colors range from blue to green to brown

Green Lacewings

They have slender, green bodies and delicate, gossamer wings, and are one of the best beneficials to release around your home. Females lay eggs, which are attached to a thin filament, on the undersides of leaves. The nymphs look like tiny brown alligators. They grab their prey with their front mandibles and suck it dry.

- Adult lacewings do not feed on Aphids, but the nymphs are ferocious eaters of Aphids, Mealybugs, Leafhoppers, Scale, Thrips, Whiteflies

Ladybugs

They're also voracious eaters of Aphids.

- After you release them, Ladybugs often fly away to search for food.
    - To prevent that, put a little honey, molasses, or yeast on strips of waxed paper. Hang the strips around the garden, next to Aphid-infected plants, and the Ladybugs should stay
    - Release them in the cool mornings. They move more slowly
    - Plant Cosmos and Tansy to attract them

Parasitizing wasps and flies

The word "parasitize" means to feed off of a host. Destructive pests like Caterpillars are essentially being eaten from the inside out by this brand of beneficial insect. These guys don't hurt humans. Make them a part of your beneficial insect arsenal.

- Braconid wasp
    - Lays eggs in Aphid or Caterpillar "hosts"
    - After eggs hatch, larvae feed on Caterpillar's body
    - When larvae pupate, cocoons emerge from the Caterpillar's back like tiny balloons
        - If you find one, don't kill it. The parasitized Caterpillar will die soon anyway and you'll be destroying many parasitic wasps, which will soon eat Aphids by the hundreds
    - If you find dried up Aphids on plants, don't wash them off. The wasps lay eggs in Aphids. They hatch and feed on the Aphid's body, the larvae mature inside the "mummy" and eventually emerge as wasps and immediately begin feeding on other Aphids. The "mummies" are dried up bodies of parasitized Aphids
- Encarsia formosa wasp
    - Favorite food is Whiteflies
    - Used in Whitefly control for more than 60 years

- - The adult wasp lays an egg inside a Whitefly egg. The wasp larvae hatches, eats the host, then matures and gobbles more Whiteflies
- Hoverfly
  - Their black and yellow bodies resemble bees or wasps
  - Adults feed on nectar and are excellent pollinators
  - Attract them by using nectar-rich plants such as Parsley, Coreopsis, other flat-surface flowers
  - Females lay eggs in the midst of Aphids. The larvae feast on the Aphids, gobbling one Aphid per minute!
- Robber fly
  - Loud buzzing insect, usually gray, with bearded head
  - Eats Beetles, Butterflies, Leafhoppers, Grasshoppers
  - The larvae eat grubs and Grasshopper eggs
- Syrphid fly
  - Yellow and black, resembling bees, except they have only one pair of wings
  - Adults are excellent pollinators
  - Predaceous larvae that spend their lives on leaves searching for Aphids, which they destroy
- Tachinid fly
  - Prey on Beetles, Caterpillars, stink bugs
  - Females lay eggs in the host insect, and the larvae mature inside the body, eventually killing it
- Trichogramma wasp
  - About one-thirtieth of an inch long, females lay eggs on top of Caterpillar eggs and other insects, preventing future damage to plants
    - Attract this wasp by planting lots of flowering herbs such as Coriander, Dill, Parsley

Praying Mantis
- Feed on Aphids, bees, Beetles, Butterflies, Caterpillars, flies, Leafhoppers, wasps, each other
- Range in size from three-quarters of an inch to five inches long, and have enlarged front legs for grasping their prey

- They are excellent camouflage artists. They can look exactly like twigs, and can change color to match green stems or brown branches
- Egg cases, available at nurseries and by mail order, have up to 200 eggs. To keep Ants from destroying egg cases, put up in branches when you release them

Spiders

Spiders have a bad rap. We often think of them as insects, but they're arachnids. They're insect predators and can be a big help to you. Don't kill them. They wait for insects to fall into their webs, or they might actively hunt insects.

   - Other arachnids such as Scorpions, whip scorpions, and sun Spiders are very effective insect eaters

True Bugs

They can be plant eaters or they can eat the plant eaters. Be certain they're causing damage before you dispose of True bugs. Here are the good guys you want to keep around.

- Encourage insect-eating True Bugs. They will search out and eat other insects
   - Assassin Bug
      - Long, slender heads with eyes in the middle, long antennae, and a long, jointed beak
      - It inserts its beak into the body of its prey and sucks it dry
      - In both larval and adult form, this brown bug searches leaves for Caterpillars, the larvae of plant-eating bugs, and other insects
   - Big-eyed Bug
      - Adult, larvae feed on Aphids, Beet Leafhoppers, Beetles, Caterpillars, Whiteflies
      - They're about one-eighth inch long and have a cylindrical head with eyes protruding on sides
   - Minute Pirate Bug
      - Even smaller than Big-eyed Bugs, they eat Spider Mites, insect eggs, Thrips

- To attract True bugs, use these flowering shrubs and herbs
  - Alyssum
  - Bachelor's button
  - Coreopsis
  - Coriander
  - Dill
  - Feverfew
  - Lemon balm
  - Nasturtiums
  - Parsley

Other insect-eating critters

- Bats are one of the best insect predators around. Try to draw one to your home, but be patient.
- The Gecko, a wall-climbing reptile, happily eats Crickets, Cockroaches, Flies, Mosquitoes. It's difficult to attract Geckos, so appreciate the ones you've got
- Lizards are super insect eaters. Provide a pesticide-free environment so they'll have all the insects they can eat
- Snakes seem to cause a lot of fear in humans. But boy do they do good work keeping Birds and mice out of the garden! They are also excellent insect eaters
- Toads are really worth their weight in . . . something. They consume 10,000 to 20,000 insects per year, including Ants and Scorpions. Be kind to this very valuable garden helper
  - For shade and shelter, turn a clay pot upside down and prop it up with a brick or board
  - Put it on the north side of house or yard to keep cool
  - Add a water source, and a Toad should be very content
  - Don't touch Toads. They ooze a chemical, called bufogen, which your skin can absorb and make you sick. Immediately wash your hands if you do handle a Toad

To attract these critters, see "Organic Animal Control."

Bug Remedies

Here are some organic ideas for keeping the bugs away. Remember, that anytime you use something for pest control (whether it's organic or chemical), you're going to also kill or damage similar bugs from the beneficial insect population. Chemicals kill everything in sight, including your insect allies. The organic recipes in here will at least isolate specific areas or insect types, without harming your family. So apply these remedies where they'll do the most good and the least harm. Target infestations, and remember to aim well.

- Bacillus thuringiensis is a naturally occurring organism. Caterpillars ingest it and die from the stomach outward. This control method is directly targeted at Caterpillars and is not dangerous to other insects, pets, or children. Order this as a dust, wettable powder, or liquid
- Bio-neem is an excellent organic control. It repels Aphids, Caterpillars, Mealybugs, Whiteflies, and many, many other pests. It comes from the Neem tree, native to India

Recipe #1 (General insect repellent including Aphids, Spider Mites, and Whiteflies)

2 bulbs of Garlic
2 hot Peppers
$1/3$ cup of water

- Mix all of this in a blender. Strain solids out, and you have concentrate. Add a quarter of this concoction to one gallon of water, and spray directly on bugs. To make it really strong, add two tablespoons of vegetable oil. Bugs hate it!

Recipe #2 (for heavy Aphid, Spider Mite, or Whitefly infestations)

2 tablespoons of blue dishwashing liquid
1 gallon of water
1 tablespoon of cooking oil

- Mix this, and add to spray bottle. Shake well, and spray on plants, especially underside of leaves. Cooking oil helps the mixture stick, while soap does the killing. Don't use yellow, soap as it contains petroleum byproducts

Recipe #3 (Ants, Mealybugs, and Aphids)

- Mix 1 to 2 cups of 70% isopropyl alcohol (rubbing alcohol) to 1 quart of water. Test spray on a small portion of one plant, and check in a day. If there is no damage to the plant, spray on insects under leaves. The rubbing alcohol dissolves insect's waxy coating, causing them to dry out and die. Use this procedure for heavy infestations only

---

Recipe #4 (Ants, Cockroaches, Fleas)

Diatomaceous Earth (DE) is one of my favorites. Buy garden-grade or food-grade (not pool-grade) DE at local health food stores or nurseries. The powder acts like millions of razor blades that cut the exoskeleton (shell) of an insect, causing it to dehydrate and die*. Sprinkle it on carpets, then vacuum. To "dust" with DE, put some in a tube sock, tie it off, then tap the sock in cracks around the house, around border areas, and at doorways. For hard to reach corners, use a turkey baster filled with DE (buy a different baster for the turkey!). Or mix two tablespoons of garden-grade DE per gallon of water, and use it as a spray to get rid of crawling insects. Use in the early morning. Dampness on the leaves causes the DE to adhere better. It can irritate your lungs, so where a mask when handling it.

Boric Acid can be found at any drugstore, and is very safe for humans. Insects, however, don't fare so well. It works a lot like DE*. Use a sock or turkey baster to spread it behind refrigerators, ovens, under sinks, at baseboards, and near pipes. Keep away from children.

*Be careful using DE and Boric Acid because they kill beneficial insects, too.

Recipe #5 (Cockroaches and Crickets)

- Mix equal amounts Arm & Hammer laundry detergent and powdered sugar in a dish or jar lid. The sugar attracts Roaches and Crickets. When they walk through the mixture, the detergent eats through the exoskeleton (shell) and kills them

- A 50/50 mix of powdered sugar and Diatomaceous Earth or Boric Acid also works. When insects come to feed on the sugar, they go back to the nest with the powder all over them. When insects groom themselves, they ingest the Diatomaceous Earth or Boric Acid and die

*Neither mixture will hurt Birds, Lizards, or Toads. Keep away from children and pets.

Recipe #6 (Ants)
- Sprinkle dry Cream of Wheat where Ants can ingest it. When cereal gets to the stomach and expands, the Ant explodes

Recipe #7 (termites)
- Bury "00" silica sand one foot down around the foundation of your home. Termites have a tough time digging through it

Recipe #8 (Mosquitoes)
- Make instant coffee and spray it on standing water
- Put disks of Bacillus thuringiensis in standing water
- Spray mineral oil on standing water to trap Mosquitoes that land
- Blend $1^1/_2$ cups of Basil leaves with one quart of water. Strain thoroughly. Spray in a room to repel Mosquitoes

Recipe #9 (any insect)
- Blend flour or buttermilk with water and spray. As the spray dries, the insect suffocates

The Vonderful Vorld of Vinegar
- I use vinegar all the time in my garden. It lowers pH, adds trace elements to the soil, plus it has lots of other benefits
- To kill weeds, spray it undiluted during the hottest time of day. Try 100% to 200% vinegar for serious jobs

- For Ant problems, find the anthill and do the same thing
- Put a tablespoon of vinegar in your pet's water, and you'll notice fewer Flea and Tick problems
- And last but not least, I add four tablespoons of vinegar to one gallon of water and wash my wilted vegetables. You'll be amazed at how well it revives them

IMPORTANT NOTE: Even though these solutions are safer than chemicals, keep them away from children.

Part Two-Damage Assessment

Maybe you've spotted some damage in your garden, but you haven't seen any insects. Assess the problem, and you can usually identify the criminal. Then get rid of him.

Here's where you get to use that magnifying glass I told you about in the first part of the book (see "TOOLS" chapter). If you see a problem with leaves, stems, branches, etc., look closely through the magnifying glass to figure out the type of damage. Elementary, my dear gardener.

Type of damage
Chewing damage

Appears as holes in leaves, around edges, and as skeletonized leaves. Insects chew, eat plant leaves

- The Suspects
  - Beetles
  - Caterpillars
  - Crickets
  - Grape leaf skeletonizer
  - Grasshoppers
  - Weevils
- Control methods
  - Predators: Birds, Parasitizing Wasps, insect-eating Beetles, Spiders, and reptiles including Geckos, Lizards, Snakes, and Toads

- o Use Diatomaceous Earth for crawling insects (see Recipe # 4)
  - o Apply Bacillus thuringiensis (see "Bug Remedies" a few pages back)

Wilting

Damage appears as limp wilted leaves, yellow leaves, or speckled discoloration or pale leaves. First check to make sure plant is properly irrigated. If so, the wilting might be the result of insects piercing the plant and sucking sap (plant juice). It can stunt growth or even kill the plant.

- The Suspects
  - o Aphids
  - o Leafhoppers
  - o Scale
  - o Spider Mites
  - o Whiteflies
- Control methods
  - o Introduce predators such as predaceous insects, Birds, Geckos, Lizards, Toads
  - o Use Recipe #1, Recipe #2, and/or Recipe #4

Holes, burrows

Damage appears as holes in branches or bark of trunk. Insects drill holes and burrow into woody parts of trees or shrubs, stunting growth or causing sudden branch dieback. The holes sometimes ooze sap.

- The Suspects
  - o Borers
  - o Palo Verde Beetles
- Control methods
  - o Because larvae are generally deep inside the wood, control is difficult and impractical
    - Keep the plant healthy and vigorous
    - Protect from sunburn
    - Protect from mechanical damage such as lawn mowers and weed-eaters
    - Don't prune from May to September, except for native plants

Part Three-Helpful Plants

Imagine you're house hunting and find the perfect place, only there's a drawback. It stinks. Real bad. The smell never lets up, unless it's to make room for another bad smell. Would you move in? I'm guessing you said "no." A bug isn't much different, and he won't stick around a place that stinks. But his definition of a bad smell is much different than ours. The beautiful scent of Lavender disgusts a Tick. The lovely fragrance of a Geranium makes an Ant turn and run.

But certain scents attract insects, too. Only these are the good insects, called beneficials, which prey upon destructive pests. Flowering Parsley and Cosmos draw beneficials like Green Lacewings and Ladybugs. Those guys feed on Mealybugs. And there are many more plants that can help you.

Encourage a wide variety of insect-eating beneficials by planting a diversity of flowering plants and herbs. This makes it difficult for one type of pest to predominate. If you plan your garden well, you won't have to worry much about bad insects. Remember to plant 18 inches away from the house foundation so the chemical termite barrier isn't broken.

Plants that repel insects
- Artemisia distracts Ants, Aphids, Mostquitoes, and Moths
- Basil wards off flies, Caterpillars, and Mosquitoes
- Bay repels Ants, Caterpillars, and Moths
  - Sprinkle Bay leaves throughout pantry and other cabinets
- Borage's blue flowers repel Caterpillars
- Calendula repels Moths
- Catnip repels Ants, Beetles, Fleas, mice, rats
- Catmint repels Beetles
- Chives repel Aphids, Borers, Crickets
- Eucalyptus leaves repel Fleas, Ticks

- Garlic is an incredibly effective insect repellent
  - Plant around Roses, stone fruit trees, throughout the vegetable garden
  - Chives and Society Garlic repel Aphids, Crickets, Grasshoppers
- Geraniums repels Ants, Moths
- Lavender
  - Repels Aphids, Ants, Crickets, Fleas, Grasshoppers, Mosquitoes, Moths, silverfish, Ticks
  - Mice and Rabbits avoid Lavender
- Leeks repel Aphids
- Marigolds repel Aphids, Caterpillars, Crickets, Grasshoppers, nematodes, Slugs, Whiteflies
  - Some say that Tagete Marigolds planted en masse exude a substance that deters bad nematodes
- Mint (including Peppermint and Pennyroyal) repels Ants, Moths, Caterpillars
- Nasturtiums repel Aphids, Moths
- Onions repel Ants, Aphids, Borers, Moths, Crickets, Grasshoppers
- Petunias repel Aphids
- Rosemary deters many insects, including Moths, Beetles, Crickets, Fleas, Grasshoppers, Mosquitoes
- Rue repels Fleas
- Sage deters mice and repels Crickets, Moths, Grasshoppers
- Santolina repels Crickets, Fleas, Grasshoppers, Rabbits
- Tansy is an all-purpose insect repellent that deters Ants, Aphids, flying insects, Fleas, Beetles, squash bugs, Moths
- Thyme deters cabbage worms, flies, Whiteflies

Plants that attract beneficial insects
- Alyssum attracts Ladybugs which in turn eat Mealybugs, Mosquitoes, Scale, Spider Mites
- Bachelor's Button attracts beneficials that eat Mosquitoes, Scale, Spider Mites

- Borage's blue flowers attract beneficial insects
- Basil attracts beneficial pollinators and other good guys
- Coreopsis attracts Hoverflies, insects that eat Mealybugs Mosquitoes, Scale, Spider Mites
- Coriander attracts Trichogramma wasps, beneficials that eat Mealybugs, Mosquitoes, Scale, Spider Mites
- Cosmos attracts Ladybugs and Green Lacewings, beneficials that eat Mealybugs
- Dill attracts pollinators as well as predaceous insects such as the Trichogramma wasp and other beneficials that eat Mealybugs, Mosquitoes, Scale, Spider Mites, Thrips
- Feverfew attracts beneficials that eat Mosquitoes, Scale, Spider Mites, Thrips
- Lavender attracts Bees, Butterflies
- Lemon Balm attracts beneficials that eat Mosquitoes, Scale, Spider Mites, Thrips
- Marigolds attract Hoverflies and many beneficial insects (also, plant throughout garden to attract Butterflies and add color)
- Nasturtiums attract beneficial insects that eat Mosquitoes, Scale, Spider Mites, Thrips (plus the flowers attract other beneficial insects as well)
- Parsley attracts Trichogramma wasps, Green Lacewings, and Hoverflies, beneficials that eat Mealybugs, Mosquitoes, Scale, Spider Mites, Thrips
- Rosemary's lovely blue flowers attract bees and other pollinators
- Tansy attracts Ladybugs (they adore the yellow flowers)

Prevent problems by planning

- Plant something improperly and you stress it out, inviting disease and pests. Put the right plant in the right place
- Are they too crowded? Some plants fight it out for water and nutrients. Allow enough space for good air circulation
- Pick up fallen fruit or vegetables before they decay, or they can become a breeding ground for insects and diseases

- Water deeply. In the summer, shallowly watered plants are stressed plants and the first to die
- Don't invite pests to dinner. Fertilize sparingly. Heavy doses of synthetic nitrogen fertilizers produce succulent green growth that is incredibly attractive to Aphids
- Plant in the correct season
  - Soil that is too cold weakens plants
  - Plant after seasonal pest populations subside, i.e., wait until September when Whiteflies taper off

Pest control for pets
- Basil repels Flies and Mosquitoes
- Catnip deters Fleas, Ants. Plant near pet runs, food and water
- Citrus bark is a great way to ward off insects
- Eucalyptus bark and leaves can be used in Dog runs and in Dog beds to deter Fleas and Ticks
- Lavender repels Ticks
- Rue repels Fleas
- Santolina deters insects
- Tansy repels Fleas

Remember
- Ugly bugs are not necessarily bad bugs
- You can't attract good bugs if there are no bad bugs to eat
- Only a few destructive pests need to be controlled
- Accept a certain amount of plant damage

ORGANIC ANIMAL CONTROL

Just like insects, there are animals that are good for your garden and animals that are bad for it. It might seem odd to find out the cuddly ones are probably doing harm to your garden while the slimy, ugly creatures are doing a lot of good. Destructive animals include Rabbits, Gophers, Deer, Cats, Dogs, and Birds — though not all Birds are bad. Now, to the helpful ones. Hold onto your seats, or for some of you, climb on top of your seats. The good guys include Snakes, Bats, Toads, Lizards, Geckos, turtles, and Frogs.

If you're like me, you love animals and hate the thought of hurting them. You don't have to invite beneficial animals into the house, but you don't want to hurt them either. Just leave them alone, let them do what they do best — eat bugs — and you're going a long way toward helping your garden. And they're doing most of the work! If you don't already have some of these critters patrolling your yard, get them.

There are natural solutions. Certain plants and homemade recipes can either keep pesky animals away or keep the good ones around. As I've mentioned, I don't use chemicals of any kind because of the significant side effects — killing beneficial animals and insects, while leaving traces that later affect pets and humans. And traps are a no-no because once the critter is released away from home, its chances for survival are slim to none.

To avoid problems, use these simple, organic remedies.

How to repel...
Birds

When my trees and grape vines come to fruit, Birds become my nemeses. They wait until the fruit is perfectly ripe, then they help themselves until everything's ruined. To keep them away, I...

- Hang fake fruit or Christmas tree ornaments before fruit ripens. When Birds don't get anything to eat from the fakes, it trains them to believe none of it's real. When fruit grows in, Birds don't bother it. Also use on Tomatoes and Grapes

- String reflective material (like strips of tinfoil or cassette tape) across plants, trees, and rooftops. It frightens Birds
- A pinwheel, child's whirligig, or any moving object scares Birds away
- Put wire, spikes, or fish line on top of the house
- A strip of hose in the grass looks like a Snake from the air. Move it every other day so Birds don't get used to it
- Use a product called Tangle Foot where Birds roost (windowsills, roof edges, etc.). Birds don't like to stand on sticky material
- Try the Nixilite system. It's a bunch of sharp spikes that Birds don't dare land on

Cats

- Mothballs repel Cats (and mice)
- Put full-sized pinecones under plants where Cats dig (they don't like the prickles on the cones)
- Plant Rue anywhere you don't want Cats — they hate the smell
- Peel the label from a plastic two-liter bottle and fill it halfway with water. Cats don't like the reflections

Deer

- Tie a plastic grocery bag to a shrub three to four feet off the ground. The fluttering bag mimics the "runaway" warning signal Deer give to one another. Move the bag often so Deer don't guess your game
- String a bar of soap (I like Irish Spring) to bushes that Deer feed on. Put it about four feet off the ground, or put the bar of soap in a piece of nylon stocking and hang from the bush
- Sprinkle blood meal around the garden
- Use a commercial Deer repellent available from nurseries or specialty catalogs

Dogs

People constantly tell me stories about neighbor Dogs that dig, do their business, or generally make a mess of yards that aren't their own. A few suggestions to keep Dogs away...

- Sprinkle full-size pinecones in areas you don't want Dogs to walk. Consider a family trip up north to collect the pinecones
- Cactus wards off Dogs
- Plant fragrant Artemisia, fragrant Santolina
- Spread rosebush clippings around (but be careful you don't scratch yourself with the thorny stems)
- Hot Pepper spray keeps Dogs away. Mix one cup of Tabasco to one gallon of water, then use spray bottle
- Grind two Garlic cloves, one teaspoon of liquid dishwashing soap, and two cups of water. Strain and spray on your plants

Gophers

As a prolific digger, he's the plague of any golf course or grass yard. The Gopher loves to eat succulent roots and plants. To get him out of your yard, read on...

- Gopher Snakes hunt Gophers. Get yourself one (a Snake, not a Gopher!), or encourage one to hang out at your place
- Thickly plant Castor Beans, Gopher purge
- Drop dry ice into Gopher hole, then quickly cover it with soil
- Leave them some Wrigley's spearmint gum. They eat the gum and it clogs their intestines

Rabbits

They seem to be a never-ending problem in desert areas. But there are several ways to keep them from coming into your garden.

- Sprinkle the ground with human hair, bonemeal, blood meal, and/or Epsom salts. They hate the smells
- Snakes scare them away. So try to attract Snakes. See below for instructions. Or buy a rubber Snake
- Plant Santolina, daffodils, Lavender, Rue around the border of your yard or garden and in flower beds. Their fragrance repels Rabbits

- Grind two Garlic cloves, and mix with one teaspoon of liquid dishwashing soap, and two cups of water. Strain and spray on your plants
- If all else fails, get one-inch mesh chicken wire that's three feet high. Bury it at least six inches in the ground to prevent Rabbits from burrowing under. Wrap chicken wire on young trees to keep Rabbits from chewing lower trunks

Raccoons
- Grind two Garlic cloves, and mix with one teaspoon of liquid dishwashing soap and two cups of water. Strain and spray on your plants

Skunks

To discourage Skunks from taking up residence around your house, use their own weapon against them — scent. Or keep them away by depriving them of a place to live.
- Remove brush piles, stacked lumber, woodpiles, and similar sources of shelter
- Build a fence around yard or gardens
- Shine bright lights up from the foundation of the house
- Leave an ammonia-soaked rag at the entrance to their den
- Sprinkle mothballs or moth flakes around the area

How to Attract...

Bats
- Install a Bat house. Like a birdhouse, it will encourage Bats to take up residence at your home. Be patient, though. It could take up to two years for Bats to settle in
    - Put the Bat house on the north or east side of your house, under the eaves
    - The chances of getting rabies from a Bat are less than one in a million
- Plant palm trees and/or flowering agaves. Bats love them

Birds and Hummingbirds

Hummingbirds eat half their weight in insects and nectar every day. Plant flowers for a daily visit from Hummers. They really like tubular flowers that hold a lot of nectar. Reds, pinks, oranges, yellows, and blues are their favorite colors.

Keep a diverse group of flowering and seed-producing shrubs to attract insects to provide Hummingbirds and other Birds with a food source. The plant life will provide cover for the Birds, too. They roost in dense bushes and trees, and hide from enemies in thick brush. Try to leave a "wild" area in your yard so Birds are protected.

- Don't trim palms, they attract Birds, Bats
- Let some brush piles, leaves, branches, and logs collect to create shelter. It doesn't have to be much
- Plants that attract Birds:
  - Agaves
  - Birds-of-paradise (Caesalpinias)
  - Brittlebush
  - Cholla
  - Desert willow
  - Fairy Duster
  - Foothill Palo Verde
  - Hopbush
  - Justicia, chuparosa
  - Ocotillo
  - Penstemon, especially the red ones
  - Prickly Pear Cactus
  - Pyracantha
  - Red yucca (Hesperaloe)
  - Ruellia
  - Sage (Salvia clevelandii, S. coccinea, S. farinacea S. greggi, S. leucantha)
  - Saguaro
  - Sunflower
  - Sweet Acacia
  - Tecoma, Orange Jubilee
  - Tecoma stans, Arizona yellow bells
  - Velvet Mesquite

Although native and adapted plant material provide the best source of food for the Birds, you can supplement their diet with the following:

- Automatic feeders
- Salt blocks
- Seed block

Butterflies
- Plant lots of flat-topped (umbel) flowers, brightly colored plants, and these flowers: bird-of-paradise, daylilies, desert Marigold, desert milkweed, desert senna, paperflower, Salvias (sages), penstemons, desert milkweed, eupatorium, fairy dusters, Lavender, Snapdragons, verbena, Zinnias
- Plant flowering herbs: Parsley, Coriander, Dill, Lavender
- Provide sheltered areas, out of the wind, with favorite plants
- Put stones in birdbath water as landing pads for them
- Construct a "seep," where water oozes into the soil to create a damp patch. Butterflies like to sip dissolved minerals and salts from small muddy areas
- In a hidden corner of your yard, plant some larval food sources (something Caterpillars can chew on)
  - Put up with some plant loss, because some Caterpillars turn into beautiful Butterflies

Lizards/Geckos
- They'll come around naturally. Your job is to NOT kill them with pesticides or chemicals

Snakes
- They like cool places, like stone or cement fences
- They like shaded areas, created by structures or plant life
- An abundance of Frogs and Toads attracts Snakes

Toads/Frogs
- To make a Toad house, partially bury a terra-cotta pot, prop up one edge as entrance, and put it on the north side of your house or yard in the shadiest, coolest place you can find

- Don't use pesticides. Toads absorb them through their skin and die very easily
- Add a water source, and a Toad should be content.
    - Build a pond and add tadpoles to the water
- Don't touch Toads. They ooze a chemical (bufogen) that your skin can absorb and make you sick. Immediately wash your hands if you do handle a Toad
- Plant Duck weeds and lily pads to encourage Frogs

If you want a beautiful and wonderfully healthy garden, plant a diversity of plants and remember, NO PESTICIDES!

AFTERWORD

MY vision for the future is full of hope that individuals will recognize the impact they can have on our environment – good or bad. When more homeowners and businesses start to take action and use earth friendly techniques and products that nurture our environment, we'll have a whole lot more to look forward to.

I predict that awareness will broaden about our own human participation and symbiotic relationships in nature. More people will come to know that we must treat the soil, with all of its micro fauna and flora, with organic types of fertilizer. Wildlife, such as Birds, bees, and small animals will be looked upon as part of our ecosystem, instead of a hindrance to our civilized progress and growth. For our own good, we need to help wildlife survive and thrive in our microsystem.

It's more than likely that down the road, local and state law will mandate the use of things like electric mowers and trimmers. Synthetic pesticides could be regulated just as carefully as our drug industry is now. It will motivate companies to take a proactive approach to dealing with pests and put more emphasis on organic types of control.

Composting might cease being an option and become a necessity: to keep our citys, towns and neighborhoods functioning, we cannot rely much longer on our overflowing landfills. Sewage and waste water systems as we know them could change drastically or become entirely obsolete. Instead, we'll use composting toilets and irrigate with a graywater system that filters and recycles water.

We might even come to embrace the lowly weed. It has a place, you know, in the polycultures that we must encourage.

In short, all members of our society will need to take a hard look at their own homes and treat them as microenvironments. We can only guide Mother Nature and we cannot do this without looking at the whole picture and how each element contributes in some way to the others. Unless we take a more simple and gentle approach, we might destroy the beautiful and life-sustaining things this planet has to offer.

If you've read about a seed, a fertilizer, or any other product in this book, there's a good chance you can get it from my website. Just log onto www.gardenguy.com to see if it's available. I'll offer organic materials and top quality products. If you don't see what you want, drop me an email at gardenguy@gardenguy.com, or you can head over to your nearest nursery or do-it-yourself center. It won't be as convenient as receiving it in the mail, but at least you'll get what you need.

-The Garden Guy

INDEX

Alfalfa, 22, 53, 63, 68, 70, 72, 82, 83, 87, 90, 91, 95, 99, 101, 134, 136, 180

All Spice, 140

Almond, 113-115

Alyssum, 29, 31, 40, 158, 182, 215, 217, 218, 219, 221, 225, 232

Ant, 29, 31, 32, 34, 35, 37, 40, 159, 162, 191, 192, 194, 196, 197, 204, 206, 210, 224, 225, 227, 228, 231, 232, 234

Aphid, 27, 29, 31, 34, 35, 36, 37, 38, 40, 49, 50, 60, 62, 65, 73, 74, 76, 80, 84, 93, 95, 96, 103, 108, 110, 131, 135, 156, 159, 163, 170, 181, 182, 187, 188, 189, 191, 194, 206, 207, 221, 222, 223, 224, 226, 227, 230, 231, 232, 234

Apple, 111, 115-117, 119, 126, 129, 141, 143, 187

Apricot, 29, 117-120

Artemisia, 29, 33, 34, 37, 39, 158-159, 182, 188, 191, 193, 206, 207, 211, 215, 216, 220, 231, 237

Artichoke, 32, 49-51

Asparagus, 36, 37, 40, 189

Avocado, 140

Bachelor's Button, 29, 36, 40, 159, 215, 221, 232

Bacillus thuringiensis, 55, 215, 221, 226, 228, 230

Banana, 141, 148

Basil, 29, 36, 38, 40, 46, 185-186, 190, 193, 207, 211, 215, 216, 218, 228, 231, 233, 234

Bats, 225, 235, 238, 239

Bay, 31, 196, 206, 211, 216, 231

Bean, 8, 11, 28, 30, 31, 32, 33, 34, 36, 37, 38, 39, 45, 52, 53, 54, 56, 57, 68, 74, 78, 82, 86, 167, 186, 188, 193, 193, 209, 237

Bee, 35, 38, 40, 100, 159, 182, 186, 187, 192, 193, 197, 213, 214, 223, 233, 242

Beet, 28, 30, 33, 35, 37, 39, 45, 54, 55, 58, 103, 208, 224

Beet Leafhopper, 208, 224

Beetle, 29, 31, 35, 36, 37, 38, 40, 53, 70, 82, 90, 93, 95, 97, 110, 118, 124, 126, 186, 193, 194, 208, 209, 210, 223, 224, 229, 230, 231, 232

Begonia, 159, 182

Beneficial Insects, 29-40, 108, 206, 208, 220, 221

Bermuda, 129, 131, 199, 201

Bio-neem, 226,

Bird, 32, 38, 70, 88, 95, 115, 117, 119, 120, 126, 128, 134, 135, 137, 157, 161, 167, 183, 184, 195, 198, 206, 208, 210, 211, 212, 214, 220, 225, 228, 229, 230, 236, 238, 239, 240

Blackberry, 111, 120, 121, 122

Black-eyed Pea, 33, 56, 57

Black-eyed Susan, 159

Black spot, 31, 34, 35, 37, 38, 178

Blood Orange, 142

Blue Elderberry, 142

Bok Choy, 30, 32, 39, 57, 58

Bonemeal, 21, 66, 87, 175, 179, 237

Borage, 30, 31, 39, 77, 186, 211, 231, 233

Borer, 31, 34, 37, 68, 74, 135, 181, 209, 210, 230, 232,

Boric Acid, 212, 213, 219, 228

Bougainvillea, 159, 214

Braconid wasp, 207, 211, 222

Broccoli, 30, 36, 39, 37, 45, 59, 60, 64, 78

Brussels Sprout, 38, 39, 61, 62,

Butterfly, 7, 29, 35, 65, 156, 158, 160, 161, 164, 188, 192, 193, 195, 198, 210, 211, 223, 233, 240

Cabbage, 28, 30, 31, 33, 35, 36, 38, 39, 40, 45, 57, 58, 59, 61, 65, 74, 75, 77, 97, 110, 162, 174, 187, 188, 191, 193, 210

Calendula, 31, 186, 209, 211, 216, 221, 231

Cantaloupe, 81, 220

Carambola, 142

Carrot, 8, 28, 29, 30, 31, 33, 35, 37, 38, 39, 45, 59, 62, 63, 64, 167, 187, 189, 191, 193, 210

Cat, 38, 90, 192, 193, 217, 235, 236

Caterpillar, 31, 32, 40, 55, 59, 59, 62, 65, 73, 76, 80, 104, 108, 159, 165, 170, 189, 196, 209, 210, 211, 222, 223, 226, 229, 231, 232, 240

Catmint, 31, 182, 209, 231

Cauliflower, 29, 30, 39, 45, 64, 65, 106

Celosia, 160

Chamomile, 30, 31, 37, 39, 40, 59, 77, 86, 164, 186, 187, 213

Chive, 30, 31, 33, 37, 39, 46, 181, 182, 207, 210, 212, 214, 231, 232

Chrysanthemum paludosum, 31, 160, 182

Citrus, 18, 19, 32, 143, 149-157, 162, 206, 210, 213, 219, 220, 234

    Bacterial disease, 155

    Fungal disease, 154

Citrus bark, 213, 234

Cockroach, 212, 225, 227

Coffee grounds, 22

Companion planting, 12, 27, 29, 96, 181, 182, 191

Compost, 19, 21, 22, 23-26, 41, 42, 46, 44, 201, 209

Coreopsis, 32, 160, 215, 217, 218, 219, 221, 223, 225, 233

Coriander, 32, 34, 37, 40, 72, 187, 188, 207, 215, 217, 218, 219, 221, 223, 225, 233, 240

Corn, 10, 19, 28, 29, 31, 32, 33, 36, 38, 45, 53, 58, 66, 67, 68, 69, 89, 90, 95, 99, 106, 167, 178, 187, 210

Cosmos, 32, 161, 215, 222, 231, 233
Cotton, 10, 181, 215, 222, 231, 233
Cottonseed meal, 21, 62, 65, 72, 87, 102, 114, 117, 119, 120, 121, 123, 126, 131, 135, 128, 157, 179
Cricket, 31, 34, 35, 37, 38, 73, 204, 212, 225, 227, 229, 231, 232
Cucumber, 30, 32, 33, 35, 36, 37, 38, 39, 45, 70, 82, 93, 167, 183, 189, 193, 197, 209

Damselfly, 207, 221
Dandelion, 28, 32
Deer, 235, 236
Design, 10-17
Dianthus, 161, 182
Diatomaceous earth, 82, 95, 97, 208, 212, 213, 214, 228, 230
Dill, 32, 40, 59, 63, 64, 72, 187, 215, 217, 219, 221, 223, 225, 233, 240
Direct Seed, 48, 60, 63
Dog, 19, 29, 90, 210, 213, 234, 235, 237
Dragonfly, 7, 221
Dutch White Clover, 33, 196

Earthworm, 22, 23, 25, 26, 199
Eggplant, 28, 29, 31, 33, 34, 35, 40, 45, 71, 72, 73, 74, 86, 93, 106, 165, 191
Encarsia formosa wasp, 163, 222
Epazote, 187, 191
Epsom salts, 22, 90, 180, 237
Eucalyptus bark, 19, 34, 220, 234
Evapotranspiration, 13, 28

Fennel, 29, 31, 34, 37, 40, 64, 88, 106, 187, 188, 213
Fertilizer, 10, 11, 21-23, 24, 42, 46, 179-180, 201, 202, 203, 242, 244
Feverfew, 34, 40, 192, 217, 219, 221, 225, 233
Fig, 122, 123, 124
Fish emulsion, 21, 23, 179, 198
Flea, 29, 31, 32, 34, 35, 38, 40, 90, 97, 187, 188, 191, 192, 193, 205, 213, 229, 231, 232, 234
Fleabane, 34, 162, 213, 217
Flowers, 7, 10, 11, 22, 23, 27-40, 41, 46, 158-184, 185-202, 221, 223, 225, 231, 232, 234
Fly, 29, 37, 38, 40, 185, 193, 194, 221, 223, 225, 231, 232, 234
Four-o'clock, 162
Frog, 235, 240, 241
Frost cloth, 104, 123
Fungus (also see Rose or Citrus), 22, 54, 69, 137, 188, 200, 206, 215

Gallardia, 162
Garlic, 22, 28, 29, 31, 34, 37, 73-74, 88, 97, 181, 182, 207, 210, 212, 214, 226, 232, 237, 238
Gecko, 212, 214, 225, 229, 230, 235, 240
Geranium, 34, 37, 162, 163, 182, 231, 232
Germination, 48, 63, 79, 96, 98, 190
Gnat, 46, 205
Gopher, 235, 237
Grapefruit, 149, 150, 154, 156, 157
Grass, 199
Grasshopper, 31, 34, 35, 37, 38, 73, 214, 223, 229, 232
Grub, 31, 93, 209, 210, 223
Guava, 111, 132, 133, 143
Gummosis, 154
Gypsum, 19, 23, 175

Heirloom, 48
Herbs, 10, 35, 40, 41, 46, 77, 182, 185-198, 218, 221, 223, 225, 231, 240
Hibiscus, 163, 220
Hollyhock, 163
Hornworm, 29, 31, 90, 186, 211
Hoverfly, 35, 188, 189, 207, 223, 233
Hydrogen peroxide, 22, 23, 220

Indian Fig, 142
Irrigation, 13-15, 19, 112, 114

Johnny-Jump-Up, 163
Jujube, 143

Kale, 39, 75, 76
Kumquat, 144, 149, 156

Lacewing, 32, 60, 163, 182, 207, 215, 217, 218, 219, 221, 222, 231, 233
Ladybug, 29, 32, 40, 60, 182, 194, 207, 215, 218, 222, 231, 232, 233
Lantana, 27, 34, 164, 220, 221
Lavender, 27, 30, 33, 34, 35, 39, 158, 168, 192, 206, 207, 211, 213, 216, 220, 231, 232, 233, 234, 237, 240
Leafcutter bee, 182, 214
Leek, 30, 33, 39, 35, 76, 77, 78, 232
Legume, 27, 86
Lemon, 32, 35, 40, 143, 151, 154, 157, 178, 192, 196, 197, 206, 213, 217, 219, 220, 221, 225, 233
Lemon Balm, 35, 40, 196, 217, 219, 220, 221, 225, 233
Lemon Grass, 192

Lettuce, 10, 28, 30, 31, 33, 35, 37, 39, 45, 61, 75, 77, 78, 79, 80, 160, 164, 187

Lime, 143, 144, 149, 151, 154, 211

Liquid seaweed, 21, 23, 46, 175

Lizard, 9, 205, 206, 212, 214, 225, 228, 229, 230, 235, 240

Longan, 144

Loquat, 144

Magnesium sulfate, 22

Mango, 144

Manure, 21, 23, 50

Marigold, 30, 31, 33, 34, 35, 37, 39, 40, 46, 60, 186, 188, 207, 211, 212, 214, 221, 232, 233, 240

Marjoram, 46

Mauget, 23

Mealybug, 29, 32, 37, 215, 222, 226, 227, 231, 232, 233

Melon, 27, 29, 30, 32, 33, 35, 36, 38, 39, 45, 80, 81, 82, 94, 184, 209

Mexican Primrose, 35, 207

Mexican Sunflower, 164

Mildew, 31, 34, 35, 37, 38, 54, 69, 82, 88, 94, 95, 99, 102, 172, 194

Milorganite, 21, 135, 201

Mint, 35, 36, 37, 39, 46, 187, 193, 197, 206, 207, 211, 216, 221, 232

Mold, 54, 129

Monoculture, 10

Mosquito, 29, 35, 37, 185, 188, 191, 192, 193, 194, 197, 215, 221, 225, 228, 231, 232, 233, 234

Moth, 29, 31, 34, 35, 36, 37, 38, 40, 145, 159, 162, 164, 191, 192, 193, 194, 196, 210, 211, 216, 221, 231, 232, 238

Mulch, 11, 13, 14, 19

Nasturtium, 27, 30, 32, 33, 36, 37, 38, 39, 40, 46, 60, 96, 103, 182, 188, 207, 209, 212, 217, 219, 220, 221, 225, 232, 233
Nitrogen, 21, 22, 24, 28, 31, 33, 56, 62, 65, 131, 135, 153-154, 179, 234
Nursery Stock, 48

Okra, 29, 33, 83, 84
Onion, 29, 30, 31, 33, 34, 35, 36, 37, 39, 50, 58, 73, 75, 84, 85, 86, 88, 90, 167, 181, 182, 187, 206, 207, 210, 212, 214, 216, 218, 232
Orange, 111, 149, 150, 151, 154, 157, 174, 213
Orange Dog, 156
Organic, 10, 11, 14, 16, 19, 21, 117, 126, 128, 148, 179-180, 201, 202, 203-241, 244

Pansy, 31, 163, 164
Papaya, 145
Parasitizing Insects, 208, 222, 229
Parsley, 31, 37, 40, 46, 72, 187, 189, 207, 209, 210, 215, 217, 219, 220, 221, 223, 225, 231, 233, 240
Pea, 11, 27, 28, 30, 31, 33, 37, 39, 40, 44, 45, 53, 56, 57, 61, 68, 74, 82, 86, 87, 88, 93, 116, 119, 165, 167, 168
Peach, 29, 124, 125, 126, 185
Peanut, 30, 33, 36, 38
Pear, 29, 127, 128, 129, 142, 216, 239
Pecan, 111, 130, 131, 132
Pennyroyal, 35, 37, 197, 206, 212, 213, 214, 216, 232
Pepper, 28, 36, 37, 40, 45, 89, 90, 97, 106, 165, 191, 226, 237
Peppermint, 61, 197, 206, 232
Petunia, 28, 31, 37, 164, 165, 207, 209, 232
Phosphorus, 62, 66, 169, 179
Pineapple, 132, 133, 146

Pineapple Guava, 132
Plum, 29, 134, 135
Polyculture, 10, 11, 12, 27, 242
Pomegranate, 135, 136, 137, 220
Poppy, 165
Portulaca, 165
Potassium, 21, 24
Potato, 30, 32, 33, 34, 35, 37, 38, 39, 49, 64, 73, 75, 81, 88, 91, 93, 94, 106, 164, 165, 167, 188, 193
Powdery Mildew, 181
Praying Mantis, 207, 208, 211, 218, 223
Predaceous Insects, 29-40
Pumpkin, 32, 36, 67, 68, 93, 94, 95
Purple Passion Vine, 146

Rabbit, 22, 35, 38, 192, 232, 235, 237, 238
Rabbit pellets, 22
Raccoon, 238
Radish, 30, 33, 35, 36, 37, 39, 53, 63, 70, 96, 97, 102, 167, 207, 209, 219
Rain Lily, 166
Recipe, 44, 115, 129, 156, 182, 206, 207, 208, 212, 213, 214, 215, 216, 218, 220, 226, 227, 228, 230
    Organic Pest Control, 204
Robber fly, 208
Rose, 22, 29, 30, 31, 33, 34, 35, 37, 38, 40, 74, 129, 158, 171-182, 189, 191, 192, 193, 194, 210, 214, 232
Rosemary, 27, 33, 37, 38, 39, 46, 59, 193, 209, 212, 213, 214, 216, 218, 232, 233
Rue, 29, 38, 185, 193, 213, 232, 234, 236, 237
Rye, 159, 199

Sage (Salvia), 27, 30, 36, 38, 39, 40, 46, 59, 70, 182, 193, 212, 213, 214, 232, 234, 239, 240

Santolina, 38, 193, 194, 213, 214, 216, 220, 232, 234, 237

Savory, 33, 46, 185

Scale insect, 29, 32, 34, 35, 36, 37, 135, 189, 197, 216, 217, 222, 230, 232, 233

Scorpion, 212, 217, 224, 225

Seedling Transplant, 48

Skunk, 238

Slug, 37, 59, 62, 73, 80, 90, 95, 170, 188, 193, 218, 232

Snail, 59, 62, 73, 80, 90, 170, 193, 218

Snake, 9, 212, 214, 225, 229, 235, 236, 237, 240

Snapdragon, 166, 240

Soaker hose, 16

Society Garlic, 38, 158, 166, 181, 182, 207, 232

Soil, 7, 8, 10, 11, 12, 13, 14, 16, 17, 18-19, 21, 22, 23, 24, 25, 26, 28, 29, 41, 42, 44, 45, 175, 176, 204, 242

Soil Probe, 17, 200

Soil Sulfur, 19, 23, 138, 175

Soil Temperature Gauge, 16

Solanaceae, 28, 106, 165

Sooty canker, 155

Spearmint, 35, 182, 197, 237

Spider, 208, 212, 214, 224, 229

Spider Mite, 29, 32, 37, 97, 108, 135, 156, 163, 182, 189, 197, 218, 224, 226, 230, 232, 233

Spinach, 30, 36, 39, 45, 98, 99, 103

Squash, 29, 30, 32, 36, 37, 38, 39, 40, 67, 68, 82, 100, 101, 102, 103, 164, 184, 188, 189, 194, 209, 220, 232

Stem Borer, 182

Stock, 48

Strawberry, 30, 31, 33, 35, 37, 39, 65, 70, 74, 88, 95, 137, 138, 139, 143, 186

Stubborn Disease, 155
Sunflowers, 27, 30, 31, 32, 33, 36, 38, 49, 53, 58, 70, 89, 90, 93, 99, 106, 160, 167, 178, 183, 184, 239
Surinam Cherry, 146
Sweet Pea, 167
Swiss Chard, 30, 35, 39, 45, 103, 104
Syrphid fly, 207, 223

Tachinid fly, 211, 223
Tangelo, 150, 154
Tangerine, 150, 154, 156
Tansy, 33, 34, 37, 40, 194, 206, 208, 209, 212, 213, 216, 222, 232, 233, 234
Tarragon, 34, 40, 191
Termite, 219, 228
Thrips, 29, 32, 86, 156, 157, 189, 197, 219, 222, 224, 233
Thyme, 30, 34, 37, 39, 40, 46, 182, 194, 208, 212, 216, 232
Tick, 29, 32, 34, 35, 192, 220, 229, 231, 232, 234
Till, 33, 41, 47
Toad, 9, 166, 205, 206, 212, 214, 217, 225, 228, 229, 230, 235, 240, 241
Tomato, 28, 29, 30, 31, 33, 34, 35, 37, 38, 39, 40, 45, 65, 69, 71, 72, 89, 90, 93, 105-109, 164, 165, 185, 186, 187, 188, 189, 193, 196, 197, 204, 208, 211, 220, 236
Tools, 14, 16, 74, 200, 229
Trichogramma wasp, 32, 187, 189, 210, 211, 233
True Bug, 189, 220, 224, 225
Turnip, 30, 33, 39, 109, 110
Turtle, 235

Vegetable, 7, 10, 11, 12, 38, 40, 45, 47-48, 229
Vinca, 28, 31, 156, 168, 188
Vinegar, 22, 23, 161, 180, 202, 206, 213, 228, 229

Watering, 9, 13-14, 17, 46, 200
Watermelon, 30, 80, 81, 82
White Sapote, 146
Whitefly, 32, 34, 35, 36, 37, 40, 108, 163, 164, 186, 188, 189,
      220, 222, 223, 224, 226, 230, 232, 234
Woolen, 38, 40, 190

Zinnia, 158, 168, 240
Zucchini, 36, 47, 100, 188